A Light to the Centurions

A Light to the Centurions

Reading Luke–Acts in the Empire

ROBERT R. BECK

WIPF & STOCK · Eugene, Oregon

A LIGHT TO THE CENTURIONS
Reading Luke–Acts in the Empire

Copyright © 2019 Robert R. Beck. All rights reserved. Except for brief quotations in critical publications or reviews, no part of this book may be reproduced in any manner without prior written permission from the publisher. Write: Permissions, Wipf and Stock Publishers, 199 W. 8th Ave., Suite 3, Eugene, OR 97401.

Wipf & Stock
An Imprint of Wipf and Stock Publishers
199 W. 8th Ave., Suite 3
Eugene, OR 97401

www.wipfandstock.com

PAPERBACK ISBN: 978-1-5326-5653-8
HARDCOVER ISBN: 978-1-5326-5654-5
EBOOK ISBN: 978-1-5326-5655-2

Manufactured in the U.S.A.   05/13/19

Unless otherwise noted, all Scripture quotations are from the New American Bible, Lexham English Bible, or New Revised Standard Version.

Stones, Stars: The Centurion Reports

"When Jesus left the tomb behind
                            he paused
upon the edge of Palestine and night
then traveled on alone; where he has gone
everyone must go, yet no one had
quite, and no one of his friends would yet.

They, his friends, had scattered under stars
of salt, of mica. Or so at first, but now
they heard the mute imperative to hide
clustered close beneath some smoky lamp
up a footworn stone stair behind a vine.

Destinies might alter, planets shift
to new and preferable alignments, soon.
But that is still unknown; meanwhile the night,
riveted across a vacant sky,
glitters
            above the twelve gates of that city."

Contents

Preface | ix
Acknowledgements | xv

Chapter One
Luke's Reader—"Most Excellent Theophilus" | 1

Chapter Two
Luke's Challenge to the Reader—"Have You No Fear of God?" | 24

Chapter Three
Luke's Text—"An Orderly Sequence" | 41

Chapter Four
Reading Luke's Gospel—"The Spirit of the Lord Is Upon Me" | 67

Chapter Five
Reading the Acts of the Apostles—"God Shows No Partiality" | 116

Chapter Six
From Edge to Center | 155

Postscript
Writer and Reader | 175

Bibliography | 179
Index | 183

Preface

- "I will give you as a light to the nations,
  to be my salvation to the end of the earth" (Isaiah 49:6).
- "For my eyes have seen your salvation
  that you have prepared in the presence of all the peoples,
  a light for revelation to the gentiles,
  and glory to your people Israel" (Simeon, in Luke 2:30–32).
- I stand here testifying to both small and great, saying nothing except what both the prophets and Moses have said were going to happen, that the Christ was to suffer and that as the first of the resurrection from the dead, he was going to proclaim light both to the people and to the gentiles" (Paul to King Agrippa and Festus the Roman governor, Acts 26:22–23).

IN MARK'S GOSPEL, A centurion responds to the crucifixion of Jesus with "Truly, this was Son of God" (Mark 15:39). The line properly belongs to a disciple, but none of the disciples are present, having abandoned the scene hours before. So the centurion is left to stand in for them, pronouncing the words they are unable to say. By contrast, in Luke's narrative in his Gospel and Acts, centurions abound. Cornelius and Julius are mentioned by name (Acts 10:1; 27:1). And the centurion of Capernaum is openly affirmative of Jesus and his works (Luke 7:4–5). Things have changed for Luke, and among these changes is a different attitude toward the Roman Empire and its military officers. That change of perspective and direction is the impulse behind the study of Luke's narrative in this book.

Ever since Joseph Tyson proposed that the centurions in Luke–Acts are intra-textual representatives of the implied reader of these works, the idea has been on the table. This proposal will be accepted here and Luke's double work read as a narrative intended for such a reader. Part of this enterprise will be to remain continually aware of what Luke changes in the narrative he received from Mark, as well as how his distinct readership might make those changes intelligible.

If the implied reader is a God-fearer, a friend of the synagogue, but unable to convert to Judaism, we then have one who is attempting to enter the narrative, not one who is out to replace it with another. Luke is finding a way into the narrative for that reader, not only by placing him in the text, but by finding a rationale within the Jewish tradition for doing so. He accomplishes that through a strategic use of the post-exilic Isaian texts, playing them against the more successfully surviving alternative tradition derived from Ezekiel, Ezra, and Nehemiah. Their policy of posting identity markers around Judaism, guarding the community that was tasked with guarding the revelation entrusted them, gives way in this Gospel and its successor, the Acts of the Apostles. But now the "light" is to be released to the gentiles.

Recent New Testament studies, inspired by postcolonial criticism, have disclosed a dimension to the New Testament writings that had otherwise remained unnoticed. Adopting the perspective of the colonized peoples, postcolonial criticism has shown the underside of imperial conquest as experienced in the nineteenth and twentieth centuries. Biblical scholars, alerted by these writings, remembered that subjection to foreign empires marked the origins of both Old and New Testaments. The trauma of the Roman Empire as the imperial overlord and eventual destroyer of both Jerusalem and its temple is recognized accordingly as an important background to the New Testament writings. As a result studies of the Gospels of Matthew, Mark, and John, as well as the letters of Paul, have undergone a profound revision of interpretation.

Nevertheless, the pertinence of empire studies to the writings of Luke has been less promising. There are five key traditional views of the purpose of Luke, with the first dominating scholarship: "(1) Luke–Acts is a political apology on behalf of the church addressed to Roman officials; (2) Luke–Acts is an apology on behalf of the Roman state addressed to the church; (3) Luke–Acts is providing legitimation for the church's identity; (4) Luke–Acts is equipping the church to live with the Roman empire; and (5) Luke–Acts is not interested in politics at all."[1] The consensus is that Luke's attitude toward the empire is ambivalent, allowing those on different sides to muster arguments that favor their position while ignoring those that do not. In each of these views, the conflict that needs negotiation is that between the Christian Church and the Roman Empire. While relations between church and empire dominate the discussion, missing from the list of views is a properly

---

1. Walton, "The State," *Rome in Bible*, 1–41. Based on the website: http://stevewalton.info/my-article-the-state-they-were-in-lukes-view-of-the-roman-empire-available-to-download/.

postcolonial standpoint. In none of them is the view of the colonized concerning empire a part of the outlook.

This omission can be explained in light of the very nature of postcolonial writing. James Scott has addressed the dynamic of hiddenness of imperial influence.[2] Resistance mounted by oppressed groups usually is, by necessity, indirect and surreptitious. The Gospel of Mark, for instance, can be shown to mount an opposition to the imperial forces, albeit nonviolently. Key terms and in-group references can be shown to relate to a common Jewish resistance to imperial occupation and cultural pressures. Luke–Acts is an anomaly in this regard, with its often positive, or at least ambivalent, attitude toward Rome, in contrast to the previous Gospels.

A postcolonial reading of Luke's work is in order, if for no other reason than to discern more clearly the author's position within the framework provided by empire studies. Forays into the territory have been made, exploring different possibilities and relevant themes—the place of the Roman military, soldiers, and centurions in Luke's work;[3] the theme of social reversals;[4] and the place of postcolonial readings in Luke's body of work.[5] What remains to be seen is how a postcolonial narrative reading of Luke–Acts succeeds as a whole. In trying to determine if a postcolonial reading of Luke can provide a coherent reading of Luke's text, my task is not to prove something, but rather to test a hypothesis.

This is the hypothesis being tested: Luke is extending the gospel he received to the gentiles. And in shifting the point of view from the Jewish to the gentile position, Luke reverses that viewpoint, away from identifying the Roman as an opponent to allowing the Roman into the fold. The general sense is this: The question is how Luke can provide a "light to the gentiles" when the gentiles have been identified as the opponent of God and the Bible.

One opening in the received gospel tradition is the nonviolent conflict resolution of Mark (and Matthew), which refuses to treat the opponent as evil and the proper target of retaliatory violence. This implies that there is room to perceive the enemy as a potential ally, and even a friend. Such a proposal helps to explain the ambivalent attitude in Luke's text toward Rome, which is both critical and approving. For this point of view, the citizen of Rome, even the Roman authorities, are potential material for conversion and discipleship. In fact, part of their story is how they use their position to further the Way.

2. Scott, *Domination*.
3. Brink, *Soldiers in Luke–Acts*; Yoder, *Representatives*; Kyrychenko, *Roman Army*.
4. Miller, *Rumors of Resistance*; Rowe, *World Upside Down*.
5. Petterson, *Acts of Empire*; Muñoz-Larrondo, *A Postcolonial Reading*.

The assumption underlying this book, then, is that Luke is showing the gentiles a way into the narrative. It is not that Luke is defending the church against Rome, or Rome against the church. The sympathetic gentiles are attracted to the community and the narrative of faith, and they would like to join it, even when conditions prohibit them from doing so. What those conditions may be is also a subject of importance investigated in the following chapters. There are six chapters, plus a summarizing postscript. The first three of them address the question of Luke's Gospel project. Each pivots off the inscription at the beginning. The following two attempt a reading of the Gospel and Acts, respectively. The concluding chapter looks back at the larger narrative arc of Luke–Acts.

Chapter One raises the question of Luke's reader, with the understanding that the implied reader of a work invites us to adopt that person's point of view and, as such, controls our reading of the work. The chapter identifies Luke's reader as a cultivated gentile, friend of the synagogue, called a *God-fearer* in Luke's account. The typical God-fearer turns out to be a centurion, which inverts the perspective of Luke's primary narrative source, the Gospel of Mark.

Chapter Two raises the question of the challenge that Luke's work makes to its reader. Noting that the inscription offers a word of assurance, the chapter details how the text itself also presents a challenge to that reader, taking matters beyond mere confirmation of settled views. In particular, the call to repentance in Luke's Gospel, placed in tension with attitudes of self-achieved righteousness, though cast in the setting of intra-Jewish disputes, raises questions for Luke's gentile reader.

Chapter Three turns its attention to the Lukan text. Noting sequentiality in Luke's narrative, as well as the apparent violations of that same concern for proper sequence, it looks at the purpose of Luke's project. Particular consideration is given to the programmatic episode of Jesus' reading from the scroll of Isaiah in the Nazareth synagogue (Luke 4:16–30). Placing that event in the historical context of the competing post-exilic traditions of Isaiah 40–66 and Ezra–Nehemiah, this chapter shows Luke's Jesus invoking one Jewish tradition against another. One looks outward beyond Judaism, presenting a "light to the gentiles"; the other looks inward, establishing identity markers to preserve the threatened community. Luke provides his reader with an entry into the Israelite narrative, beyond identity markers.

Chapter Four is an exercise in reading Luke's Gospel as a God-fearer might. Noticing how Luke has adapted his source in Mark, we discover how he has reconstructed the narrative to serve his needs. The result is an account that presents Jesus as a prominent teacher and healer who takes his liberating ministry in Galilee to another level by bringing his movement to the central forum of Jerusalem. The extended period of teaching during the long journey to the city (Luke 10-19) is carefully shaped to present three conversations with different parties—his disciples, the Jewish teachers who oppose him, and the crowds. The arrival in Jerusalem shifts the terms of the conflict. Jesus spends a period of time teaching in the city as the Sanhedrin, the Jewish authorities, plot to quiet him. Ironically their success in having him removed is undone when his movement, animated by the Spirit, revives after his resurrection. The disciples remain in Jerusalem, waiting for the next part of the story.

Chapter Five turns to the Acts of the Apostles and to a narrative that begins in Jerusalem and moves out from there. After reviewing the "rhetorical" plan of that narrative—tracing the Spirit-guided movement from Jerusalem, through Judea and Samaria, out to the ends of the earth—the chapter proposes a fresh approach based on shifting character sets and conflict alignments. Two major narrative thrusts are proposed. One is directed to the synagogues (Acts 8-20), the other to the Roman courts (Acts 21-28). For reasons already discussed, both have significance for the God-fearing reader. The move toward the synagogues, addressing the Jewish tradition, removes obstacles to the gentile believer. However, the move to the Roman court, while welcoming to the gentile believer, also intimates a subversion of Graeco-Roman cultural values, as the teaching of Jesus extends into the empire.

Chapter Six proposes an alternative narrative arc that plays against the more overt pattern of Luke-Acts, as moving out toward the wider world. A move from edge to center, seen in the Gospel narrative as it goes from Galilee to Jerusalem, is repeated in the move from Judea to Rome, as seen now in Acts. The general narrative pattern of moving from the margins and the marginalized toward the center is given a geographical image. This in turn informs the resolution of narrative conflict in Luke-Acts, as Mark's pattern of nonviolent confrontation is transmuted in Luke to an invitation to the antagonists toward conversion. The centurion emerges as the Lukan image of the Roman opponent called to discipleship.

Acknowledgements

THIS BOOK WAS PROMPTED by an offhand suggestion of Sharon Ringe following a panel discussion at an SBL (Society of Biblical Literature) Conference, to the effect that it would be useful to explore the notion of Luke's reader as a God-fearer. Along with that, the need to preach on the Third Sunday of Ordinary Time in the C Cycle forced the generating idea of the book. The lectionary pairs two passages, from Nehemiah 9 and Luke 4. Superficially similar, these are seen on reflection to represent two opposed Jewish traditions. The reform of Ezra that set the norm for the post-exilic colony of Judea competed for dominance with the contrasting world-mission vision of the Isaiah tradition. It was this alternative tradition, in the form of Isaiah 61:1–2, that Jesus invokes in the synagogue of Nazareth, setting the program for Luke's writing project.

As before, thanks must go to those who joined in animated discussions of these matters—Amy Lorenz, John Waldmeir, Jean Beringer OSF, Mona Wingert OSF in particular. Deep appreciation also for the editing skills of Marilyn Gorun, which did so much to improve the book. Mention must also be made of the generosity of Sue Davis, allowing use of the back table in her bookstore, River Lights Second Edition. And again, Dustin Bartels, was willing as usual to give us the corner table at One Mean Bean coffeehouse. It was during these lively exchanges that much of the present book took shape.

CHAPTER ONE

Luke's Reader
"Most Excellent Theophilus"

I. THE QUESTION OF THE READER

IMAGINE THIS SCENARIO. An envelope with another address comes in your mail. Noticing it, you dutifully set it out for the mail deliverer to retrieve so it can be forwarded to the right person.

Or maybe you don't. Maybe this envelope was buried in a stack of envelopes that you methodically slit open and then began to read, and only then discovered that one was not intended for you. Having begun to read it, you have a sense of unease, knowing you are looking in on a message meant for someone else. The name on the letter establishes a right. This writing is another person's property, and that person has the right to withhold or share the contents. And you are violating that right. If not exactly an intruder, you are at least an eavesdropper, and you recognize it. Luke is aware of eavesdropping and makes it a feature of his writing. In the middle section of his Gospel, where Jesus is journeying toward Jerusalem, we find eavesdroppers. Jesus will be speaking to a certain group, for instances, disciples, and a third party, perhaps Pharisees, will interrupt, responding to something that was said, but not said to them.

Whose name is on the text makes a difference. Even when, as in pursuing historical research, public permission is given to read private conversations—say Abraham Lincoln's correspondence with his wife, preserved in the national archives—even then we have a sense of trespassing on another's personal territory. And while the sense of intruding on another's privacy is not an issue, even in public statements we are conscious of the time and place, and the persons addressed. The Gettysburg Address takes much of its meaning from such circumstances. For us, Luke's writing is part of the biblical canon. But it was not always so, and it did not begin that way.

At the very beginning of Luke's Gospel, readers discover a reader already there in the text, one who is awarded particular attention. In the first four verses, for convenience called the *Prologue,* the author addresses this individual as "most excellent Theophilus."

> I too have decided, having carefully investigated everything from the beginning, to write it down in an orderly sequence for you, *most excellent Theophilus,* so that you may know the certainty of the things you have been taught (1:3–4).[1]

And we encounter this same name again at the beginning of the Acts of the Apostles, Luke's other volume. Furthermore, the work is written specifically for him, to meet his particular needs. The language is formal, but the focus is personal. The author states his intention, and it doesn't include us.

For most of us, most of the time, this doesn't seem to be a problem. But it is. We come to the work expecting to read Scripture, part of the biblical canon. To find another reader with his particular needs addressed here is a matter to be noticed. It speaks to the purpose of the author. When the author refers explicitly to the need of the reader in describing his writing project, the wise reader takes notice.

It invites us to specify more closely the identity of the reader. For Luke, or any biblical author, this is difficult to do, but attempts have been made. For example, following the reasonable assumption that Luke sees himself as writing history, genre studies compare this to other early historical writing and view this as a typical dedication of a work. In this vein the author acknowledges Theophilus as the sponsor of Luke's project.[2] Theophilus, for Luke, may be dedicatee and sponsor, but he is also most explicitly a reader of the work, with an agenda spelled out by the author.

What does it mean to find a reader in the text? Grammarians of narrative distinguish the intended, the inscribed, and the implied readers in a

---

1. This translation attempts to bring out the features related to the following reading of Luke's narrative.

2. Among the examples cited, the most commonly mentioned are the works of Flavius Josephus, the Jewish historian and contemporary of Luke. In his *Antiquities of the Jews* and the two volumes of *Against Apion,* Josephus acknowledges a certain Epaphroditus, who prompted and supported his writing. Was Epaphroditus a reader of the works, as Theophilus is for Luke? Possibly, but not explicitly so.

text. We can get an idea of the *intended* reader only by way of the text. So when we question the text, we may find that the reader is actually named there, *inscribed* in the text. In Luke's case this inscription is "Theophilus." However, it remains unclear whether this Theophilus is an actual historical person or not. The name may be a cipher intended to suggest the kind of reader Luke had in mind. And this may even be true if the dedicatee is an actual person, perhaps given a symbolic name for the occasion.

In contrast, the *implied reader* is suggested by a reading of the text itself, as opposed to making deductions from the inscription at the beginning. This too has mixed results. Some scholars think that the range of experiences reflected in the Gospel and Acts is too wide to expect a single reader, despite the fact that Theophilus is invoked at the beginning of each book. For others, this very range leads to the conclusion that a specific kind of person is intended—a cultured gentile who is sympathetic and knowledgeable about Judaism as well as about his own cultural Graeco-Roman tradition.

The Implied Reader as God-fearer

Contemporary studies suggest there is one category of reader that fits this description—the God-fearer. The title refers to an attitude of reverence toward God, as in the old idiom of "a good, God-fearing person." Throughout Scripture, "fear of the Lord" characterizes the faith posture of the true Israelite. In Acts 9:31, Luke sketches a picture of the early church at peace, as it "was being built up and walked in the fear of the Lord." The title *God-fearer* then denotes due reverence toward a transcendent God. What is unusual in Acts of the Apostles is that the title is also given to gentiles. And that happens only here. Which is to say, the term is not unusual, but its *application* is.

The findings of critical discussions concerning the God-fearers can be summarized under three headings. First, the God-fearer is a socially prominent *gentile*, in a position of authority or influence. Second, the God-fearer is a *believer* in the one God—one who "fears" God. Third, and this is what most conspicuously defines the status, the God-fearer *does not convert* to Judaism. These three, then—gentile status, true belief, and non-conversion—provide us with three talking points for considering the reader inscribed and implied in the text of Luke–Acts.

1. The God-fearer is a Gentile.

The inscription at the head of the Gospel naming Theophilus calls him, "Most Excellent" (*kratistos*), an honorific shared by Luke only with Felix and Festus, the procurators of Judea (Acts 23:26; 24:3; 26:25). For the title to make sense, Luke implies that Theophilus is a gentile of considerable influence. In addition, he is associated with prominent Roman officials. This takes us some distance from the Markan point of view, with its resistance to the imperial occupation. These two procurators are not only gentiles in a prominent social position, but are exemplars of the ideological far extreme from the perspectives of the Gospels of Mark and Matthew, as their writings have been explored in empire studies. The Roman procurators are governors of the army that occupies the land, an army that had in fact destroyed Jerusalem and its temple. We get a preliminary glimpse of the dramatic reversal of viewpoints as we turn from the previous Gospels to this one.

Furthermore, both Luke and Acts name the same person. The implied reader of Luke–Acts, if a single person, as noted, fills the same profile. Joseph Tyson, after noting the rich information given in the text about Jewish tradition and the paucity of similar information provided the reader about gentile religious life, concludes,

> Thus, our implied reader would appear to be someone who has a limited knowledge of both pagan and Jewish religious practices, as well as an aversion to polytheism and the worship of humans. By contrast the reader seems to have an attraction to Jewish religious life but not an easy familiarity with all aspects of it. In terms of the implied reader's knowledge of religious practices, we can describe him as sympathetic with some significant Jewish beliefs and practices but not a full-fledged participant nor a fully integrated member of a Jewish community.[3]

Both inscribed and implied reader theories lead us to a hypothetical reader of Luke who is a prominent and cultured gentile, open to the revelation of Scripture and a friend of the synagogue. In Acts, the term *God-fearer* appears as a name for such a person. Similarly, the name *Theophilus* seems to move in that direction, insofar as *loving God* is not so far from *fearing God*.

2. The God-fearer is a believer in the one God.

Since *Theophilus* itself means "God-lover," this inscription might well describe any reader who picks up the work to learn from it. Furthermore, Theophilus is presented as being reassured in his faith ("so that you may realize the certainty of the teachings you have received"). However, such a

---

3. Tyson, *Images*, 34.

line of approach inevitably leads to a comparison with the similar designation, "God-fearer." If the name *Theophilus* is intended to be symbolic, as many think, then once again we have an indication that Luke has in mind as his reader a friendly gentile, one who is devout and can be addressed in language otherwise appropriate to faithful Jews.

Due to inscriptions found at ancient synagogues in the Mediterranean basin, along with extra-biblical literature, we know that the attribution of God-fearer to gentiles has an historical basis, apart from Luke's use of the term. And so the discussion of the God-fearers has turned toward their presence in the background of New Testament writing, particularly in light of the work of Paul. Studies investigating the title *God-fearer* as designating a class of persons in the first century have produced mixed results.

Extra-biblical instances of the term suggest a variety of reasons for being a God-fearer. For us, two representatives will serve. First, in their book, *In Search of Paul*, John Dominic Crossan and Jonathan Reed propose a theory of Paul's mission as "poaching" the God-fearers from the diaspora synagogues, angering the local Jews who depend on these gentile supporters for both financial and political benefits.[4]

Crossan and Reed depict a group of gentiles who are sympathizers of the synagogues. They are believers but haven't converted to Judaism, "not full Jews but no longer pure pagans."[5] "Through Acts, Luke not only speaks of 'Jews' and 'pagan gentiles,' but also of a third group, an in-between group who are both/and rather than either/or."[6] The reason given for non-Jews to associate themselves with the synagogue is ultimately a religious one: "Why were some pagans attracted enough to Judaism to be 'God-fearers' or 'God-worshipers'—semi-Jews by whatever name one chooses to call them? Apart from social, political, economic, or personal reasons, there was one very special religious factor. Greek and then Roman thinkers appreciated and admired Jewish aniconic monotheism, that is, the belief that there was but one transcendent and un-image-able divinity."[7] The key idea here is the opposition to idols—the aniconic tradition of Judaism. It is central to this view. A primary value of this study is to foreground the role of idol-rejection in the configuration of the God-fearer.

In contrast, Paula Fredriksen describes God-fearers as *pagans*. In *Paul: The Pagan's Apostle*, she bases this opinion on various extra-biblical literary examples, which present a different view of these gentile friends of the

---

4. Crossan and Reed, *In Search of Paul*.
5. Ibid., 16.
6. Ibid., 36.
7. Ibid., 25.

synagogue.⁸ Describing the major transformation that conversion to Judaism would require—adherence to the full law, she notes that religion in the ancient world was embedded in one's social identity and ancestral custom. "A pagan's 'becoming' a Jew in effect altered his past, reconfigured his ancestry, and cut his ties with his own patrimony, both human and divine."⁹ Consequently, Fredriksen prefers the concept of *inclusion* rather than *conversion* for those sympathetic gentiles who frequented and supported synagogues. Citing the presence of the term in various inscriptions on votive tablets and memorial steles, she notes, "These donor inscriptions provide us with glimpses of another population involved with Jewish communities: some of these synagogue benefactors were pagans."¹⁰ She also makes reference to examples of prominent Roman ladies, such as Julia Severa, Roman aristocrat, priestess of the imperial cult, and supporter of the synagogue in Acmonia, in Phrygia. These were synagogue friends, but not aniconic non-pagans. "Epigraphical 'god-fearers,'" in other words, may relate straightforwardly to "pious" pagans or Jews or (eventually) to Christians, rather than to the actively "cross-ethnic" pagans whom we meet here: gentiles who, as pagans, were involved (variously) with the Jewish community and thus with Jewish ancestral customs ("religion"). She also cites Josephus, who called Poppaea Sabina, Nero's consort, a "god-fearer" because, "though a pagan, she sympathized with Jewish causes."¹¹

3. *The God-fearer has not converted to Judaism.*

In Fredriksen's view, for this and similar instances, the God-fearers are sympathizers and friends of the synagogues who remained pagans, however, in the sense that they added Israel's God to their pantheon of deities without

---

8. Fredriksen, *Paul*.

9. Ibid., 54–55.

10. Ibid., 55. Also: "From Acmonia in Phrygia we learn about a contemporary of Paul's, Julia Severa. A Roman aristocrat as well as a priestess of the imperial cult, Julia built the *oikos* ("house," meaning synagogue) for Acmonia's Jews. Two centuries later, another wealthy Roman lady, Capitolina, epigraphically identified as a *theosebēs* ("God-fearer"), refurbished a synagogue interior in Tralles in Caria. Like Julia, she too came from a distinguished pagan family: Capitolina's father was the proconsul of Asia, her husband a Roman senator and a priest for life of Zeus Larasios. In nearby Aphrodisias, a Jewish inscription currently dated to the fourth or fifth century indexed benefactors by affiliation: some donors are born Jews, with Jewish names (Theodotos, Judas, Jesus); some are listed as "voluntary" Jews, that is, as "converts" (e.g., Samuel *prosēlytos*); and still others—fifty people, among whom are nine members of the city council—are given as "God-fearers" (*theosebeis*)" (55–56).

11. Ibid., 56.

abandoning the idols. They did not convert. Neither did they profess faith in one God alone. Non-conversion, then, is what sets these believers apart, whatever the quality of that belief. Non-conversion is the distinguishing mark of the God-fearer, while the rejection of idols remains uncertain.

In the literature the reasons given for not converting vary. A frequently encountered view is that circumcision was a serious difficulty for Roman citizens. At one level, there is the matter of the circumcised attending the public baths. The *Jewish Encyclopedia* notes, "Hellenistic and Roman culture found circumcision to be cruel and repulsive."[12] At another level, circumcision represented a considerable risk of serious infection before the discovery of antibiotics.

Such cultural motives are extended by a fuller notion of conversion, and what that meant in ancient times. In the ancient world, one's religion was a part of one's ethnicity, part of the social fabric of your community. Unheard of in the ancient world, conversion historically first appears, it seems, in relation to Judaism, which experienced a surge of growth in the post-exilic period.[13] Furthermore, "Forging an exclusive commitment to a foreign god, however—an act unique to Judaism in the pre-Christian period—was tantamount to changing ethnicity."[14] Elsewhere, Fredriksen explains, "Conversion accordingly meant ceasing traditional pagan worship altogether, thus cutting oneself out of the social and religious fabric of the ancient city. This was a serious and consequential step."[15] To reject your native heritage and adopt another was a matter for profound consideration. Conversion in our modern sense is a fresh reality, and what began in Judaism continued into Christianity, but with differences. This is the territory into which Luke takes us.

In terms of Luke's *inscribed reader* concerning conversion, the inscription regarding Theophilus, sharing his title with the procurators Felix and Festus most certainly indicates he was not a convert to Judaism. In fact, aligning him with the Roman procurators indicates a point of view that is diametrically opposed to that of Mark or Matthew. For them, the Roman was the unclean occupier of the land. Not so in Luke. We can connect this change of perspective to Luke's purpose for his project, and in turn to an explanation of the purpose stated in the prologue—"so that you may realize the certainty of the teachings you have received." Not only does Luke take the gospel beyond the Jewish community to the gentiles, but he takes

---

12. "Circumcision," *Jewish Encyclopedia*.
13. See, for instance, Blenkinsopp, *Isaiah 56–66*, 137.
14. Fredriksen, *Paul*, 54.
15. Fredriksen, *Jesus*, 130–31.

it to the far extreme of the gentile world as Judeans might perceive it—the structure of Roman authority. This move consequently would require some justification. The prologue provides that justification. Reworking Mark's text, Luke provides an assurance that the gospel can reach the most distant gentile.

As far as the *implied reader* is concerned, Fredriksen offers another reason for not converting. In her discussion of Paul's mission to the gentiles, she cites the eschatological vision of Judaism which looks forward to the fullness of time when the gentiles will abandon their idols and turn to the one true God. But, for the promise to be fulfilled, the gentiles must come to the final gathering *as gentiles,* and not as converts to Judaism. For the proselyte, the convert, would then be counted as Jewish. Among her examples is the diaspora Jew, Tobit, who prays on his deathbed for the fulfillment of the promises. Tobit prays: "All the nations of the world will turn and reverence God in truth; all will cast away their idols, which have deceitfully led them into error" (Tob 14:6). Fredriksen brings into her argument other testimonies, namely, the classical prophets (Isa 2:2–5; Zeph 3:9), *The Sibylline Oracle* (3.616, 716), as well as the "Aleinu" prayer recited at Jewish services.[16] For Paul, the argument runs, the gentiles must remain gentiles if the vision is to be fulfilled. It is for this reason he insists on refusing circumcision to the gentile followers of Christ, for then, circumcised, they would no longer be gentiles, and the promise would be void.

Paul's vision is apocalyptic, and, though Luke does not subscribe to Paul's apocalypticism, he does retain the broader commitment to eschatology. Jesus' invocation of Isaiah 61:1–3 in the Nazareth synagogue cites a text generally accepted as referring to the eschatological era. Concerning it, Jesus affirms, "Today this scripture passage is fulfilled in your hearing" (Luke 4:21). Thus it begins. But later we read, in the teaching about the destruction of the temple and city and the final times, that before all this the "times of the gentiles" must be fulfilled" (Luke 21:24). For Luke, it would appear, the final times have begun, but are by no means near their completion.

What these studies provide for us is a general image of a "God-fearer" as *a literate socially prominent gentile, a sympathizer and active supporter of the local synagogue.* However, and this is a defining note, this sympathizer *remains a gentile,* declining to convert to Judaism. Non-conversion sets this category of person apart from all others, Jews or gentiles. Furthermore, we can expect this to be a fair description of Theophilus, the reader inscribed in Luke's text. He too, whether a historical individual or a symbolic reader, can be described as a literate and prominent gentile, sympathetic to Judaism.

---

16. Ibid., 133.

However, we also recognize that the commitment of the God-fearer to exclusive belief in the one God—the *aniconic* monotheism of Judaism—is disputed today. In this, it is important to remind ourselves again that thus far we have been looking at studies in terms of extra-biblical historical categories, conducted for the purpose of understanding of Paul's ministry and letters. We are interested in what Luke intends by the term. While the historical information assists our understanding, it is basically supporting evidence for his literary perspective.

II. GENTILES IN THE TEXT

We now turn to the implied reader of Luke's text and how God-fearers enter into the narrative. If Luke's reader is a literate gentile who is a friend of the synagogue, yet not a convert, how would he read Luke's work? When we turn from the historical evidence of the God-fearers and interrogate Luke's text itself, what do we find?

More narrowly: How do the God-fearers read these passages. Or better: How do we read them with the eyes of the God-fearers. If we read with the eyes of Theophilus, what we see most notably in the text are *versions of himself*. An array of cameos—some called God-fearers (or God-worshipers), some simply meeting the description of the God-fearer—appear in Luke-Acts, as if to present a composite portrait. Despite some disputes, a roster of such "God-fearers" include the Gospel account of the Capernaum centurion (Luke 7:1–10), along with the series of figures in Acts of the Apostles: Ethiopian eunuch (8:26–40), Cornelius the centurion (10:1–49), Lydia (16:14–15), and Titus Justus (18:7). Read as an unfolding narrative, what does this sequence say to our reader?

The Centurion of Capernaum

The story of the Capernaum centurion (Luke 7:1–10) shows us a sympathetic gentile. He is not called a God-fearer, yet he fits the usual description. Luke shares this story with Matthew, clearly drawn from their shared source, the Q document. However, they treat it quite differently. Matthew 8:5–13 has the centurion himself coming to Jesus in Capernaum with a plea for him to restore his sick slave. But when Jesus volunteers to accompany him to his house, he demurs, with the famous line, "Lord, I am not worthy to have you come under my roof; but only speak the word, and my servant will be healed" (Matt 8:8). He supports his plea and deferral with a saying about his experience of possessing authority and his ability to recognize the authority of another. In response, Jesus effects the cure from a distance. Matthew then elaborates his account with lessons directed to his disciples concerning authority and faith. On the whole, Matthew's account is simple and direct.

In Luke's account things are more complicated. Luke adjusts the story by reporting two delegations, one of Jews and one of gentiles, each sent to Jesus with a message from the centurion. These adjustments make the point that the centurion is a friend of the synagogue, just as the typical profile of a God-fearer would have it. The delegation of Jews first urges Jesus to come, attesting that "he loves our people, and it is he who built our synagogue for us" (Luke 7:4). This is entirely in line with what we have learned about God-fearers. The second delegation, of friends—presumably gentiles, though that is not specified—meets him when he arrives at the house. They deliver another message, the one that Matthew's centurion delivers in person: "Lord, do not trouble yourself, for I am not worthy to have you come under my roof; therefore I did not presume to come to you. But only speak the word, and let my servant be healed" (Luke 7:6–7).

Here we have an account that threatens to undo itself. The two delegations cancel each other out. The Jews invite him to come, but when he comes, the gentiles ask him not to enter. And both are messages from the centurion himself. He invites *and* disinvites. The gentiles who carry his message of "no entry" undo the Jewish delegation's invitation to come to his house, which is now seen to be purposeless. His contradictory invitation represents his own sense of being called—the gentile centurion finds himself in a paradoxical position in which he is both invited and excluded. His blocking of Jesus reflects his own qualms about overcoming the blocks that he himself, as a gentile, faces. The sympathetic gentile reader would recognize not only the centurion's attachment to the synagogue, but also the frustration of being attracted and blocked at the same time.

In this position, his authority is also paradoxical, in that he can command others, but in contradictory ways. And yet the solution that Jesus brings to the situation overcomes the difficulties. Luke not only describes it with features of a God-fearer, but as one who finds the solution in Jesus— and, later, his movement. It is directly related to his faith in what Jesus can do. The centurion does not feel worthy to have him enter. But Jesus' authority can make up the difference.

While Luke's Gospel makes no mention of God-fearers, this centurion fits the description. His story presents both the dilemma of the God-fearer and the solution. However, it is in Acts of the Apostles that Luke provides the narrative that will fill out the meaning of the God-fearer in his work.

While the narrative presents the problem, it also suggests the answer to the problem. In this sense, it anticipates the narrative journey of Acts.

The Ethiopian Eunuch

In Acts 8:26–40, Philip encounters an Ethiopian pilgrim, a court eunuch, returning home from Jerusalem. The pilgrim is reading from the scroll of Isaiah, but he needs help in interpreting it. Philip provides that assistance.

It is not made clear whether this Ethiopian was a Jew or gentile, a convert or a sympathizer.[17] We learn that he came to Jerusalem to worship. It was the temple, of course, that made Jerusalem a site for pilgrimage. But what would be his experience in Jerusalem? A gentile would be allowed to enter the outer court of the gentiles. If the Ethiopian is not a Jew, the prohibition would be a reminder of his outsider status. And the Ethiopian is not only a foreigner, but also a eunuch, it is even more doubtful that he would be able to worship at the temple. So why did the Ethiopian go to Jerusalem? Again we find contradictory directives. The eunuch made a pilgrimage to the temple, where he cannot enter, and is now reading the scriptures, which he cannot interpret. At this stage of Luke's narrative, the eunuch again represents the plight of the God-fearer. Once more Luke has complicated an account so that the story fights against itself. He is called, and yet he is blocked. Like the Capernaum centurion, we have someone who is attracted to the Jewish revelation but is stymied in his desire.

This reader of scripture is devoted enough to have obtained his own scrolls, which in this case, as in the quotation, would be the Greek Septuagint. His attraction to the Septuagint represents the synagogue experience of the God-fearer. However, the meaning of the text eludes him. He is reading from the Book of Isaiah, and Philip arrives just in time to interpret

---

17. The Ethiopian in Acts 8:26–40 is not identified in the text as a gentile or a Jewish convert. The commentators are divided on this. See, for instance, Fitzmyer, *Acts*, 410–11. The main problem exegetes have with viewing the Ethiopian as a gentile is that the storyline that leads up to Cornelius, the major example of mission to the gentiles, would be short-circuited. Furthermore, if this were the actual narrative announcement of the inclusion of gentiles, why would a minor character like Philip get the glory? As Peter notes in Acts 15:7, he is the one through whom the revelation comes. Fitzmyer (speaking of Cornelius): "The spread of the Word to the gentiles, however, begins only in chap. 10 with Peter's evangelization of them and in the conversion of Cornelius, after the call of Saul, 'a chosen instrument of mine to carry my name before gentiles,' has been narrated" (410). The position taken here, however, is that neither this story nor that of Cornelius counts as the beginning of the storyline of release from identity markers, but rather that the story of the God-fearer begins with the first chapters of the Gospel.

its mysterious message for him. The passage in question is Isaiah 53:7–8, quoted from the Septuagint.

> Like a sheep he was led to the slaughter,
> and as a lamb before its shearer is silent,
> so he opened not his mouth.
> In [his] humiliation justice was denied him.
> Who will tell of his posterity?
> For his life is taken from the earth.
> [because of the iniquities of my people he was led to death.]

Philip interprets the passage for him, showing him how it points to Jesus. While we rightfully understand that this particular passage serves Luke's theological purposes, we might also ask if he did not see rhetorical value in the eunuch reading this particular passage.[18] As indicated by the bracketed line above, Luke's quotation stops short of the last line—the line that would best serve Philip's Christological interpretation. Instead, it concludes with the thought that his life is taken away from him. Does this name the humiliation of the eunuch as well? The problem for the eunuch is that he has no place in the historical narrative of God's people, since he has no offspring to continue his story—" . . . the nation in the future would not include their seed."

Luke wants his reader to remember another passage from the Book of Isaiah. In Isaiah 56:3–7, foreigners and eunuchs are specifically identified as being admitted to the temple in the fullness of time.

> The foreigner joined to the Lord should not say,
> "The Lord will surely exclude me from his people";
> Nor should the eunuch say,
> "See, I am a dry tree."
> To the eunuchs who keep my sabbaths . . .
> I will give them, in my house
> and within my walls, a monument and a name
> Better than sons and daughters . . .
> And foreigners who join themselves to the Lord,
> to minister to him . . .
> Them I will bring to my holy mountain
> and make them joyful in my house of prayer;
> Their burnt offerings and their sacrifices
> will be acceptable on my altar,
> for my house shall be called
> a house of prayer *for all peoples.*

---

18. As cited in *Jewish Study Bible*, 896, commenting on Isaiah 56:4.

The convergence of the story of the Ethiopian eunuch and the passage from Isaiah 56 suggests Luke intends to speak of overcoming prohibition. He is blocked, both at the temple and in the scripture, but Philip opens the scripture by way of Jesus. In this regard, this passage finds its antecedent in the promise made in the synagogue in Nazareth, at Luke 4:21—he said to them, "Today this scripture passage is fulfilled in your hearing." The sympathetic gentile again would identify with the predicament of the eunuch, although there is no indication the eunuch is a God-fearer, or even a gentile.

At that point the eunuch is baptized at his request. Elsewhere in Acts, baptism is reserved to Jews and God-fearers. In his baptism, the eunuch finds his difficulty resolved. Coming at this point in Luke's narrative, the baptism of the Ethiopian eunuch anticipates a solution for what has not yet been developed fully in the unfolding account. While there are parallels between this story and the Gospel account of the Capernaum centurion, especially in the way of exemplifying the frustration of the non-Jewish believer, the narrative locations differ. The Gospel story of the Capernaum centurion provides the whole in a nutshell—difficulty and solution; the episodes of Acts unfold in a dramatic storyline, which begins with this eunuch. Questions are raised, leading up to the story of Cornelius. With this story, the stage is set for the unfolding drama of Acts and the gentile reader.

The Centurion Cornelius, and the Language of "God Fearing"

Told in exceptional length and detail, the story of Cornelius signals its importance to Luke's narrative project. Initial scenes of Cornelius being visited by an angel and Peter being given a vision indicating all foods are clean generate the action. As in the case of the Capernaum centurion's encounter and the Ethiopian's request to be baptized, Cornelius is presented as the initiator. But, in this case, we are not told what Cornelius wants or even if he knows why the mandated meeting is to take place.[19] The two come together at Cornelius' house in Caesarea Maritima. The essential action takes place there, with Peter's decisive proclamation: "In truth, I see that God shows no partiality. Rather, in every nation whoever fears him and acts uprightly is acceptable to him" (10:34–35). In that word, *acceptable,* we detect an allusion to the similar emphasis in the programmatic Lukan scene of Jesus in the Nazareth synagogue (Luke 4:19, 24). Now it is being fulfilled.

---

19. However, note Peter's statement in 11:14, where the motive is given—"your household will be saved."

With that, Peter delivers his customary resurrection *kerygma* speech,[20] followed by the Spirit visiting the household of Cornelius in a version of the Pentecostal experience. Peter then concludes that nothing stands in the way of his baptizing them, which he does. The story does not end with chapter 10, however, since Peter is required to return to Jerusalem and explain to the community why he did as he did. The account concludes with everyone, including the circumcision supporters, agreeing to this move. They make a general pronouncement: "God has then granted life-giving repentance to the gentiles too."

With that affirmation, we notice something peculiar about Cornelius's drama. It combines two plots. We can call it the story of the *Vision* and the *Visit*. The Vision, recounted again in the explanation Peter gives in chapter 11, concerns food laws. The Visit, begun with a message from an angel, concerns Jews mixing with gentiles. While Peter's vision serves to establish that all *foods* are clean (10:15), this is not explicitly applied to the household of Cornelius. Rather, an analogous lesson is drawn, that all *persons* are clean (10:28, 35).

The link between the two is tenuous, not made explicitly until 11:2–3. When Peter returns to Jerusalem, the charge leveled against him makes the connection between the two: "You entered the house of uncircumcised people and *ate with them*" (11:3). Which is to say, that Peter joined their meal, rather than they being required to conform to his practices. Peter defends himself by citing the Pentecostal visit of the Spirit upon the family: "If then God gave them the same gift he gave to us when we came to believe in the Lord Jesus Christ, who was I to be able to hinder God?" (11:17).

Luke's reading is clearly about ritual purity. That is the message behind the vision establishing that all foods are clean. But purity issues were already a concern with the eunuch. There we saw that ritual prohibitions kept the foreigner in the outer court of the temple. But now, at least initially, those ritual prohibitions are encountered in the context of food laws. Considerable energy is devoted to this point, with the elaborate vision followed by three invitations to take and eat, and three refusals. "But Peter said, "Certainly not, sir. For never have I eaten anything profane and unclean" (10:14).[21]

But upon arrival at the household of Cornelius, Peter testifies not to food, but to the persons gathered there: "Then Peter proceeded to speak

---

20. The *kerygma* pattern shapes Peter's speeches in Acts—2:22–36; 3:11–20; 4:10–12; 5:30–32; 10:36–43. The *kerygma*, or "proclamation," has the character of an early credal formula, used by Luke to provide Peter with an appropriate announcement for his resurrection witness.

21. This is despite the problematic cleanness of Simon the Tanner, who is mentioned three times.

and said, 'In truth, I see that God shows no partiality. Rather, in every nation whoever fears him and acts uprightly is acceptable to him'" (10:34–35). This is not only the third instance of the mention of fearing God, but it also contains a key word—*acceptable*—that links back to the synagogue reading of Jesus in Nazareth (Luke 4:19, 24). The main point is that the primary issue addressed is *purity laws*, not *food laws*.

Luke amply buttresses this momentous turning point. Three kinds of authorization are brought to bear. (1) The visions of Cornelius and Peter establish the divine initiative for the event. (2) In addition, the coming of the Spirit on the family connects the event to the overall narrative program of Luke-Acts.[22] The example of John's baptism, contrasted with that of the Spirit through Jesus (Acts 10:47; 11:16) and the connection with the initial Pentecostal event both present this story as integral in fulfilling the narrative program of this author. (3) Finally, the confirmation of the Apostolic Council, both in the report of Peter in Jerusalem (Acts 11:18), as well as in the Apostolic Council (Acts 15:7–8), seal the occasion with the official approval of the community.

Cornelius is emphatically presented as a believer who prays to God and to whom God is willing to send an angel. The baptism of Cornelius and his household brings his part of the story to a conclusion. It aligns him with the Ethiopian, also baptized. But it also brings him into the fold of those multitudes mentioned in Acts 2:41, 47; 4:4; 6:1, and so forth. Those, however, were Jews, many of the Diaspora. Now, however, we unambiguously have a non-Jew incorporated into the community of believers in Jesus.

God-fearers in Luke's Text

With the story of Cornelius, the language of *God-fearing* becomes explicit. Although it is first used here, we find it does not end here. Luke's use of the term brings synonyms into play, and that development will involve the accounts of the two other explicit gentile believers in the text—Lydia and Titus Justus.

Three times (10:2, 22, 35) the centurion is described as "God-fearing," in each case accompanied by supplementary terms —"devout" (*eusebēs*, 10:2) and "righteous" (*díkaios*, 10:22, 35). In other words, the term is being defined as equivalent to worship of God and righteous living. Each of these has a fuller career. "Worshiper" continues in this book of Acts; "righteousness," as we shall see in chapter two, defines the repentant in the Gospel. The term appears again, in Paul's preaching in Pisidian Antioch (13:16, 26), as

---

22. See Moessner, "Appeal and Power of Poetics (Luke 1:1–4)," 84–123.

part of his address to his hearers. After that, other terms and other language serve the narrative.

In this chapter, another term is introduced—*worshiper* (*sébomai*, 13:43, 50), which will continue in the subsequent narrative, as Paul visits the cities in his itinerary. In Philippi (16:14), Thessalonica (17:4), and Athens (17:17), Paul encounters Israelites and non-Israelite "worshipers," who are the equivalent of the God-fearers mentioned earlier. They are identified by worshiping the one God, but not converting to Judaism. These two features set them apart from everyone else. They are devoted to the one God, and yet they do not convert. They are unique.

What we see in the text so far is that the term *God-fearer* is restricted to the speech of the *characters* in the narrative. The one exception is the initial introduction of the term in Acts 10:2, as a description of Cornelius. After this, the *narrative voice* prefers the more conventional term, *worshiper*, with the understanding that this refers to non-Jews who worship the one God. Along with this understanding, a scattering of references to *prominent* people among them, typically women (13:50; 17:4, 12), confirms the picture of the God-fearer as a person of some status, and of some benefit, financial or influential, to the synagogue community.

This in turn gives way to an even simpler reference, *Jews and Greeks*, likely reflecting the views of the author, which clearly intends the same coupling of Israelites and gentile worshipers, but in a convenient format. This term already appears at the event at Antioch Pisidia (14:1) and continues into the later mission of Paul at Thessalonica (17:4) and finally, Ephesus (18:4; 19:17). Along the way, the inclusion of Timothy in the mission allows mention of his father as a Greek (16:1, 3), helping to identify what Luke understands by the term.

Mapping this in a chart helps show how the concept unfolds in the narrative:

Pericope	God-fearers	Worshipers	Prominent w/m	Jews & Greeks
Cornelius	10:2, 22, 35			
Antioch Pisidia	13:16, 26	13:43, 50	13:50	
Iconium				14:1
Philippi		16:1 (Lydia)		
Thessalonica		17:4	17:4	17:4
Beroea			17:12	
Athens		17:17		

| Corinth | | 18:7 (Titus) | | |
| Ephesus | | | | 18:4; 19:10, 17 |

Some conclusions: The Cornelius episode follows upon the predicament illustrated by the Ethiopian eunuch, and before that the Capernaum centurion of Luke 7. At this point, the language of *God-fearing* becomes an explicit title for the gentile believers who are friends of the synagogue. Notably, only five instances of the term occur in Acts, all uttered by characters in the narrative except for the first, at 10:2, where the narrator introduces it to the reader.

The event in Antioch Pisidia consolidates this and moves the idea to a new vocabulary item—God *worshipers*. The missionary excursion into Pisidia, shared by Paul and Barnabas, effects the transition (Acts 13–14). This term is favored by the narrator, as opposed to *God-fearers*. Worship implies a commitment to the one God. It suggests that while others use the designation *God-fearer*, this narrative would prefer *God-worshiper*. Paul's speech in Pisidian Antioch is transitional between Peter's encounter with Cornelius in Acts 10 and Paul's own mission to Greece, which will follow in Acts 16–20.

A subsidiary term refers to *prominent* women and men. This suggests a social class for the God-fearers, whose support for the synagogues proves to be significant. It fills out the picture of the God-fearer/worshiper as a person of some influence, signaled by the company he keeps.

The final set, *Jews and Greeks*, appears to be shorthand for the terms that preceded it. The synagogue, as far as Luke is concerned, is home to Jews, the proper adherents, along with certain "Greeks," or God-fearers. Beginning with Lydia's story, the term becomes a convenient reference, useful later, in Paul's mission to Greece (Acts 16–20). As we will note, it charts the move from synagogue to house (and eventually lecture hall) as Paul's typical venue.

Lydia, of Philippi, and the Pagans

According to Acts, Paul's first stop, in today's Europe, is in Macedonia, at the Roman colony of Philippi. Perhaps there was no synagogue in Philippi, since that Sabbath Paul heads to a "place of prayer," which he suspects to be on the riverbank. There he encounters Lydia, a "worshiper of God." Lydia is described as "a dealer in purple cloths," implying that she ran a business that catered to wealthy customers, including royalty. She would seem to be a person of some wealth herself, insofar as she is in a position to provide hospitality to Paul and his entourage.

Encounters with Lydia, in Luke's narrative arrangement, provide a positive frame to the other events taking place at Philippi. Lydia welcomes Paul to Philippi (Acts 16:14–15) and sends him on his way at the end of his stay there (16:40). In between, events include an impulsive exorcism of a demon from a slave girl (16:16–18) and the outrage of her owners (16:19). Tellingly, the demon in the girl keeps announcing "These men are slaves of the Most High God, who are proclaiming to you the way of salvation" (16:17). This event echoes a Gospel motif, in which the demons announce the identity of Jesus, only to be rebuked by him. Here the trope serves to bring into explicit expression the authentic faith in the one God, contrasting Lydia with the pagans. Paul's command invokes Jesus: "But Paul, becoming greatly annoyed and turning around, said to the spirit, 'I command you in the name of Jesus Christ to come out of her!'" (16:18).

The narrative of the subsequent jailing of Paul and Silas (16:19–24) and deliverance from prison, including the baptism of the jailer (16:25–39), is extended and elaborate. Along with Silas, Paul is jailed, after being beaten with rods. In the night, an earthquake provides the opportunity to escape, but they do not. The jailer, believing they have, despairs for his life. After Paul and Silas call out that they have not left, he bows to them in gratitude and asks to be saved. The result is that he and his household are baptized, and he takes Paul and Silas to his house for a meal. And "and with his household he rejoiced at having come to faith in God" (16:34).

The next day, the magistrates give orders that Paul should be released, but Paul objects to their treatment. We discover for the first time that Paul is a Roman citizen. It is not clear why, apart from narrative purposes, he did not reveal this before he was beaten and jailed. Paul demands the magistrates come in person and deliver them from their confinement. The two then stop at Lydia's house before leaving the town.

God-worshipers and the Pagans

The Philippi incident is one of three accounts that describe a pattern. In the first, the missionaries have an encounter with pagans that does not turn out well. Paul and Barnabas are shown in Lystra dealing with the aftermath of Paul's restoration of a crippled man who was afflicted from birth (14:8–20). The pagans respond by hailing Barnabas and Paul as Zeus and Hermes walking among them. Paul protests and begins to preach the one God:

"We proclaim to you good news that you should turn from these *idols* [worthless things][23] to the living God, 'who made heaven and earth and sea and all that is in them.' In past generations he allowed all gentiles to go their own ways; yet, in bestowing his goodness, he did not leave himself without witness, for he gave you rains from heaven and fruitful seasons, and filled you with nourishment and gladness for your hearts" (14:15–17).

The account sharply distinguishes the truth of the one God from the chaotic world of pagan idols. The lesson for Paul and Barnabas is that faith in God needs to be established first, before the further invitation of becoming a follower of Jesus, the risen one, can be extended.

The second instance is this moment in Philippi. Lydia, a worshiper of God, is placed in vivid contrast to the world of pagan idols. Luke insists on the aniconic faith of the God-fearer in "the living God." The entire narrative of the time in Philippi makes this case, but especially in the encounter with the demon-possessed slave girl and her owners. Paul's interaction with the jailer involves three elements of interest—faith in the one God, belief in the Lord Jesus, and baptism. When the jailer asked what he should do to be saved, Paul and Silas responded: "Believe in the Lord Jesus and you and your household will be saved." Later, he took them to his house, where he and his family were baptized. Finally, he and his household "rejoiced at having come to faith in God" (16:34). Merged in the story, these three are later distinguished in Acts when Paul comes to Athens. There faith in God will emerge as a requirement for belief in Jesus. But here the faith in God is presumed, included at the end as a component of the event.

The third instance, occurring at Athens, clarifies the distinction between pagans and God-worshipers. Here we find Paul making a program of the impromptu speech at Lystra. This episode is famous for Paul's decision to depart from his usual message, namely, the good news of the risen Messiah. Instead, appalled at the number of idols in the city, he decides to preach the more basic message of the one God. But this follows a period of time when "he debated in the synagogue with the Jews and with the worshipers [God-fearers], and daily in the public square with whoever happened to be there" (17:17). After this, Paul makes a major speech in the Areopagus, focused entirely on the one God, without mentioning, until the end, the message about Jesus, the risen Christ. The hearers have first to be believers in God—that is, the equivalent to God-fearers—before the message about Jesus can be delivered to them.

---

23. "Worthless things," often translated "idols" (14:15); elsewhere the actual word appears: Acts 7:41; 15:20, 29; 17:16; 21:25.

The consequence of this set of episodes is that the encounter with idols is placed in contrast to the God-fearers, or God-worshipers, here represented by Lydia. Whatever the historical status of the God-fearers, prominent gentiles in contact with the synagogues, Luke clearly portrays them as faithful believers in the one God. While historical records can show God-fearers as sympathetic to Judaism, though reluctant to break with the customs and rituals of their pagan upbringing, for Luke they are God-*worshipers*, having abandoned idols for the "aniconic" God of Judaism.

Titus Justus, of Corinth, and [the Move Beyond] the Synagogues

Titus Justus is the last gentile "worshiper" that Luke mentions explicitly. He repeats the hospitality of Lydia, but, putting it to new purpose, he provides a venue for Paul to shift his preaching away from the synagogue. With this, a new series begins, ending in the "lecture hall of Tyrannus" (19:9). While the pattern of moving from the synagogue to an alternative site is not evidenced in the Pauline letters; it is a theme in Acts, helping to shape Luke's larger narrative project.

We read that upon leaving Philippi, Paul follows the main routes, visiting primary cities. First Thessalonica, followed by Beroea, Athens, and then Corinth. From Corinth he will go to Ephesus. Throughout, the God-fearers remain part of the story. But it is in Corinth that we encounter another person explicitly named as such. When Paul encounters opposition in his Sabbath discussions in the synagogue, he leaves that location for the house of Titus Justus, who lived next to the synagogue and is described as "a worshiper of God" (Acts 18:7). We do not learn much more about him, except that his hospitality shown to Paul reminds us of Lydia.

However, in this case the offer is not of a place to stay, but rather a place to preach, in lieu of the local synagogue:

> When Silas and Timothy came down from Macedonia, Paul began to occupy himself totally with preaching the word, testifying to the Jews that the Messiah was Jesus. When they opposed him and reviled him, he shook out his garments and said to them, "Your blood be on your heads! I am clear of responsibility. From now on I will go to the gentiles." So he left there and went to a house belonging to a man named Titus Justus, a worshiper of God; his house was next to a synagogue (18:5–7).

This shift is part of a larger pattern in this section of Acts, in which Paul is gradually leaving behind the synagogue to turn to other venues. It is shown in Luke's tagline, "discussing in the synagogue" (*dielègeto én te sunagōgē*), which he uses to describe Paul's activity in the cities he visits—Thessalonica (17:2), Athens (17:17), Corinth (18:4), and Ephesus (18:19).

17:2	discussing in the synagogue—Thessalonica (Titus Justus)
17:17	discussing in the synagogue—Athens
18:4	discussing in the synagogue—Corinth
18:19	discussing in the synagogue—Ephesus
19:8	discussing in the synagogue—Ephesus (on a later date), to . . .
19:9	discussing in the lecture hall of Tyrannus—Ephesus

This pattern sets up a pattern that finds a fulfillment later in Ephesus. In Acts 19:8–9, Luke describes Paul's activity in the synagogue in these typical terms (v. 8). But in the next verse, after meeting opposition, Paul shifts the base of his operations. Now he is "discussing" in the lecture hall of Tyrannus, signaling the completion of a pattern first seen with the description of the God-fearer, Lydia.[24]

However, there is no indication outside of Acts that moving from synagogue to alternative sites was the historical practice of Paul. We see that this pattern serves Luke's purpose: a rhetorical figure for his larger narrative. The shift, depicted as accomplished in Ephesus, is a key moment in the larger movement of Acts, facilitating, at this point, its program of moving out to the gentiles. Furthermore, the God-fearers are shown to have an important role in this larger movement. With Titus Justus, then, we see a "God-worshiper" who signals a new move in the direction of Luke's story. Where Lydia, who provided Paul with a place to stay, dramatizes the contrast of the worshiper with the pagans who revered idols, Titus Justus helps to initiate the move to the gentile world by providing Paul with a place to preach.

Conclusions

The survey of the God-fearers *in the text* produces certain findings. Each of the God-fearing figures in the series makes a specific contribution to the larger meaning of the narrative.

24. "He entered the synagogue, and for three months debated boldly with persuasive arguments (*dialegomenos*) about the kingdom of God. But when some in their obstinacy and disbelief disparaged the Way before the assembly, he withdrew and took his disciples with him and began to hold daily discussions (*dialegomenos*) in the lecture hall of Tyrannus" (Acts 19:8–9).

- The Capernaum centurion (Luke 7): An implied God-fearer personifies both the predicament and the solution that is dramatized in Acts. Invited but blocked, the centurion finds his difficulties solved by Jesus.
- Ethiopian eunuch (Acts 8): The dramatization of the obstacles of the God-fearer (or the gentile, or the foreigners and eunuch) begins here. It picks up the predicament on the Capernaum centurion in Luke 7 and moves it to the drama that will unfold in Acts. The baptism of the eunuch illustrates the solution to his problem. However, the meaning of this is yet to be played out in the narrative.
- Cornelius (Acts 10–11): The language of *God fearing* is introduced to the narrative. The story addresses the purity laws that represent barriers encountered by the gentiles. But it is extended to an invitation to the gentiles in general. The theme of the promise is extended: the gentiles *as gentiles* will be part of the promise.
- Lydia (Acts 16): The God-fearer contrasts with the pagan. For Luke, the God-fearer is not a pagan, as the historical record may prefer. The God-fearer's devotional side has already been presented in Cornelius. But the point here is that the pagan is someone different entirely and that Paul does not go to them. The point is made through three episodes—the healing of a cripple in Lystra, the exorcism of the slave girl in Lydia's town of Philippi, and the preaching of Paul in Athens. In this set, the term *idols* seems to be important.
- Titus Justus (Acts 18): While this brief mention builds on the Lydia story, it also introduces a new theme—the transfer of Paul's preaching from the synagogue to the lecture hall. This can be demonstrated with the sequence of "reasoning [discussing] in the synagogue."

In this way, each of the figures in this series in Acts offers a chance to open up the narrative in a different way.

More generally, we have a clearer picture of what Luke means by his God-fearers and God-worshipers, and how they may impact the reader. First, Luke's God-fearer is a believer, not a pagan. The point is made emphatically with the dramatic contrast occurring in the Lydia sequence (Acts 16) and elaborated on in the various accounts of pagans with their idols. This aniconic devotion is also indicated by the title *worshiper* favored by the narrator, as opposed to that of *God-fearer,* attributed to the characters within the narrative. Language accompanying these critical terms—devout, righteous, etc.—also underline the authenticity of the devotion of the gentiles singled out here.

Unlike Fredriksen's reconstruction in his historical version Crossan and Reed's view of Luke's God-fearer is not as a pagan, since he has put aside idols and exhibits a laudable devotion to the one God. Further, this God-fearer believes in the aniconic God of the Jews. However, Crossan and Reed seem to represent Luke's particular take on it, rather than that of the historical record, as Fredriksen has demonstrated. The Crossan and Reed reconstruction depends heavily on Luke, but disregards the program behind the narrative freedom of Luke. An important instance is the shift from synagogue to lecture hall as a feature of Luke's narrative, but this shift is not noted in the historical record.

Luke presents the God-fearer as one who wishes to join the faith community; that is, the God-fearer is attracted to the faith community, but does not join it. He is devout and does what he can without joining the community. He frequents the synagogue, where he hears the narrative of God's people, as provided in the Greek translation. He identifies to some extent with this narrative, but he remains outside of it. The reader recognizes this predicament or situation and finds himself in the same quandary as the God-fearer. The Lukan text provides an entry into the narrative he wishes to join.

The narrative of the God-fearers in Acts demonstrates a process of entering the narrative by way of a growing involvement. Two major movements can be discerned. First, the outsider comes inside. The Capernaum centurion and the Egyptian eunuch find themselves outside the faith community, wishing to be inside. With Cornelius, the gentile is brought inside, by way of his commitment to the risen Christ. This movement suggests that the goal of the God-fearer is to find an avenue of entry into "salvation." It implies a narrative program of *joining* the community of Judaism, rather than *replacing* it. In a second move into the narrative, the one-time bystander is given an active role. With Lydia, we find a God-worshiper who provides hospitality, contributing to the welfare of Paul and his friends. But with Titus Justus, we find the God-worshiper actually providing an alternative venue for preaching, using his position in the synagogue, but also peripheral to it, to take the movement beyond the synagogue to the wider world.

Finally, it must be noted that the most prominent God-fearers in Acts (and the only one in the Gospel) are Roman centurions. If the main God-fearers are officers in the occupying army of Rome, this implies an inversion of the postcolonial perspective of Mark.

CHAPTER TWO

Luke's Challenge to the Reader
"Have You No Fear of God?"

IN HIS PROLOGUE, LUKE provides Theophilus with assurances. He has been instructed in certain matters, and Luke's document serves to support that instruction.

> I too have decided, having carefully investigated everything from the beginning, to write it down in an orderly sequence for you, most excellent Theophilus, so that you may *know the certainty of the things you have been taught* (1:3–4).

And yet, Luke's fuller text includes challenge as well as confirmation. In addition to the expressed announcement that his reader is secure in decisions already made, the Gospel text also issues a call to repentance, a note of invitation to further choices as yet undecided. So we have a counter to any suspicion that Luke is making it easy for the God-fearer, simply removing obstacles to conversion. For although "people will come from the east and the west and from the north and the south and will recline at table in the kingdom of God," this announcement is coupled with an admonition, "Strive to enter through the narrow door" (Luke 13:24, 29).

The Apostle Paul famously pushed back against those who claimed that he was preaching an easy gospel ("seeking favor") in arguing against circumcision for the gentile converts (Gal 1:10; 5:11).[1] A similar accusation

---

[1] "It would be quite natural for missionaries, who were themselves devout Jews, to draw the conclusion that someone who was preaching faith in the Jewish Messiah Jesus to gentiles, but without making clear the covenant obligations of that faith, was guilty of softening or cheapening the gospel," Dunn, *Galatians*, 49.

can be leveled against Luke's program. The signature trait of our God-fearing gentile is the decision not to convert to Judaism. And this in turn raises certain questions. The removal of the Jewish practices of circumcision and kosher food laws is a prominent part of Luke's narrative in Acts, but affects his Gospel as well. If he is removing prescriptions of the Law from required practice, he must be choosing an easy path for gentile God-fearers.

I. SCENARIOS OF REPENTANCE

The presentation of God-fearers shows us how Luke pictures the gentile believer, the God-fearer, and this has implications for his reader. The God-fearer in Luke's text exhibits a profound devotion to the one God. This is not a friend of the synagogue who remains a pagan. Meanwhile, the signature trait of this God-fearing gentile is the failure to convert to Judaism.

However, it is not the case that Luke makes no demands of the believing God-fearer, and the key is repentance. The portrait series of God-fearers in Acts is set off against another in Luke's Gospel, also found only in Luke, which describes certain scenarios that suggest a set of demands made on the believing reader. There we find certain *figures of repentance*—an unnamed repentant woman who washes Jesus' feet with her tears (Luke 7:36–50), the prodigal son (Luke 15:11–32), Zacchaeus the tax collector (Luke 19:1–10), and the "good thief" (Luke 23:39–43). These scenarios conclude with a signal to the God-fearing reader, as the good thief rebukes his fellow criminal: "*Have you no fear of God . . . ?*" (Luke 23:40).

In addition, the four figures of repentance are paired and contrasted, directly or implicitly, with a *foil* who remains unrepentant: the unnamed repentant woman and Simon the Pharisee (Luke 7), the prodigal son and the other son (Luke 15), Zacchaeus and the parable of the Pharisee and tax collector (Luke 19, 18), and the good thief and the other thief (Luke 23). The lesson of repentance is configured in the picture of its absence as much as in the positive figures representing it. These moments lead to a change of life for the persons involved. For the God-fearer, then, non-conversion to Judaism is replaced by another experience very much like it, presented as constitutive for the follower of Jesus—repentance.

A Nameless Repentant Woman and Simon the Pharisee (Luke 7:36–50)

The first of the four repentance scenarios is found in Luke 7:36–50—the story of a woman who washes Jesus' feet with her tears. The story has similarities with the account of Jesus' "anointing" at the beginning of Passion Week, found in all the other Gospels, but missing in Luke's; thus this is this author's version of the story. While the woman commands our attention here, the story is also about Simon the Pharisee. In fact, the text devotes most of its time to Simon the Pharisee; albeit he is discussing the action of the woman with Jesus, including a parable about love and forgiveness. It is helpful to see how the narrative is apportioned to each of the main characters.

7:36	Invitation to the meal
7:37–38	The woman washes Jesus' feet with her tears and dries them with her hair.
7:39–47	Jesus speaks at length with the Pharisee.
7:48–50	Jesus pronounces forgiveness to the woman, worrying the guests.

The narrative of the woman consists of only four verses (7:37, 38, 48, 50). However, her action is the topic of the ensuing conversation between Jesus and the Pharisee.

Simon's invitation to Jesus is not followed by the courtesies that would be expected of a host. One gets the impression that Jesus was invited to provide entertainment for Simon's other guests. The woman repairs the failed courtesies by washing Jesus' feet. In a way, just as Jesus was a display for Simon (for his guests), so the woman is a display for Jesus (for Simon). The brief parable is delivered during the exchanges between Jesus and Simon, drawing a lesson contrasting small and large love. The parable addressed to Simon elicits the correct answer.

41	Two people were in debt to a certain creditor; one owed five hundred days' wages and the other owed fifty.
42	Since they were unable to repay the debt, he forgave it for both. Which of them will love him more?"
43	Simon said in reply, "The one, I suppose, whose larger debt was forgiven."

The exchange enters the narrative as an illustration of the parenthetical verse found in the story just preceding. In 7:29–30 we read:

> All the people who listened, including the tax collectors, and who were baptized with the baptism of John, acknowledged the righteousness of God; but the Pharisees and scholars of the law (*nomikoi*), who were not baptized by him, rejected the plan of God for themselves.

The two parties are distinguished by their willingness to listen to John. The Pharisees and the scholars of the law (*nomikoi*) are identified as not calling for baptism, not feeling the need. Their sense of well-being and their standing before God is satisfactory—or, in a word, they are righteous, having achieved that righteousness on their own merit. John's baptism of repentance is the criterion. As the principle is enacted in the story of Simon and the woman, his claim to virtue becomes a detriment, since he believes he has nothing for which to be forgiven, and therefore he cannot enter the community of the forgiven. But the nameless woman receives approval.

This account is not so much a story of conversion as it is a story of repentance. Simon is a negative example of one who resists repentance. The unnamed woman repents, but we do not learn about a life change on her part. Jesus simply tells her, "Your sins are forgiven." Repentance is presented as a change of state, perhaps internally, but not a conversion.

The Prodigal Son and His Older Brother (15:11–32)

Again we have a parable—perhaps the best known parable in this Gospel. Two brothers are set in contrast—the repentant prodigal is approved over the obedient elder brother. In this case, the contrast is between two kinds of response to the father's love. As before, the one who has a clear sense of a need for repentance is promoted over the one who does not, not recognizing any need to do so. The compliant brother is denied the opening into self-awareness experienced by the prodigal in his debasement. A consistent pattern so far is the assumption of virtue blinding one to the need to repent. The older brother justifies his anger by referring to his own record. "Look, all these years I served you and not once did I disobey your orders . . . " (15:29). Here we have an explicit appeal to merit, in the form of obedience and fidelity. The other son bases his claim on the dutiful actions which amount to a ledger of righteousness. On the other hand, the prodigal places himself entirely upon his father's mercy.

The introduction to the chapter is a narrative setting for the parable (along with the Sheep and the Coin):

15:1	Now all the tax collectors and the sinners were drawing near to hear him.
15:2	And both the Pharisees and the scribes were complaining, saying, "This man welcomes sinners and eats with them!"

We learn that the contrast of Pharisees and sinners, established in the previous instances, still holds. What is added to the record is the statement of the elder brother, which details his rectitude. His statement makes the case for virtuous action; however, it fails to move him to repentance.

Although the parable suggests a life-change on the part of the prodigal, it does not talk about that. The focus is on the comparative receptiveness of the two brothers. One is open, one is not. The difference between the two is their relative set of experiences. The prodigal in his exploration has reached the far end of his resources and found an abyss. The elder brother has not; thus he maintains his proper behavior, expecting a reward for that. The one begs for mercy; the other demands proper recognition for his righteousness.

Zacchaeus (19:1–10)

A third scenario is found in the story of Zacchaeus. He stands at the end of Luke's account of Jesus' public life, having displaced the blind man of Jericho from that role. He is a character in the main narrative, and he is mentioned only by Luke. Furthermore, Zacchaeus undergoes a repentance that leads to a change of life. He is also rich, and in that regard may be a Jewish representative of the socially-prominent God-fearer reader.

Zacchaeus demonstrates a life change in the extravagant way in which he distributes his goods for the benefit of others.

8	But Zacchaeus stood there and said to the Lord, "Behold, half of my possessions, Lord, I shall give to the poor, and if I have extorted anything from anyone I shall repay it four times over."
9	And Jesus said to him, "Today salvation[1] has come to this house because this man too is a descendant of Abraham.
10	For the Son of Man has come to seek and to save what was lost."

The "son of Abraham" would seem to restrict this to a Jewish audience. But if we have gentile readers, this might have another meaning—i.e., this represents the true heritage of the tradition to which the gentile is attracted and to which discipleship to Jesus will admit him.

In this case, there is no direct comparison with a contrasting character. As in other instances, however, we have a nearby text that offers a contrast that explains the story. The parable of the Pharisee and the tax collector

(Luke 18:9–14), addressed "to those who were convinced of their own righteousness and despised everyone else," puts the same values in contrast. On the one hand, the Pharisee recounts his numerous spiritual accomplishments; on the other hand, the tax collector simply beat his breast and said, "O God, be merciful to me a sinner" (18:3). The connection between the parable and Zacchaeus is not immediately obvious when we take them as individual stories. But, shortly after the parable, we come across Zacchaeus. The connection seems inevitable, with Zacchaeus as the embodiment of the penitent tax collector. Unlike the Pharisee, the tax collector recognizes his need for mercy.

Jesus' pronouncement upon the affair is "Today salvation has come to this house." What it is that Jesus brings to the tax collector—and the reader—is named in various ways. This is the only instance of the term *salvation* since the canticle of Zechariah in Luke 1. As the story continues, other names will describe what Jesus brings to people.

The Good Thief and the Other (23:39–43)

In a culminating position in the story of Jesus, we have the good thief. He also is paired with the other; traditionally they are known as *Dismas* and *Gestas*. The good thief finds a contrast with the other, and the episode brings together a number of lines of narrative development.

On the one hand, this is the culmination of the series of scenarios of repentance. "Dismas" is an example of repentance, while "Gestas" is not. Of course, the latter is not a paragon of self-achieved virtue, like the Pharisee. However, he does represent the value of human acts, considered on their own, unleavened by the mercy of God, so there is no appeal to meritorious deeds. Instead, we have the opposite: Their deeds condemn them. However, the good thief knows that they are not condemned if they are repentant. And so the final part of the interaction shows his repentance (conversion) and the response from Jesus:

> Then he said, "Jesus, remember me when you come into your kingdom." He replied to him, "Amen, I say to you, today you will be with me in Paradise" (23:42–43).

On the other hand, the good thief stands at the end of a mounting series of taunting opponents—a prominent feature of Luke's Passion account. Mocking is attributed to those gathered in the courtyard, to Herod, and to the rulers, soldiers, and bad thief at the crucifixion (Luke 22:63; 23:11, 35, 36, 39).

The other thief joins in the mockery of Jesus: "Are you not the Messiah? Save yourself and us." Given that *King of Jews* is a messianic claim, it could be said that the mocking of Jesus is a heightened questioning of whether Jesus is Messiah.[2] In Luke's trial scene there is no mocking, but simply attempts to convict him by his words. The Messiah references in the Gospel raise the question, and in the Passion account this is intensified.

But the good thief does not mock; in fact, he chastises the other:

> The other, however, rebuking him, said in reply, "Have you no fear of God, for you are subject to the same condemnation? And indeed, we have been condemned justly, for the sentence we received corresponds to our crimes, but this man has done nothing criminal" (23:40–41).

The good thief stands last in line among those Lukan figures who dramatize repentance. His rebuke of the other thief uses the sensitive phrasing—"Have you no fear of God. . .?"—alerting the God-fearing reader that these examples of repentance apply to any who would follow Jesus.

II. SCENARIOS OF CALL

Peter and Paul, Called to Be Apostles

A second, and related, set of scenarios involves *apostolic calls*. While the calls of Peter and Paul seem to fit the category just reviewed, they also transcend it. Peter's call is paradigmatic, standing at the beginning of the narrative of Jesus' works. The moment is given special prominence by separating it from Jesus' first encounter with Peter. The healing of his mother-in-law has already occurred (Luke 4:38–39), displaced from its role as a response to Peter's call (Mark 1:16–20, 29–31). Luke has other plans for this event.

The story of Peter emphasizes his repentance. Peter's response resembles that of the tax collector in the parable: "Depart from me, Lord, for I am a sinful man" (Luke 5:8). But here the recognition of sinfulness does not involve specific misbehaviors, as we see with Zacchaeus, who makes reparation. Instead, we have a sense of Peter having a transcendent experience, bringing home his own fragile mortality. This is more than regret for past actions; it is a sudden deep insight into his very being as a creature, provisional and frangible.

---

2. The proofs that are suggested for him are these: saying who "struck" him (*prophet*, 22:64); "save yourself" (*messiah, king*, 23:35, 37, 39).

The stories of Paul's call offer a similar exemplary function. His experience on the road to Damascus is emphasized by a three-fold repetition, first by the narrator (Acts 9:1–30), and then twice by Paul (Acts 22:1–21; 26:1–23). All three accounts emphasize the radical about-face occurring in Paul's life as a result of this experience. This is different from simple repentance of past sins and errors. It is much more! Luke aligns awareness of one's insignificance before the transcendent God with repentance. The narrative progress in Acts moves from removal of blindness to baptism in the initial report, adding witness to resurrection in the second instance and mission to the gentiles in the third. Paul is selected to be a witness to the gentiles of the resurrection of Jesus.

In his final speech, to Agrippa, Paul says, "But now I am standing trial because of my hope in the promise made by God to our ancestors (Acts 26:6). While this promise to Abraham is often taken to refer to the promise for Israel's future, in context, and with Luke's reader in mind, it now refers to the promise to Abraham that "In your offspring all the families of the earth shall be blessed" (Acts 3:25; Gen 12:3; 18:18; 22:18).

Here the resurrection is primary and central to the event. However, in some ways the same can be said of Peter. Luke has arranged for the call of Peter to evoke the resurrection stories. His use of *Lord,* as well as other features in line with John 21:1–11, suggest that Luke saw Peter's call, like that of Paul, aligned with an experience of the risen Christ. In Jesus, both Peter and Paul recognize the transcendent God. In Paul this occurs through the encounter with the resurrected Christ. What the two calls have in common is the window on transcendence that the resurrection provides for them. And in each case they are overcome.

The Spirit, a gift to the community, is properly explored in Acts. But already in the Nazareth synagogue, Jesus announces that "the Spirit of the Lord is upon me." The Spirit has come upon Jesus, and later Jesus will be heading to Jerusalem, where the Spirit will be released to the people. It is the Spirit in Jesus that reveals the transcendent God. It is proleptic in Peter, but in proper order with Paul.

We have now witnessed two stages in Luke's understanding of repentance—a two-phase movement involving repentance and conversion. This movement is seen, for instance, in the appearance of Apollos in Acts 18:24–28. Johnson has this to say about Apollos and his knowledge only of the baptism of John: "Luke consistently portrays John's baptism as a preparation for the baptism in the Holy Spirit that connects with Jesus (Luke 3:16; Acts

1:5; 11:16). The connection will be stated thematically in the next passage (19:3–5)."[3]

The first phase, involving *repentance*, is associated with the baptism of John. John's baptism, a baptism of repentance, is rejected by the Pharisees (Luke 7:29–30), who see no need of repentance. The Gospel shows Jesus involved in stories of refusal of repentance, and the repentance that leads to awareness of one's need. The second phase is the *baptism of the Holy Spirit*. Repentance prepares the ground by its awareness of inadequacy of one's self, the futility of relying solely on one's self. But it is in the coming of the Spirit, a consequence of the resurrection, that the fullness is achieved. Baptism becomes the completion of the quest, the need fulfilled. Furthermore, baptism is a public act, moving repentance beyond personal conviction to social statement. Consequently, we discover that Luke shows the God-fearers rejecting a conversion to Judaism that would involve adhering to Jewish laws and practices in a public manner. And yet, at the same time, Luke enlists the same God-fearers in a conversion that is made public by the baptism of households, sealed with the visitation of the Spirit.

And with this, certain questions present themselves concerning the matter of *conversion*. We have considered why the gentiles did not convert to Judaism. But symmetrical with this is another question: Is not their entry into the Jesus movement itself a form of conversion? It may be a private, personal moment, but with baptism it becomes a public commitment. Are these two different but equivalent forms of conversion, or are different kinds of transition involved? A second, and related, question in Luke's program concerns the dismissal of *ritual regulations*, such as the food laws and circumcision, and what their removal as a requirement means in the relationship of gentile and Jew in the Jesus movement. Is this a matter of replacing Judaism with another religion called *Christianity*? Or is it, as is held here, an accommodation for the gentiles entering the narrative of Judaism, but in their own way?

III. A LIGHT TO THE GOD-FEARERS

We come to understand that Luke's narrative program, with its invitation to the God-fearers and release from certain restrictions of the law, is the eschatological promise of the final ingathering of Jews and gentiles—a mission to the gentiles requires that they remain as gentiles. Furthermore, this program is firmly grounded in texts foundational to Luke's project, the exilic

---

3. Johnson, *Acts*, 332.

and post-exilic writings of Second and Third Isaiah. They provide Luke with the opportunity to spin out his narrative.

This is foreshadowed early on, with the pronouncement of Simeon looking to a light to the gentiles, in the manner and language of Isaiah 49:6, "I will make you a light to the nations, that my salvation may reach to the ends of the earth."

> "Now, Master, you may let your servant go
> in peace, according to your word
> for my eyes have seen your salvation,
> which you prepared in sight of all the peoples,
> a light for revelation to the gentiles,
> and glory for your people Israel" (Luke 2:29–32).

It finds its fullest expression in the mission of Paul, citing the same passage: "For so the Lord has commanded us, 'I have made you a light to the gentiles, that you may be an instrument of salvation to the ends of the earth'" (Acts 13:47).

Second-Isaiah was pivotal in moving Israelite theology to new insight. Rainer Albertz notes how the exile experience took some of the Judean believers beyond the former more limited universalism in which God's rule of the nations was to protect Israel by defeating their enemies. Now it moved to a greater universalism in which Yahweh was God of the other nations as well as of Israel. Inclusion of foreigners moved from forced subjection to inviting the free consent of the other.

As always, the transition to the new understanding is hesitant and incomplete, but still visible. Passages calling for God to defeat the enemies of Israel stand alongside others that recognize that God is God of those nations as well. A purified monotheism saw Yahweh not simply as the one God of Israel, but as the one God of all the nations. Encounter, often friendly, with outsiders elicited a sense of shared suffering and a need to be freed of domination. "So the concept moved from conquest to conversion, from force to voluntary adherence. In addition, the vision became one of opposition to domination—arrogant political rule is stripped of its power, and its victims are freed."[4]

As a way of understanding belief in the coexistence of the two conceptions of God, as God of Israel as well as God of the nations, Albertz offers an image of two concentric circles. In the inner circle we find the relationship of Israel and its God. Here God is seen as defending Israel against the nations that would defeat and dominate it. But in a larger circle we find Israel

---

4. Albertz, *History*, Vol. II, 420.

and its God in dialogue with the nations.[5] Here Second Isaiah's "light to the nations/gentiles" finds its proper place.

But Israel's sojourning among the nations changed minds in both directions. In addition to a new Jewish view of the nations, the foreigners were exposed to the religion of Judaism, with its one God, leading to "voluntary adherence." In discussing the important passage, Isaiah 56:1–8, Joseph Blenkinsopp points to the growth of Judaism in the post-exilic era and how this had to do with exposure to Judaism and its belief in the one God. "And indeed, it would be difficult if not impossible to explain the remarkable demographic expansion of the Jewish people throughout the Second Temple period without taking account of proselytism."[6]

The writings of Third Isaiah (Isa 56–66) reflect conditions encountered once the exiles were back in the land. In discussing the post-exilic experience, Albertz notes how the promise of the exilic (and post-exilic) Isaian tradition was sidelined, giving way to a more "realistic" approach to the new Judea. The promises of a mission to the world, a light to the gentiles, was deferred, consigned to a distant, eschatological future.

In the meantime, however, it was important to close ranks in order to protect the revelation entrusted to the Judeans. Confessional signs of membership in the community, such as circumcision, Sabbath observance, and kosher food laws, probably developed during the time in Babylon in order to preserve the group's identity in alien environments. In the post-exilic return to the land, these observances and laws continued to be important as the returnees struggled against those who did not welcome their return.[7] The covenant renewal of Ezra made official the principle of separation from the surrounding peoples, and established the social markers that identified the chosen people. Meanwhile, the outward-looking promise of the light to the gentiles, the outreach to the ends of the earth, was set aside, kept on the books, but deferred indefinitely.

Luke picks up the story in the time of the Messiah Jesus and the God-fearers. Luke's eschatological thrust continues as an expression of Second Isaiah, but puts it in terms of the intervening time of the gentiles (Luke 21:24), which is the time of gathering the gentiles *as gentiles*. For Luke, the coming of Jesus on the scene marks the arrival of the eschatological era, the time of the gentiles ("Today this scripture passage is fulfilled in your hearing" Luke 4:21). Luke narrates the initial movement out to the nations.

---

5. Ibid., 421.
6. Blenkinsopp, *Isaiah 56–66*, 137.
7. Albertz, *History*, Vol. II, 407.

But the God-fearers represent a new phase in the story of conversion to Judaism. While they are attracted to the revelation of the one God, and in Luke's view are authentic believers, for one reason or another they do not convert to Judaism. The mark of the God-fearer, as believer, is non-conversion. This anomalous position conforms to the end-time expectation that gentiles, as gentiles, will be gathered into the fold. But they represent a new stage in the revelation to the gentiles.

And yet we have seen that Luke makes a considerable demand on the new adherent to the Jesus movement. It involves repentance, dramatized as a complete and sobering realization of one's place as a sinner. This repentance is identified as relating to John's baptism. But there is a fuller transformation that comes with the visitation of the Spirit, and that is sealed with baptism. The examples of Peter and, especially, Paul have caused us to speak of these transformations as "conversions." However, this is distinct from, and contrasted to, the conversion to Judaism that has not taken place for these individuals.

With Albertz's example, we can shed some light on the troubling contrast between the two kinds of conversion presented in Luke's work, which also can be imagined as a pair of *concentric circles*. In the first, outer circle, the legal and ritual practices of Judaism, its "identity markers," guard the community. But the community in turn guards the heritage it has been delegated to preserve and hand on. This is the inner circle. It contains the "light" that Judaism has historically been given to guard. The community is the guardian of the light. The outer circle is the set of identity markers—circumcision, food laws, marriage laws, etc.—that are put in place to preserve the community and, in so doing, preserve the sacred revelation.

Conversion to Judaism is the act of joining that community. However, the conversion offered the God-fearer by Luke is an opportunity to have access to the "light" that is guarded by that community, even though the God-fearer stands apart from membership in that community. The desire of the God-fearer is to tap into the Jewish tradition of true worship, to enter the sacred narrative. In offering a light to the gentiles, the Isaian vision releases the heritage to the nations, apart from the community—the "light" that is offered to the gentiles, as gentiles.

And so the question becomes this. What is this "light," this "salvation," this "paradise" offered to the gentiles? What is it that the Jewish tradition has preserved, now available to gentiles for their benefit? Not too long ago, Adam Kirsch, in an article in the *New Yorker* magazine called "Tales of the Tribe," put a name to this as "ethical monotheism and Messianic hope." The phrase certainly helps to orient the inquiry. The same question has been asked by Jewish historians, such as Heinrich Graetz. In the view of those like Graetz, Kirsch's two themes name the necessary heritage and gift that the world needs and which Judaism has historically preserved, somewhat in the manner of an ark.

The first, *ethical monotheism*, names the heritage of the past. It is contained in the narrative of Judaism. In a trenchant phrase, Graetz says, "The worship of paganism was for the most part orgiastic. If Zeus is a god, licentiousness is no sin. If Aphrodite is a goddess, chastity cannot be a virtue."[8] We recognize in "ethical monotheism" language that commentators have typically used to describe the God-fearers. This is what brought them to the synagogue in the first place.

But the theme of *messianic hope* is one that looks to the future. Again, Graetz: "'Judaism is not a religion of the present but of the future,' which looks 'forward to the ideal future age . . . when the knowledge of God and the reign of justice and contentment shall have united all men in the bonds of brotherhood.'"[9] Here we find Judaism's sense of an unfulfilled, unsatisfactory present, looking forward to a future fulfillment, one promised by God, who teaches the reader to look and work toward that fulfillment. It is presented in the eschatological texts of Isaiah and others that spoke of a future in which the gentiles would put aside their idols and believe in the one God. It is the messianic hope, the promise of Judaism that Luke (and Paul) believe finds fulfillment in Jesus of Nazareth and brings the God-fearer beyond the synagogue to the Jesus movement.

At the same time, it shows that in Luke's presentation of Isaiah's light to the gentiles we have a vision of the gentiles finding a way to enter the admired narrative of Judaism. Within the Jewish tradition there is an Isaianic theme that includes the gentiles, as gentiles. In this depiction of both a past and a future, we find a narrative of the human family. It is this narrative that the God-fearer wishes to join.

To Judaism's "light to the gentiles," we must add a third dimension that gives shape to that ethic and content to that hope: *justice for the poor*. Speaking of the proclamation in Isaiah 61:1–3, cited in Luke's programmatic scene in the Nazareth synagogue, Blenkinsopp says, "To whom is this good news addressed? . . . [The] prophetic 'preferential option for the poor' is perhaps the most significant contribution of the Hebrew prophets to the moral traditions of Judaism and Christianity."[10] Here Third-Isaiah is inheritor of a prophetic tradition that reaches back into the story of the Israelite community (Amos 2:7; Isa 3:14; 10:2).

8. Graetz, "Significance of Judaism," *Jewish Quarterly Review*, 9.
9. Graetz, *Ideas of Jewish History*, 226.
10. Blenkinsopp, *Isaiah 56–66*, 223.

The ethical aspect of monotheism includes care for the vulnerable. It is embedded in the covenant code of Exodus 22:21–27[20–26], summarized in "the cry of the poor." One must not molest the alien in the land, the widow and orphan, or the poor neighbor (*'ani*). It they cry out to God, he will answer them, for he is a God of both wrath (22:24[23]) and compassion (22:27[26])—compassion for the vulnerable and wrath for any who use their very vulnerability against them. The poor are to be protected from exploitation, laborers paid promptly (Deut 24:14–15), gleaning rights maintained (Lev 19:10; 23:22). Ruth, the gleaner, and her mother-in-law Naomi are prominent examples of the concern for the poor. The Book of Ruth is a dramatization of Exodus 22.

Meanwhile, the hopeful part of messianic expectation is the conviction that injustices endured will be ultimately overcome and an era of justice will prevail. The long-suffering Anawim will at last find release and relief. This is the promise that Luke's Gospel announces is in the process of fulfillment. Guided by the scene in Nazareth (Luke 4:16–30), along with the reinforcement in the response to the Baptist (Luke 7:21–23), we understand that the entire Galilean ministry of Jesus in Luke is revealed to be the fulfillment of the messianic hope. We can assume, then, that an option for the poor is among the attractive characteristics that draw the gentile to the Jewish tradition.

Judaism's gift to the nations, as represented in ethical monotheism, messianic hope, and care for the poor, can represent for us the "light to the nations" that many gentiles found compelling. Many people were thus attracted to and converted to Judaism; these are the "proselytes" mentioned by Josephus and Luke in the Acts of the Apostles. But Judaism also attracted those gentiles who didn't convert, and yet frequented the synagogues, the God-fearers to whom Luke directs his writing.

IV. A CHALLENGE TO THE EMPIRE

But we cannot ignore the fact that the gentiles selected by Luke to represent the mission to the nations prominently include Roman authorities. This is true whether we look at the inscribed reader, as identified by Theophilus, or the implied reader represented most conspicuously by the two centurions of Capernaum and Caesarea. Theophilus is not a centurion, but he and the centurions—military personnel—point the direction that Luke intends for indicating the reader.

Furthermore, as the Gospel scenarios we just reviewed indicate, Luke presents repentance as a demand of discipleship. Therefore he includes his reader among those who are, or were, called to repent, including soldiers. At the very beginning, he says, "Soldiers also asked him, 'And what is it that we should do?' He told them, 'Do not practice extortion, do not falsely accuse anyone, and be satisfied with your wages'" (Luke 3:14). As Laurie Brink notes, in her study of military figures in Luke's narrative, the surprising thing is that the soldiers asked in the first place. "Could these soldiers, known for their harassment, be actually interested in repentance?"[11] It contradicts their literary stereotypes.

For Luke, the "light to the nations" leads to Rome. The universal world arena in New Testament times was in fact the Roman Empire. Rome is the imperial capital of the nations. The empire sets the scope, the horizon of their worldview. But when we compare Luke's Gospel with that of Mark, his narrative source, we discover dramatic differences. Empire studies have shown that Mark is to be read in the context of the resistance movement against Rome.[12] Luke's project not only takes him to the gentiles, but to the farthest extreme from Judean sensibilities. The conversion of the gentiles, whose world is centered in Rome, includes the military order that has placed Judea, Jerusalem, and its temple in dire straits and led to its eventual destruction. These are officials and officers in the Roman army that occupied the land of Judea, eventually executing the destruction of Jerusalem and its temple to the one God. We begin to understand the reach of Luke's project in his version of the mission to the gentiles.

And while the repentance demands made of the soldiers by the Baptist seem minimal, asking only that they act fairly and humanely, the same cannot be said of the call to conversion for the larger work of Luke–Acts. Here what is at stake is the set of cultural values that define the Roman world. Among those cultural values are the social hierarchy that would separate elites from the humble masses, the *honestiores* from the *humiliores*. "The privileged *honestiores* included the three aristocratic orders and veterans, rewarded for their service in protecting the social order. The remainder of the free population fell in the category of *humiliores* . . . If the advantages of high rank were conspicuous and real, so also were the disadvantages of

---

11. Brink, *Soldiers*, 102. Commentators note (as with Fitzmyer, *Luke I-IX*, 470) that the soldiers are Herod's and not Roman. That responds to the historical question, but not the literary. An answer to the literary question tells us that Luke is developing a notion of repentance that includes even the military, for that is where the thread leads in his narrative. But see Brink, 100–01.

12. See, e.g., Myers, *Binding Strongman*; Horsley, esp. the seminal *Jesus and Spiral of Violence*; Horsley, *Hearing Whole Story*; Carter, *Matthew and Margins*; Carter, *John and Empire*.

falling outside the circle of privilege."[13] The aristocratic orders include senators, equestrians, and decurians, all of whom were expected to have respectable birth, wealth, and moral worth. To these are added notable military, who offered valuable services and security.

So it is that the Roman system made a radical distinction between *honestiores* and *humiliores*. While the evidence comes from the second century, the system was clearly in place earlier. As the Acts account of Paul's appeal to citizenship demonstrates, the legal protection enjoyed by Roman citizens, first won under the Republic, continued into the time of the empire. "However, as the *honestiores/humiliores* distinction came to supersede that between citizens and non-citizens, the privilege of exemption from corporal punishment came to be reserved for *honestiores*, and, in a parallel development, cruel penalties associated with slaves were extended to the humble free."[14]

A stronger sense of the demand made on the gentile reader is gained from Friedrich Nietzsche's protest against the "transvaluation of values" effected by the influence of Judeo-Christian morality on classic Graeco-Roman cultural ideals. Nietzsche railed against what he viewed as the historical defeat of the values of the strong by those of the weak. In his book, *On the Genealogy of Morals*, he plays off the resentment of the priestly class against the knightly aristocratic values of the warrior.[15] The warrior ethic strives toward excellence, which by nature is not a common property. It gives rise to a "noble morality"[16] valuing strength, will, and the dictates of honor.

However, the Judeo-Christian morality that came to replace it was not concerned with excellence, but with egalitarianism. Nietzsche characterized this as an invention of the priestly caste and traces the Christian adherence back to its roots in Judaism, for which he has little sympathy. However, we might posit, from our point of view, that this strain of ethical concern derives from the prophetic tradition as much as from the priestly tradition.

Beginning from different suppositions and fueled by resentment against the higher classes, in Nietzsche's view, the focus is on the negative valuation of sin, as violation of the wellbeing of others. This focus values human equality, humility, and community. It posits that each human person has an equal claim to respect, in sharp tension with the honor culture of the ancient world. And for Nietzsche it was unnatural, humanly invented,

---

13. Garnsey and Saller, *Roman Empire*, 116–17. For the aristocratic orders, see 112–14.

14. Ibid., 117–18.

15. Nietzsche, *Genealogy of Morals*, Essay 1, sect. 6.

16. Nietzsche, *Good and Evil*, 260.

and a product of resentment of the higher classes, an expression of "slave morality."

Nietzsche concludes his broadside, *The Anti-Christ*, with a famous appeal: "I call Christianity the one great curse, the one great innermost corruption, the one great instinct for revenge for which no means is poisonous, stealthy, subterranean *small* enough—I call it the one immortal blemish of mankind . . . Revaluation of all values."[17] And with that, we find a passionate and eloquent case made for the ethic of the Roman Empire, ultimately to be superseded by Christian values.

We also find an eloquent expression of what Luke, perhaps most clearly among the New Testament writers, was requiring as a reconsideration. While we are accustomed to viewing Luke's proposed moral system with ethical commonsense, Nietzsche helps us see that this is not necessarily the case. We begin to see what is under assault by Luke's interpretation of the gospel. It is at the center of his call to repentance and conversion. And it is articulated in his emphasis on reversals coming into being—his version of the beatitudes (Luke 6:20–26), and the canticle of Mary—

> He has shown might with his arm,
> dispersed the arrogant of mind and heart.
> He has thrown down the rulers from their thrones
> but lifted up the lowly.
> The hungry he has filled with good things;
> the rich he has sent away empty (Luke 1:51–53).

---

17. Nietzsche, "Conclusion," *Anti-Christ*, 656.

CHAPTER THREE

Luke's Text
"An Orderly Sequence"

I. PROPERTIES/FEATURES OF LUKE'S TEXT

When Luke begins his Gospel, not only does he identify Theophilus as the reader, but he specifies how the work will benefit him.

> I too have decided, after investigating everything accurately anew, to write it down in an *orderly sequence* for you, most excellent Theophilus, so that you may realize the certainty of the teachings you have received (1:3–4).

And yet, we may question just how "orderly" Luke's account really is. Anomalies in his text are not difficult to find. In fact, commentaries commonly question Luke's information or his judgment. Often these departures from the expected are seen as "mistakes," due to lack of information or simply carelessness. Typically, they concern departures from the historical facts as we now determine them. But what if we give him the benefit of the doubt and adopt a provisional confidence in Luke as writer, allowing for other intentions to surface? Rather than assuming that Luke failed to accurately account for historical facts, we might instead assume authorial control on his part and suspect other goals were at work in his arrangements.

Examples of Luke's Approach

Here, for example, are some instances in the initial chapters of the Gospel, confronting us as we first open his text:

Chapter 1: Mary Returns Home

A riddle for the careful reader is the announcement in Luke 1:56 that Mary, having completed her time with Elizabeth, returns home to Nazareth, which seems to be shortly before the birth of John (1:57–80). It seems unlikely that one so solicitous as to spend months assisting the expecting mother would not stay to see the birth through. *However*, Luke seems to favor completing one story before setting out on another. He does not imply that Mary does not stay for the birth, but rather that he needs to complete one topic before raising a different one. Luke's episodes have themes which are not allowed to bleed over into another.

Chapter 2: Timing of the Births of John and Jesus

At the beginning of the second chapter of his Gospel, Luke sets the context of Jesus' birth in the time of Caesar Augustus, when Quirinius was governor of Syria (2:10–12). However, in the previous chapter, he had set the birth of John in the time of Herod the Great (1:5). We have an anomaly: The narrative leads us to understand that John and Jesus were born six months apart. And yet, Herod died in 4 b.c.e., succeeded by his son, Archeleus, who ruled Judea for ten years. It was only after his removal from the position that Quirinius (Cyrenius) appears as governor of Syria, with the census of the leading landowners.[1] And yet, it is not likely that Luke was ignorant of the basic imperial history, of which he elsewhere seems to have a firm grasp. And we also remember that those events are not that far removed from Luke's own time. *However*, Luke appears to be placing the two figures in their narrative contexts. John's story belongs to the world of Judeans. It does not extend beyond that world. Jesus' story, on the other hand, will be set by Luke in the context of a larger world, the world of the Roman Empire. Here we have another example of the Gospel anticipating the Acts of the Apostles.

---

1. Josephus, *Antiquities*, Chap. 1: "Cyrenius came himself into Judea, which was now added to the province of Syria, to take an account of their substance. . .." (see 47–661).

Chapter 3: Timing of John's Baptism of Jesus

Luke adjusts the account in Mark 1:9–11, where Jesus is baptized by John. There Jesus receives a commission from the voice from heaven, but he does not take it up until after John is arrested (Mark 1:12–13, 14–15). Luke confuses things by reporting John's arrest *before* he gives the account of Jesus' baptism (3:19–20, 21–22). Granted, he finesses the account. John is not mentioned at the baptism, which is told as having taken place earlier. And yet, the inversion of the sequence can be awkward. *However*, much as in the story of Mary and Elizabeth, we can see here the need to complete the narrative attending to John before we begin that concerning Jesus. The time of John is shown to be over before that of Jesus begins.

Chapter 4: Delaying the Exorcism at Capernaum

Luke has moved Mark's account of Jesus' rejection at Nazareth to the front of his narrative of Jesus' public life. This moved the account of the expulsion of the demoniac at the Capernaum synagogue, which Mark uses to open this phase of the story, to second place. Since Jesus hasn't been to Capernaum yet, it is confusing when Jesus anticipates the inhabitants of Nazareth saying, "Whatever we have heard that took place in Capernaum, do here in your hometown also!" (4:23).[2] *However*, we see Luke's interest in providing a programmatic episode for his narrative, intentionally replacing that of Mark. By now we are accustomed to witnessing Luke's freedom in rearranging episodes to serve his purposes. Those purposes include "that you may know the certainty concerning the things about which you were taught" (1:4).

Also Chapter 4: The Geography of Judea

After the initial days of his mission, Jesus expands it to the territories around. Mark says, "And he went into all Galilee preaching in their synagogues and expelling demons" (Mark 1:39). Luke adjusts this, replacing Galilee with Judea: "And he was preaching in the synagogues of Judea" (Luke 4:44). The change is clearly deliberate. And while some commentators decry Luke's lack of knowledge of the territory, that doesn't explain the deliberate nature of the change from Mark. *However*, by means of the geographical indicator, Judea, Luke situates the gospel narrative of Jesus in the world of the Jews,

---

2. For one possible solution, see Tannehill, *Shape of Luke's Story*, 7–8.

leaving the larger implications of worldwide mission to be related in Acts.[3] In a manner consistent with the timing of the births of John and Jesus, *Judea* represents the arena of the gospel story, opening into the larger arena of the empire in Acts.

Chapter 5: Peter's Call

Luke has rearranged the sequence found in Mark that has Peter bringing Jesus to his mother-in-law in response to his experience of being called. A parallel is that of Levi, called (Mark 2:13–14) and inviting Jesus to his house (2:15–17). But Luke has this sequence reversed, with the story of Peter's mother-in-law (Luke 4:38–39) preceding his call (5:1–11). *However,* here too we find a programmatic purpose for the call of Peter, much like we see with the episode in the Nazareth synagogue (4:16–30). In fact, these two may be contrasted, with Peter demonstrating the positive response of the disciple, in contrast to the negative response of the Nazareth villagers who try to throw Jesus from the cliff. Moreover, we have seen how he initiates a series of scenarios of repentance, which trace a thread through the Gospel.

Some Inferences

What do these "mistakes," these anomalies, tell us? First, Luke exhibits an utter freedom in *relocating episodes* to new positions where they work better for him. Far from a close fidelity to his narrative source, Luke shows a remarkable willingness to rearrange events to his purpose. Notable instances of this are the programmatic episodes of the Nazareth preaching and the call of Peter. The account of the rejection at Nazareth (Luke 4:16–30) clearly builds upon Mark 6:1–6, which occurs deep into the narrative. But Luke reworks it, elaborating considerably, to use as the programmatic episode in the public life of Jesus. Similarly, the story of Peter's call (Luke 5:1–11), as noted, reverses the sequence of the call and the healing of Peter's mother-in-law, as found in Mark. But Luke has a paradigmatic purpose for Peter's call and builds a story with overtones of resurrection experiences on the Lake of Galilee.

Four of the six instances listed here alter the source we have at hand—Mark's Gospel. And we see that these changes are *deliberate*, not

---

3. Fitzmyer, *Luke*, 558: "However, it should most probably not be understood as the specific area of Palestine (in constant to Galilee), but rather in the comprehensive sense of all the country of the Jews, a sense that it sometimes has elsewhere (1:5; 6:17; 7:17; 23:5; Acts 10:37)."

coincidental. They are intended alterations that we can presume contribute to Luke's project. With that, we might also consider the others, where we lack a source to compare, to be equally as intentional. In addition, these changes speak to certain features of Luke's text. We see that he arranges his narrative to take up *one topic at a time*. We see this particularly in Mary's visit to Elizabeth, with the apparent contradiction of the solicitous Mary, coming from a distance to assist her elder kinswoman in her need now making an unfeeling departure before the grand event occurs. But—one topic at a time. First the visit; then the birth. And likewise, the account of Jesus' baptism is told without mentioning John, since this account of his arrest has just been given in the preceding verse. First the era of John, then that of Jesus. This aspect of Luke's writing results in a certain sequential quality to his narrative, separating it into distinct segments.

Along with the adjustments in the time frame, we see revision of the *space* in which Luke's story unfolds. Luke expands the horizon of the story as found in his narrative source to include the much vaster imperial world. This was made evident in the contrast between the births of John and Jesus, which placed John within the horizon of the Judean world, only to follow with Jesus in the much larger world of the imperium. We further see his use of *Judea* to name the original mission of Jesus as it takes place in the Gospel, set in contrast to the larger implications of Jesus' influence as realized in the book of Acts.

Taking these movements up in turn, we will look at the character of Luke's narrative, first in terms of his use of time, and then in terms of his use of space. In the first case, his preoccupation with sequence attracts our attention, in particular in the way it shows in his adaptation of his Markan source. This will direct us to look at the spacial dimensions of Luke's narrative. We will turn to the expanded horizon of Luke's narrative world, enlarged from his source from Judea to the Roman Empire. This in turn will lead us to look at Luke's freedom in rearranging the narrative, with special reference to the considerable reworking of Mark's plot.

Sequentiality in Luke–Acts

Luke is insistently linear in his presentation. In translating the term *kathexes* as "sequence" (1:3), we are interested in Luke's use of the term to describe his own work. The word contains an undeniable element of sequentiality, rather than simply arrangement. Aspects of sequentiality are linearity and segmentation—both characteristic of Luke's narrative. Linearity is apparent in Luke's concern with calendar time. Not only does he give us the forty days before the ascension and the fifty days of Pentecost, he also tells the story in distinct segments.

Of course the most obvious of Luke's adjustments is this addition of a second book, the Acts of the Apostles, as a continuation to the Gospel narrative. For Matthew, in contrast, the narrative of Jesus borrowed from Mark and the drama of the times of the evangelist are collapsed into a single story with a double focus—the "inclusive story" of Matthew.[4] For Luke, however, these two times are given separate accounts. They are not simply two books of similar materials, but are to be considered a single narrative. David Moessner, employing the poetics of Luke's time, has shown how an inner "logic" determines the unity of the *one narrative* in the double work. Interpreting *kathexes*, "sequence" is seen as the meaning, but understood as "logic." Thus, to follow means to follow the steps in the argument—connect the dots.[5] These logical connections operate across the entire narrative of the two books. To be clear, the Acts of the Apostles is not the result of a later decision to extend the narrative beyond the story of Jesus—a sort of sequel to the main act. On the contrary, the single narrative in the double work is part of the original conception of Luke's project.

While this is, in a sense, extraneous to the editing of the Gospel itself, the addition of a further narrative has resulted in removing and adjusting some items in the Gospel account, also indicating Acts was in the plan as the Gospel was being composed. An example would be the martyrdom of Stephen. It takes up the theme of the temple displacement (Acts 7:47–50), removing it from the Gospel trials and allowing the Gospel account of Jesus' trial and death to focus on the high priest's charge of messianic presumption. Another example is the treatment of the Gospel narrative as an "object" which turns out to be the topic of preaching in Acts. This objectifying presents the Gospel as a complete and finished item in itself, comparable to a creed. This finished aspect is signaled by the closure achieved by the ascension as the end of the time of Jesus.

In terms of Luke's relation to Mark, his narrative source, we see that he already is involved in a serious reconceptualization of the story. Not only does he expand it by an additional book, but he also thoroughly reorganizes the Gospel account itself, as seen in the effort to create coherent segments,

---

4. Howell, *Matthew's Inclusive Story*.

5. Moessner, "Appeal," 98: ". . . *kathexes* in Greek literature often bears a sense synonymous with *ephexes*, 'in order in a row, one after another.' But when we see that 'logical progression'—whether within temporal, or spatial, or textual contexts—can be the primary referent for its sequential sense, then we must investigate more precisely what Luke is referring to." Moessner shows how indications given through the course of the narrative are to be added up to draw a conclusion about Luke's message.

each with its own set of themes. Episodes are kept distinct, even while clustered with related examples. For instance, once we leave the infancy narratives of the first two chapters, we come to John the Baptist. As earlier noted, his part is finished before we begin with Jesus. In the introduction of Jesus, we have a series of three pericopes. The baptism (Luke 3:21–22), the genealogy (3:23–38), and the temptation in the desert (4:1–13) are distinct episodes, but they are clustered together under the concept of Son of God (3:22, 38; 4:3). This kind of clustering continues throughout the double work.

In addition, the *scope* of the story is radically expanded. In Mark's Gospel we have a narrative covering less than a year. It moves from a time in the villages of Galilee, with Jesus healing individuals and restoring community life, on to the city of Jerusalem. It moves from edge to center, from symptoms of the malaise to the cause. It has more the shape of a campaign than of a biography. Luke vastly extends the time covered by the narrative. He begins his narrative with the conception of John and of Jesus, and then moves on to their births. He continues the narrative beyond the resurrection through the time of the early Christian movement to conclude the Acts of the Apostles with Paul in Rome. The time frame of Luke's narrative is the life of Jesus, followed by the movement that he generated.

Narrative Horizon

The extension of the narrative line is not the only feature that distinguishes Luke's revision. The horizon of the story world also widens immensely. Observing the "anomalies" seen earlier, we saw that the contrast between the births of John and Jesus signal to the reader a shift of the narrative horizons for the entire double work from the Gospel's Judea to Rome's world empire.

The contrast can be seen clearly in the *shape* of the two narratives. Mark's account moves from the edge to the center. It begins in Galilee, where Jesus is working among the villages, and in the second part of his Gospel moves to Jerusalem, where he is shown confronting the authorities. The narrative horizon of Mark is the Judean world of Galilee and Judea, and its context is the Judean crisis that culminated in the destruction of Jerusalem and its temple. The shape of Mark's story underlines the message of resistance, as the protagonist moves from the peasant villages to the capital city, from edge to center.

The shape of Luke's narrative includes that of Mark, but opens it immensely. Luke's Gospel indeed takes us from edge to center in the manner of Mark's, moving from Galilee to Jerusalem. However, Luke adjusts the narrative arc considerably, in extending the time on the road to nine chapters, from Mark's two. The result is that the narrative generates a Jerusalem-directed momentum that makes the reader feel the growing significance of the final arrival there. Meanwhile, Luke also extends the story to include the Acts of the Apostles. He widens the horizon to bring into the mind's eye the long reach of the Roman Empire. And here again we have a passage from edge to center, as the Jesus story in the territory of Judea moves out into the imperial world, to end in the imperial capital, Rome. In this regard, the double work imitates, in its own fashion, the narrative shape of the Gospel itself.

The report of large crowds attending Jesus from the very beginning offers another illustration of this expansion. In Luke 3:14, in contrast to Mark (and Matthew), the moment Jesus returns to Galilee from his time in the desert, the news of his return spreads throughout the surrounding region, as if he were being awaited. In 4:42, after the healing of Peter's mother-in-law, the crowds are seeking him. By contrast, in Mark the healing event prompts Peter to look for him, but Jesus announces that others need him as well. The crowds are yet to come. Luke concludes this exchange announcing Jesus' activity of preaching in the synagogues of Judea, with *Judea* representing the gospel phase of the story, with Jesus of Nazareth (Luke 4:44). The notice of crowds continues through the Galilean ministry. On the road to Jerusalem, the crowds become a dominant presence, as they (along with the disciples and the Pharisees) represent one of the groups interacting with Jesus. As the city nears, the crowds increase. In contrast to Mark's account of a provincial Galilean carpenter challenging the courts of power, Luke gives us a popular and widely-known figure.

II. PROGRAMMATIC EPISODES

One way Luke organizes his narrative is by way of frequent foreshadowing. Jesus publicly anticipates what will happen in Jerusalem, the city that kills the prophets and stones those sent to it (Luke 13:34–35). The prophet Agabus foresees Paul's arrest (Acts 21:10–11). Theologically, this procedure of Luke's can be enlisted as a pattern of *prophecy and fulfillment*. Johnson, for instance, makes this case, showing how Luke is working within a biblical tradition that favors such a way of proceeding.[6] This certainly fits Luke's scheme of including the gentiles in the promises of Scripture. On the other hand, programmatic episodes can be discussed in terms of narrative structure as well. David Moessner, working from a survey of first-century

---

6. See, for instance, Johnson, *Prophetic Jesus*, 24–26.

poetics, speaks of the importance of beginnings.[7] His interest is affirming credentials for the writer in the prologue, situating for the reader the account to follow.

This discussion involves the use of prologues. But Luke also articulates his narrative by beginning the different sections with programmatic episodes. Here we can see him exercising considerable latitude in "arranging" his texts, borrowing episodes from other contexts or relocating them from their original positions. In certain cases, we see this in his adaptations of his Markan source. With this in mind, we can also detect similar activity where an available source is lacking.

In the first category, reworking the source, Jesus' pronouncement in the Nazareth synagogue (Luke 4:16–30) serves as the preeminent example. Mark's account of Jesus' rejection at Nazareth (Mark 6:1–6), is adapted and supplemented to serve as a programmatic piece for the first part of Luke's Gospel narrative—and, as we will see later, as the narrative contract for the entire double work of Luke-Acts.

Again, the dispute over the great commandment, found among the debates that occur during the final week in Mark's account (Mark 12:28–34), is now moved to the beginning of Luke's long road to Jerusalem. There it serves to introduce the conflict that will interest us in this part, the debates between Jesus, on the one hand, and the Pharisees and the *nomikoi*, or lawyers who have joined up with the Pharisees, on the other. At this point, the question of the law enters the account and is raised by Jesus himself (Luke 10:26).

In other examples we have evidence of a similar operation at work. For instance, Luke Timothy Johnson points to the "parable of the Kingdom" (Luke 19:19–27),[8] usually called the "parable of the Pounds," or "the Ten Gold Coins," now positioned by Luke at the end of the journey to the city, which prepares for what will occur in Jerusalem. Luke pushes the story beyond the inherent message of the use of *talents* (as in Matthew's version) to questions of delegation and violent opposition. At the Supper, the apostles receive their delegation for the action in Acts. On the other hand, the farewell of Jesus prepares for his Passion and death at the hands of his opponents. While these aspects are indicated in the parable, there is an excess of meaning that suggests the parable is being repurposed for its present task within Luke's account.

In a similar manner, the Pentecost story (Acts 2:1–11) establishes the program for the subsequent narrative. The account of Acts 2:5–13 has two

---

7. Moessner, *Jesus and Heritage*, 88–96.
8. Johnson, *Luke*, 288–95.

elements—a list of nations and the repeated refrain to the effect that "each heard them speaking in his own language" (2:6, 8, 11).[9] The account of the disciples speaking in tongues borrows the phenomenon of *glossolalia*, as featured in 1 Corinthians 12–14, where it has been described as "fluid vocalizing of speech-like syllables that lack any readily comprehended meaning."[10] Luke, however, takes it beyond its inherent meaning to adapt it for his narrative purposes. More properly, as related in Acts, the phenomenon is *xenoglossia*, the ability to speak in a language not acquired in the normal manner. In this form, it serves to prefigure the expansion into other lands in the narrative of Acts.

Similar observations can be made of the Apostolic Council in Acts 15:1–35. Joseph Fitzmyer, for instance, detects a conflation of reports about two apostolic events, one determining the church position on circumcision, the other attending to diet and marital unions.[11] Again, a programmatic episode sets the stage for the next part of the narrative; a letter is issued for the account that follows regarding Paul's mission to European territory (Acts 10:22), reminiscent of that issued to him by the high priest in an earlier part of his life (Acts 9:2; 22:5).

The story of the apostolic gathering in official council brings together the previous strands of Peter's encounter with Cornelius (and its message about food laws) and Paul and Barnabas's experience in abstaining from circumcision among the gentiles. Brought together in the form of an official letter, this establishes the terms for Paul's mission. Upon his return to Jerusalem, following his mission, the content of the letter is again mentioned, with its commission for the gentiles (21:25).

III. NAZARETH AND THE NARRATIVE CONTRACT OF LUKE–ACTS

The account of Jesus reading the scroll of Isaiah in the Nazareth synagogue introduces a section of the Gospel narratives, namely, the time in Galilee. But it also has a predictive character for the entire narrative of Luke's double work. In terms of current narrative studies, the approach taken in this book, the theories of narratologists are helpful. A. J. Greimas posits such a structure: an initial narrative sequence is seen to set the terms for the following narrative. Taking the narrative as a whole, the initial sequence can be

---

9. See, for instance, Haenchën, *Acts*, 169–71.
10. See https://en.wikipedia.org/wiki/Glossolalia.
11. Fitzmyer, *Acts*, 553.

conceived as a *narrative contract*[12] in which the protagonist accepts a task, which is in effect the topic of the narrative to follow.

The narrative contract is a moment at the beginning of a narrative. It takes the form of a contract establishing the task of the protagonist, who accepts it. The task agreed upon is what will happen in the ensuing story. In effect, the narrative contract alerts the reader or viewer to the terms of the narrative plot to follow. It also gives us the information for knowing when it is over. In crafted narratives, such a moment comes at the beginning when the plan is laid before the reader or viewer, as in the case of films. The prototypical instance is in detective fiction. When the client arrives at Sherlock Holmes's door, the story is about to begin, and the job he accepts is the rest of the story, which may include surprises. In the recent incarnation of that genre by Robert Galbraith, the name J. K. Rowling adopts for her Cormoran Strike novels, the narrative contract itself becomes an issue in *The Cuckoo's Calling*. It calls attention to itself by being the crux of the enigma.

The narrative contract is especially useful in examining the narratives of the four Gospels. In Mark's account, it is the voice at the baptism of Jesus that presents his calling and sets his task (Mark 1:11). In Matthew's account, the dream of Joseph defines the task of the protagonist—"he shall save his people from their sins" (Matt 1:21). In the narrative of Luke, this is the special function of the particular programmatic episode of the Nazareth synagogue in Luke's narrative (4:16-30). The episode itself, as noted earlier, elaborates the account of Jesus' rejection at Nazareth, as given in Mark 6:1-6. Differences from Mark are numerous, but certain items are useful to note. These include the quotation from Isaiah 61:1-3; the play between the quotation and the proverb, with special reference to the term *acceptable*, and the interplay of acceptance and rejection; along with the introduction of the prophets Elijah and Elisha into the account.

As narrative contract, the episode establishes Jesus as protagonist, whose task is presented in the words of Isaiah 61:1-3. One aspect of this passage is its allusion to Leviticus 25:10 and the Jubilee Year, shown in the phrase *proclaim liberty*: "He has sent me to *proclaim liberty* to captives" (Luke 4:18).[13] In Leviticus 25:10 we read:

12. Greimas, *Sémantique*, 172-89. Wright shows an example of this in *New Testament*, 74. The initial sequence is distinguished from the topical sequences that make up the larger narrative. The initial sequence is the narrative contract.

13. *Jewish Study Bible*, 95, on the phrasing of Isa 62:1 "*Proclaim release*: The phrasing comes from Lev. 25.10, which discusses Israelite farmers who lost their land and were forced into indentured servitude. Leviticus rules that they may leave their servitude and regain their land every fifty years. Deutero-Isaiah applies this concept to the nations as a whole: In 586 it lost its land and was forced to live elsewhere. Fifty years later, its period of service ended when the Edict of Cyrus allowed them to leave

> You shall *proclaim liberty* in the land for all its inhabitants.
> It shall be a jubilee for you,
> when each of you shall return to your own property,
> each of you to your own family.

The passage from Leviticus concerns Israelites who have lost their farmland when they were forced into indentured servitude. It rules that they should be released from their servitude every fifty years. Isaiah 61:1–3 extends this to the nation as a whole. After the destruction of Jerusalem and its temple in 587 b.c.e., Judeans are forced into exile in Babylon. But when Cyrus of Persia allows them to return to their land, the prophet Third Isaiah sees a parallel, as their servitude is over and they return to regain the land of their ancestors.[14] Luke certainly is playing upon these levels of meaning.

The reference to the year of Jubilee, and that part of Jesus' work, is elaborated by Sharon Ringe. These elements can be seen in the first part of the story—Jesus' activity in Galilee (Luke 4:14—9:50). Ringe explores in depth the relationship of these passages and concludes that "the beginning of God's eschatological reign is to be marked by the proclamation of a 'release' from all the experiences of enslavement or imprisonment that characterize human life."[15]

While the healing works of Jesus are present throughout his story, the greater majority of them, by far, are found in the Galilee part of the Gospel, which establishes the *praxis* of Jesus. The following section on the road to Jerusalem (9:51—19:44) lays the foundation of that activity in theory, as Jesus debates his opponents along the way. The practice of Jesus is to free people from their various confinements, whether illness, demon possession, or distorted self-regard. Meanwhile, as in the case of the leper, Jesus shows the community that survives by expelling some of its members another path to communal health, as the excluded are reintroduced into the community. The program of liberation is especially evident in the Galilee section of Luke's Gospel, and part of the purpose of the Nazareth encounter is to prepare for Jesus' mission of healing and liberation in Luke 4:14—9:50.

But the Nazareth story has levels. While it introduces the ministry of liberation in Galilee, it also establishes the terms of the entire double work of Luke. This can be seen in the two epigrammatic elements at the heart of the Nazareth account: a quotation and a proverb—a prophetic *quotation* from Third Isaiah and a *proverb* on prophets from Mark. Each is adequate to generate a story as illustration. They interact in Luke's use of the word

---

Babylonia and to regain their ancestral land."

14. Ibid., 903–04.

15. Ringe, *Jesus, Liberation*, 30.

dektos, acceptable. It is first encountered in the final line of the quotation from Isaiah 61. In Luke, it follows the translation of the Septuagint: "and to proclaim a year *acceptable* (*dektos*) to the Lord" (Luke 4:19; Isa 61:2 [LXX]).

The quotation is taken straight, but Luke adjusts the proverb to fit. In Mark 6:4 (as in Matthew 13:57) the pertinent line reads: "A prophet is not without honor except in his native place and among his own kin and in his own house." But Luke changes it: "Amen, I say to you, no prophet is *accepted* (*dektos*) in his own native place." Not only is the proverb brought into relationship with the quotation, but they are put at odds. What is acceptable to the Lord is *not* accepted in Jesus' native place.

But this little contest between sayings finds a larger context with Peter and Cornelius. The term *dektos* appears only three times in Luke (and only five times in all of the New Testament),[16] and this third time is in Peter's statement upon arriving at the house of Cornelius: "In truth, I see that God shows no partiality. Rather, in every nation whoever fears him and acts uprightly is *acceptable* to him" (10:34–35). This is a heavily loaded passage, as the episode also is the site for declaring all foods clean, along with naming Cornelius one who "fears God." Each point made is an important aspect of Luke's program. Here the rejection of Jesus is thematically linked to the acceptance of those who are not Jewish. What is *acceptable* to God does not seem *acceptable* to the villagers of Nazareth.

In this way, countering the talk of acceptance is the meaning of the episode itself—namely, *rejection*. In this episode rejection takes the rather extreme form in Nazareth of following up the villagers' objection to what Jesus is saying by trying to kill him. The reaction seems wildly overdone, if their concern is simply that a native son is moving beyond their world. But this too looks ahead. The ensuing narrative will indeed tell of Jesus being killed, and in Luke it is because of what he has to say. In this Gospel the opposition is against him as a teacher, one who is seen as presenting views subversive to the interests of those who are tasked with managing the affairs of Judeans.

There is a larger sense in which this is the case as well. The reaction of the Nazarenes points to something more than what is on the surface. The real objection to what Jesus is saying and doing carries unspoken implications which they find intolerable. That premonition is not yet actualized, but it will be in the narrative to come. It is only suggested here. But what is involved in the declaration of Isaiah 61 is an implication that bears upon the self-definition of Judaism, as seen in the identity markers that define Jews to others as well to themselves.

---

16. Also 2 Cor 6:2 and Phil 4:18.

In this way, the narrative contract of the Nazareth event in the synagogue anticipates the action to follow, as the teaching and practice of Jesus, positioned to activate the acceptance of the outsider and the gentile into the community, leads to his death—*acceptance moves to rejection*.

However, the dynamic of Luke-Acts also moves in the other direction—*rejection leads to acceptance*. We see this particularly in the move from the Gospel to the book of Acts. At the immediate level, we've seen that the "acceptance" of Nazareth, twisted into rejection, leads to the acceptance of the gentiles in the story of Cornelius in Acts 10. In the larger arc of the drama, the rejection of Jesus in the Gospel leads into the mission of the Spirit in Acts. Here acceptance takes the form of mission to the gentiles, who Peter declares acceptable to God. In this sense, the overall move is from rejection to acceptance.

In the Nazareth story in particular, this is indicated by the introduction of two figures—the prophets Elijah and Elisha. It might be noted first of all that Luke's treatment of Elijah differs from that of Mark (and Matthew), for whom Elijah is a predecessor of John the Baptist. Mark, to concentrate on the Gospel that is Luke's narrative source, presents John as the fulfillment of the prophecy of Malachi 3:1, an Elijah reference, given Malachi 3:21 [4:2]. He appears clothed like Elijah (Mark 1:6; 2 Kings 1:8). In response to the disciples' question after the transfiguration, Jesus suggests the Baptist is the expected Elijah (Mark 9:13).

However, in Luke's account these references are omitted[17] and replaced with others that place Jesus in the role of Elijah. In addition to Luke 4:25–27, we have a cluster of passages in both the Gospel and in Acts. Among these are the story of the raising of the widow of Nain's son (Luke 7:11–17), a story that has echoes of Elijah's revival of the son of the widow of Zarephath (1 Kings 17:17–24)—in its story form, its geographical location, and its declaration: "A great prophet has arisen in our midst." Elijah is commonly seen as the great prophet, and references recur on the road to Emmaus (Luke 24:19). In Acts, the theme of Elijah raising the dead continues in Peter's raising of Dorcas in an upper room (9:36–41) and Paul's raising of Eutychus, also in an upper room (20:7–12). And the Ethiopian eunuch in Acts 8:26–40, not only shows Philip as appearing suddenly in the manner of Elijah (2 Kings 1:1–8), but also involves a chariot, an unlikely mode of transportation, which again evokes Elijah.

The mention of Elijah and Elisha in Luke 4:25–27 is there to illustrate the proverb, " . . . no prophet is accepted in his own native place." Ostensibly, the main point of introducing these two figures is their success outside the

---

17. Albeit another is *added* in reference to John—Luke 1:17.

land of Israel, foreshadowing the movement of Luke's Gospel and Acts. The addition of Elisha to the roster of prophets attending to foreigners expands the category of foreigner to include a commander of an opposing army during a time of war: Naaman was not only a Syrian, but a commander of the king's army, who had captured a young Israelite woman in a raid (2 Kings 5:1–3). It was she who alerted Naaman to the possibility of consulting Elisha. So this is no mere foreigner who is evoked as the objective of Jesus' mission, but his mission includes even those who are considered militant enemies. Already here we see intimations of Luke's centurions, and, with that, implications for the implied reader.

IV. READING THE SCROLL OF ISAIAH IN THE POST-EXILIC COMMUNITY

When Jesus reads from the scroll of Isaiah in the Nazareth synagogue, Luke says, "He unrolled the scroll and found the passage." The choice is deliberate and, for Luke's purposes, programmatic. The passage has a history, and the full meaning of what Luke is doing with this text from Isaiah 61 becomes clearer when we consider the story behind it. For this, a brief review of that history will serve us.

The event evoked by the quotation is the Babylonian Exile and the time after as the people return to the land of Judah. The exile itself, from the defeat and deportation in 587 b.c.e. to the Edict of Cyrus in 539 b.c.e. permitting a return, was a time of considerable reassessment and gathering of traditions. Older texts were collected and edited, new texts were composed to account for their dislocating experience. For those who were exiled, it also was a time of scrambling to construct a social framework as an alternative to the monarchical state which had previously defined them. Among these efforts were a reworking of the clan system, reflecting what they left behind, but on different terms. Also, it occasioned a concerted theological clarification. Their identity, which had been centered in the kingship, now gone, needed new mooring. This was accomplished by shifting to the temple, now idealized, and the One God who dwelt there.

Second Isaiah

The primary witness to these developments is Second Isaiah—the name we give to the anonymous prophet of the exile, whose writings, along with those of his followers, were appended to the Isaiah scroll in chapters 40–55.

While these determinations are still under discussion, the received opinion is that Isaiah 56–66 represents a separate prophet or school of prophets, and the time of the writing is after the exiles' return to the land of Judah, or Yehud, as the critical literature commonly names it in this period of history.

The writings of Second Isaiah present us with a double focus. In the first place, we find certain theological strategies developed to sustain the exiles and their faith. These include parodies of pagan gods, who might be seen to offer competition to the faith of the defeated Judeans. Along with this, providing a positive balance, we find a clarification of monotheism. Faced with the defeat by a people who worship Marduk, the prophet preaches a greater universalism of God Yahweh, seen to be still in charge, even though the Israelites are outside their land. With this change, a positive role for the exiles is sketched out to explain their abrupt removal into foreign territory—they are to be a "light to the nations" (Isa 42:6; 49:6). This important theme is picked up by Luke and exploited by him.

Second Isaiah's openness to the gentile world differs from earlier views in which God Yahweh is in control of the other nations only in the interest of defeating them in defense of the Israelites. A new assessment of God's relationship to the nations no doubt is occasioned by the new experience of those other peoples. Albertz describes a situation in which the exiles encounter other exiles from other nations, recognizing in them a common predicament.[18] The exile experience not only softened their view of the other nations, but now that they were among them, it provided them with a mission, at least as far as the prophet was concerned.

Meanwhile, the influence worked in the other direction as well. Exposed to the dignity and appeal of a purified monotheism, pagans converted to Judaism. Estimates say that the Jewish community in the diaspora grew as much as tenfold in the time from the exile to the time of the Romans,[19] as hinted in the late verse appended to the writings of Zechariah:

> Thus says the Lord of hosts: In those days ten people from nations of every language will take hold, yes, will take hold of the cloak of every Judahite and say, "Let us go with you, for we have heard that God is with you" (Zech 8:23).

The demographic expansion of Judeans during the time of the diaspora stands in the background of Luke's writing as well, with its invitation to the God-fearing reader. That reader is for Luke a current representative of that very movement toward the one God.

---

18. Albertz, *Israelite Religion*, II, 420.
19. Blenkinsopp, *Isaiah 56–66*, 137, and *Judaism*, 25–26, 145.

In addition to a purified monotheism, a second kind of teaching is proper to Second Isaiah: the call to return to the land of Judah, once the opportunity is offered to the people. The political event that prompts this turn of fortunes is the Edict of Cyrus. This theme may be said to shape Isaiah 40-48, the first part of Second Isaiah's writings. The message begins with a call to return (40:1-11) and continues through the Edict of Cyrus, who the prophet describes as doing the work of God (45:1-13). The prophet envisioned a revival of the Judean kingdom, which now, in his idealized vision echoing Isaiah 2:2-4, is the recognized center point of the world. In this regard, he modifies the promise to the house of David (2 Sam 7:11-16) to have it refer to the entire people of Israel (Isa 55:3).

The prophet's message about Yahweh's role in restoring captive Israel is illustrated in a particular image, the metaphor of the *goel* or "redeemer." The *goel*, a figure in Israelite tradition, epitomized by Boaz in the Book of Ruth, was the kinsman charged with retrieving the fortunes of a relative who had fallen on hard times.[20] The work of redemption had specific obligations, each of which finds its parallel in the activity of Yahweh the Redeemer of Israel. The *goel* was tasked with buying back from slavery the relative who had sold himself into servitude; the Lord God delivers the exiles from captivity (Isa 40:1-2). The *goel* repurchases the property of the relative who sold it because of poverty; the Lord God restores the land to the exiles (43:5-13). The *goel* avenges the blood of a slain relative; the Lord God oversees the fall of Babylon (43:14-15; 47:1-15). And the *goel* restores the family name, producing a child for a dead kinsman; the Lord God restores the community of relocated Judeans (43:1, 7), reestablishing his own name as well. While we are accustomed to a spiritualized interpretation of the term, in the writings of Second Isaiah, Yahweh as Redeemer has specific meaning for the exiled community—redemption from captivity and restoration in the land.

Third Isaiah

Upon the exile's return to the land, the school of prophecy associated with the writings of Second Isaiah continues in Third Isaiah, 56-66. In the core section of this part of the scroll, chapters 60-62, we are given a nationalist vision in which Zion becomes the bright central city and the abode of God, to which the nations of the world bring their treasures, and to which the

---

20. After Lev. 25:25, 26 and Num. 5:8; 35:12, apart from the ten instances in Ruth and the nine in Second Isaiah, the term *redeemer* appears only five times, in the Psalms and Proverbs, where it has the spiritualized meaning we commonly associate with the title.

children of Israel are allowed to return. As mentioned earlier, in Second Isaiah the promise to the family of David, of kingship in an eternal kingdom (2 Sam 7:11–16), is transferred to the people themselves (Isa 55:3). No doubt the prophet is trading on the vision of the ingathering of nations in Isaiah 2:2–4, when sword will be beaten into plowshares, and all nations will gather for instruction from the Lord. However, in Third Isaiah this nationalist hope finds an arresting new image, shifting from kingship to priesthood. The relation of Israel to the rest of the nations is spoken of as analogous to that between the priests and the people in Israel (Isa 61:6). Just as the priests provide spiritual guidance to the people and the people support the priests in return, so Israel will be to the nations of the world. Here we have a picture of Judaism in the role of mediating the revelation of the true God to the rest of the nations—the gift of Judaism as a "light to the nations." It is also the interpretive context of Luke's project. It is pertinent that this portrayal of Judaism as the world's priesthood is a continuation of the quotation from Isaiah 61 with which Luke begins his narrative, as Jesus reads it in the synagogue of Nazareth.

But in Third Isaiah we find the tone muted, idealized. A grounding in political events, so central to the writing of Second Isaiah, is absent here. Or, to use a term favored by Albertz, the text is "eschatologized," its events projected onto a distant future.[21] In a similar vein, Blenkinsopp writes in his commentary:

> One of the most characteristic themes of chs. 56–66 is the assurance that the present unsatisfactory situation will be reversed by a divine intervention in the affairs of the Jewish community that will bring history as we know it to an end. At this point [Isa 61:1–7] the reversal is from mourning to comfort, and assurance of its ultimate fulfillment is continued from the prophetic witness of chs. 40–55 (40:1; 49:13; 51:3, 12, 19; 52:9).[22]

The themes of Second Isaiah remain—but without the ballast of political referents. Nevertheless, the promise remained on the books, available for Luke to show Jesus reading it in the synagogue of Nazareth. What Luke presents is the arrival of the long-deferred time—"Today this scripture passage is fulfilled in your hearing" (Luke 4:21). The last age has begun, though for Luke it will not conclude until the time of the gentiles is completed (Luke 21:24).

But for Third Isaiah, the time was not ripe. Certain events had intervened. The Edict of Cyrus in 587 b.c.e. allowed the exiles to return and

---

21. Albertz, *History*, 456.
22. Blenkinsopp, *Isaiah 56–66*, 225.

rebuild. The Persian policy was to encourage local identity, including rebuilding the temple and gathering the traditions of the tribes. They faced the task of compiling and redacting those texts for what would eventually become the Hebrew Bible. During all of this they also faced the prospect of rebuilding their temple and their common life. The initial efforts in 520–515, under the direction of the governor, Zerubbabel, and Joshua the high priest, with support from the prophets Haggai and Zechariah, saw the second temple built, along with an effort to return to an independent monarchical state.

However, in circumstances that are somewhat obscure, the governor and royal descendant of David, Zerubbabel, was removed from the scene, and the move toward independence, no doubt as a vassal state, was thwarted. The satrap Tattennai, governor of the province west of the Euphrates River, got wind of the independence objective and put an end to it. A vestige of that event in Zechariah 6:11 shows that Zerubbabel's name was later removed and replaced by that of Joshua, son of Jehozadak, the high priest. Perhaps it is a sign of the turn of events that the prophets Haggai and Zechariah, active in forwarding the cause of the temple rebuilding, also are not heard from after initiating the temple project.

Albertz sees two developments here that set the terms for the following social reconstruction.[23] On the one hand, the repressive regimes of previous empires—Assyrian and Babylonian—are replaced by the policies of Persia, which includes greater support of local cultures. This encourages the Judean community to back away from overt expressions of nationalist revival, as given in the Isaian texts. On the other hand, as illustrated in the disastrous turn of events with Zerubbabel, the new imperial regime does not tolerate attempts toward self-government that reject the dominance of the empire. So an interest in survival suggests that nationalist hopes were best deferred to the eschatological dream of a far-off day. On the one hand, the attempt to restore the kingdom fails. On the other, the more supportive policies of the Achaemenids reduces opposition and invites cooperation with the empire. While this makes much of the revival possible, it also threatens assimilation to the culture of the empire in the views of some. For the returned exiles, this means seeking to construct a social framework as an alternative to the monarchical state which had defined them prior to the exile in Babylon.

---

23. Albertz, *History*, 444.

Ezra and Nehemiah

An alternative program for survival in the new conditions appears and prevails in the reforms of Ezra and Nehemiah. The dates given for Nehemiah are 445–433 b.c.e., while the dating for Ezra is more fluid, although the most favored date for his arrival in Jerusalem is 458 b.c.e.[24] The approach of Ezra and Nehemiah contrasts dramatically with that proposed in the Isaiah texts. Abandoning the idealized Isaian vision of an invitation to the gentiles, it opts for strong boundaries as a security against threats from outsiders. While at one level it is an expression of conflict over land disputes for the returnees attempting to recover their lost properties, questions of identity also are at stake. The language that dominates is that of purity of the faith, which also implies purity of the authentic community. While these barriers were erected against other expressions of Judaism deemed too relaxed, they also serve to preserve identity in lieu of other political structures. The program of Ezra and Nehemiah, which constructed boundaries to preserve the faith, was designed for a colonial existence, where a cohesive state no longer supplied the terms of identity, as in the former days of the Judean state. The social structures developed during the Babylonian Exile served as models for the new colony.

Among the prophets of the exile, *Ezekiel,* an alternative to Second Isaiah, provided a vision of return in the law of the temple (Ezek 44–46). Blenkinsopp speaks to the "roots of the ideology" in Ezekiel's law of the temple, and concludes, "The agenda which, in their different situations and according to their different functions, Ezra and Nehemiah drove to implement was incubated in the Babylonian diaspora and was a product of its history going back to the earliest deportations."[25] The most pronounced expression of this approach is seen in the dissolution of marriages with outsiders (Ezra 9:1—10:44; Neh 13:23–31). The language of cleansing prevails throughout the accounts and shows the concern for a pure essence of the community. Tellingly, Nehemiah is quoted as saying, "So I cleansed them of all foreign contamination" (Neh 13:30). He draws a clear line between persons inside and outside; not only are outsiders not invited in, but any "contamination" with outsiders is condemned. A firm boundary is set.

Along with clarifying marriage alliances, other identity markers become important—Sabbath worship, the rite of circumcision, and food laws. Sabbath worship was a part of Ezekiel's prescription (Ezek 46:1–7) and was strictly enforced by Nehemiah (Neh 13:15–22). Ezekiel's emphasis

---

24. Blenkinsopp, *Ezra-Nehemiah,* 60.
25. Blenkinsopp, *Judaism,* 158.

on circumcision (28:10; 31:18; 32:19–32) has been explained as a mark of distinction for the community in exile, since it was a practice rare in Mesopotamia. Similarly, food laws seem to have emerged as a way of establishing identity in the exile, as the exiles discovered that their dietary customs were not shared, and therefore provided a mark of distinction. These practices become a natural way of distinguishing the returning community of true believers.[26]

Postcolonial Criticism

Postcolonial critics recognize familiar themes in the experiences of the Babylonian exiles. If we accept Declan Kiberd's dictum that postcolonial writing occurs not only when a colonizer withdraws, but whenever "a native writer formulates a text committed to cultural resistance," we can detect similar moves in the Jewish texts written during and after the captivity.[27] And the categories that best show the situation are those of *authenticity* and *identity*.

Inasmuch as colonized peoples during foreign occupation experience their identity as determined by the colonizing power, the task of an occupied people is to retrieve, or even invent, an identity that expresses who they are. The quest for an "authentic identity," as opposed to the false identity imposed on them, risks the distortion of essentialism, in which a set of character traits are named as the permanent and authentic identity of a people. But this self-defining in an absolute way turns into a caricature as inevitably as that imposed upon it and, thus, also bears the marks of inauthenticity.

Kiberd, for instance, traces the journey of establishing an Irish identity, showing how the three stages articulated by Franz Fanon—occupation, nationalism, and liberation—operate in modern Irish literature.[28] This allows him to identify stages in the Irish effort toward cultural self-determination. The struggle toward cultural self-discovery involves identifying the extent to which the colonized peoples have accepted the caricature bestowed upon them by the colonizer. This is followed by the adoption of a national identity in the manner of the imperialist model, though self-designed. Finally, it carries through to the full grasp on one's own cultural identity among the other peoples of the world. And throughout, the overriding concerns are for authenticity and identity.

26. Albertz, *History of Religion*, 407–08.

27. Kiberd, *Ireland*, 6: "In my judgement, postcolonial writing does not begin only when the occupier withdraws: rather it is initiated at that very moment when a native writer formulates a text committed to cultural resistance."

28. Kiberd, *Ireland*, 184; Fanon, *Wretched*, 222–23.

Authenticity in the Ezra and Nehemiah Narratives

These categories of post-colonialism can be mapped onto the political terrain of the returned exiles, often called the *golah*—the Hebrew term for the exilic community, and subsequently applied to those returning from exile, as distinct from those who had never left the land. They serve to distinguish those returning to the land from those who never left. The confidence in being the community of true believers, the *authentic* expression of Judaism, is pervasive in the moves made in the reform. But perhaps nowhere is it more vivid than in the requirement that marriages with anyone outside the community be dissolved and replaced with marriages with members of the community. The concern for legitimacy, as represented by various census lists (Neh 7:4–72), as well as the genealogies of 1 Chronicles 1–9, are expressions of the same social anxiety. The returning *golah* had a difficult case to make in claiming that they, and not those who were in the land throughout the time of exile, were the true Judeans.

A firm wall is erected between the authentic community and the threat of diluting it by syncretistic elements. Nehemiah's mission to rebuild the wall of Jerusalem may have multiple motives, including the need for such if Jerusalem is to return to being a regional capital. But it also expresses vividly the desire to separate the *golah* from the others. It is a symbolic as well as a practical construction. The concern for purity, with the consequent need to cleanse the community of "abominations" (e.g., Ezra 9:1, 11), demonstrates the degree of anxiety involved in this social reordering.

Identity of the Post-exilic Golah

Matters of identity are related to those of authenticity, but identity and authenticity are conceptually distinct. Authenticity characterizes the true community; identity proclaims it—to others and to the members themselves. *Identity markers* provide boundary posts to charter the social territory of the authentic community. Albertz names *circumcision*, *dietary regulations*, and *Sabbath observance* as the markers that developed during the Babylonian Exile.[29] These practices developed in the tighter context of family traditions and proved important in the return to the land as well, in order to distinguish the restored community. The construction of an alternative social structure, in lieu of the state structure that has been denied the colony, serves the need of an otherwise amorphous collective.

---

29. Albertz, *History*, 407–09.

This perspective is not intended to diminish the religious motivations animating the *golah* community. Rather, it is an attempt to distinguish this religious response from others that do not share these traits, or at least not to this degree. For this is only a partial view of the movement. We should note that Nehemiah's demand for justice against those who exploit the poor also expresses an integral dimension of the reform (Neh 5:1–13). Some complained that they were forced to sell their sons and daughters into slavery or sell their lands to others in order to survive. Nehemiah bitterly protested against those who were "selling your own kindred," as if it never happened that "we bought back our Jewish kindred who had been sold to gentiles" (5:8). Here we find a dedication to the vulnerable that is shared with the Isaian tradition, although it may not have been applied as widely.

And, of course, at the center of all of this is a faith in the one God, preserved as a sacred trust that permits no compromise. One aspect is the heightened role of the temple. Now that the kingdom, and the kingship of David, are no more, the center of the common life was the temple, the concrete symbol of their faith. Here again, the temple law of Ezekiel 44–46 was a crucial part of the *golah's* plan for reform. And behind that is the sacred revelation of the one God, the monotheism that Judaism was concerned to preserve, and what constituted its gift to the nations of the world.

And at this point it is useful to recall the twofold concentric circles that describe the safeguards of the community. It would not be fair to give the impression that there was nothing more at stake than the preservation of the community alone. The community had a mission, and that mission was of ultimate importance. One wall of defense guarded the community, and this is represented by the identity markers. The other defense was the community itself, tasked with the mission of guarding the sacred deposit, the revelation of the one God—what Graetz called *ethical monotheism*.[30] For clarity, it is useful to present this nested set of circles in a simple graphic:

---

30. See chapter one, 35–36.

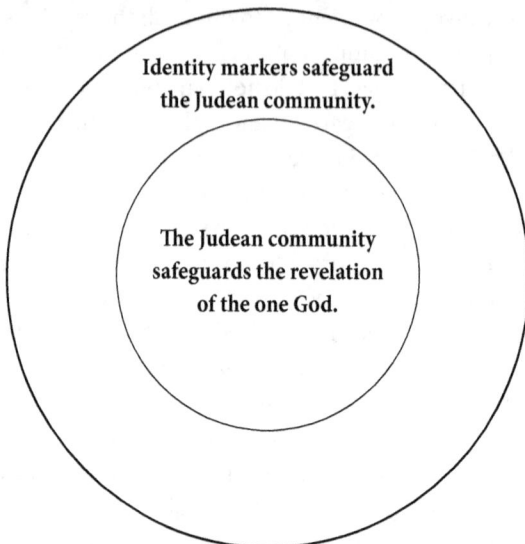

In this double circle we locate the distinction between (1) the essential task of preserving the sacred trust and (2) the practical peripheral operation of securing the community that is given that task. However, any interference with the identity markers necessarily will be interpreted as an attack on the faith itself, despite the distinction between the two tasks. It is this difficulty that Luke will encounter in writing his Gospel for the gentiles.

Here we run up against the rationale for mission. The worship of the one God was to be shared, was it not? In the Isaian vision, it was preserved for the welfare of the nations, inviting them to the fuller life of liberation from injustices as well as from false gods. In fact, they were invited to see the connection between these two. But this invitation was both secured and inhibited by a system of barriers and boundaries. The conundrum faced by the community was stark—there would be no revelation to share if the community itself did not survive. Caught in this dilemma, they postponed the Isaian invitation to the gentiles until the time was ripe, and in the meantime concentrated on preserving the community of believers.

V. LUKE AND THE NAZARETH SYNAGOGUE

In the tension between these two post-exilic expressions of Judaism, one deferred to an end-times vision, the other put in place to survive a colonial existence, Luke writes his Gospel and Acts. That is, Luke's narrative acts as an arena in which the struggle between these two traditions is played out, with Luke looking to announce a path to the gentiles. Or better, Luke finds a path for the gentiles to enter the narrative, that of the biblical people of God. When Jesus makes his declaration in Luke 4:21—"Today this scripture passage is fulfilled in your hearing"—it signals that the eschatological time of Third Isaiah has arrived. For Luke, it is now the time of the gentiles. Though this is a time of conquest by the gentiles (21:24), it is also (as in the exile) an opportunity for conversion. Just as the unasked-for thrust into the foreign land of Babylon was read as an opportunity to be a "light to the gentiles," so the foray into the Roman world is an unprecedented opportunity for mission, also precipitated by circumstances (Acts 8:1).[31] And in this narrative, as the programmatic scenario in the Nazareth synagogue makes clear, the tension between the traditions plays out in terms of *acceptance* and *rejection*. The openness to the gentiles leads to the rejection of Jesus, foreshadowed at Nazareth. The rejection of Jesus, which is the Gospel story as predicated in Nazareth, leads to the mission to the nations, in Acts.

In the narrative that follows, Luke shows the removal of the identity markers, carefully identified as relating only to the gentiles. Each receives its due attention. The *Sabbath* is highlighted, and questioned. Not only is the narrative contract enacted in the synagogue on the Sabbath, but Luke amplifies this theme. The Markan episode of the withered hand (Mark 3:1-6), which concludes the initial week of Jesus' ministry in this Gospel, ends with the Pharisees' and Herodians' firm decision to oppose him. Luke not only includes this event in the Galilee part of the story (Luke 6:6-11), but he supplements it with similar incidents on the road to Jerusalem, each with its ensuing discussion about the meaning of the Sabbath (13:10-17; 14:1-6).

A prevailing topic of concern in the debates with the Pharisees and lawyers on the road to Jerusalem is the *law* itself, as Jesus asks, "What is written in the law? How do you read it?" (10:26). Meanwhile, the *temple* receives its own critique, with references removed from the scenes of Jesus' trials and crucifixion, and the theme transferred to the story of Stephen in Acts 6:8—7:60. In Acts, of course, this is followed by the encounter of Peter with the household of Cornelius and the pronouncement of all *foods made clean* (Acts 10:1—11:18). This in turn is followed by the practice of Barnabas and Paul of not requiring their gentile converts to be *circumcised* (Acts 13-14), and then the two issues are brought to the Council of Jerusalem (Acts 15) to settle the issue for the gentile mission. Thus the obstacles in the path of the gentiles are removed.

But this in turn seems to represent an attack on Jewish tradition. If we do not appreciate the distinction between the two safeguarding concentric

---

31. Acts 8:1: "On that day, there broke out a severe persecution of the church in Jerusalem, and all were scattered throughout the countryside of Judea and Samaria, except the apostles."

circles mentioned earlier, then a profound gap opens between the aspirations of the gentile mission and the identity (and security) concerns of the Jewish community. In this way, the apparent overreaction of the Nazareth villagers to Jesus' announcement, in Luke 4:29—"They rose up, drove him out of the town, and led him to the brow of the hill on which their town had been built, to hurl him down headlong"—is justified in what this announcement of his implies for the entire double work of Luke–Acts.

Furthermore, we see this reaction perpetuated in the narrative of Luke–Acts by the Jewish authorities, though not so much by the people themselves. But now we understand that this tension is already in place when Luke comes on the scene with his writing mission. He is attempting to negotiate a path through its pitfalls. But the inherent instability of such an effort will allow later readings to see his attempt as describing the displacement of Judaism with gentile Christianity.

CHAPTER FOUR

Reading Luke's Gospel
"The Spirit of the Lord Is Upon Me"

IF LUKE'S PROJECT IS to provide the God-fearing gentile with an entry into the Jewish tradition, he does so by means of a narrative about Jesus of Nazareth as the fulfillment of that tradition. In service of this objective, he reworks the narrative he has at hand, that of Mark, and turns its viewpoint around 180 degrees. With an implied reader on the far side of the divide that establishes Mark's narrative conflict, Luke manages to construct a plausible narrative that looks in the other direction. It is this narrative, its transformation, and its literary effect that is the subject of this chapter.

While Luke's narrative is continuous, it is also divided into two books— the Gospel and the Acts of the Apostles. Although this division has allowed them to be separated in the New Testament, it is a current opinion, and one that is followed here, that a single continuous narrative is intended by the author, albeit consciously divided into the two books. With that continuity in mind, the two will be treated separately here, without suggesting they are to be considered independent of one another. This is not simply a matter of convenience, but also because there are distinct features of each that need to be perceived in its own right. In addition, of course, Acts deserves its own distinct attention, which can be lost in a discussion of the Gospel.

Luke constructed his gospel narrative by adapting Mark's. While there are numerous borrowings from the Q Document that Luke shared, unknowingly, with Matthew, as well as similarities to John's account, as in the resurrection appearance in the upper room and the story of Peter's call, with its resurrection overtones, the narrative thread itself comes from Mark.

So one way to read Luke's narrative is to observe its construction as Luke makes his adjustments.

Apart from frequent small, subtle changes, often with considerable consequences, Luke made three major surgical changes. First, he added an infancy narrative, which operates something like an overture in that it previews themes of the coming narrative. This addition establishes a new context for the narrative Luke is producing. A second thing Luke did was to excise approximately two chapters in Mark's account of Jesus' Galilee ministry (Mark 6:45—8:26). In these chapters Mark shows Jesus briefly extending his mission into gentile territory, Luke wishes to save this theme for Acts, and removes it from here. Third, Luke vastly extended the central part of the Gospel in which Jesus shifts his focus and journeys to Jerusalem. Here Luke replaced the twenty-two verses of Mark 9:41—10:12 with nine chapters: Luke 9:51—18:14. In this way, a short section of Mark's narrative—a little over two chapters—was converted into a major part of Luke's narrative.

As a result, Luke ended with the four distinct sections to his gospel narrative that will provide the divisions of this chapter. *The Anawim,* commonly identified as the infancy narrative, includes all of the first two chapters except the first four verses of the Prologue. The section here called *Galilee* presents the mission of Jesus recounted from 3:1 to 9:50. The *Road* shows Jesus intentionally marching into the city of Jerusalem, taking his retinue with him (9:51—19:27). The narrative climaxes with *Jerusalem* (19:28—24:53), where this gospel narrative concludes. Each of these is clearly marked with a beginning and an ending, and each has its distinct character set.

This chapter will consider the Gospel of Luke in post-colonial terms. The Anawim narrative describes the faithful of Israel waiting on God to deliver his people, much as Third Isaiah had promised. This prepares the reader for the announcement at Nazareth that the day has arrived. The Galilee mission fulfills the program announced at Nazareth, presenting the *praxis* of Jesus. Here the Jubilee message of the announcement is actualized in the narrative by healings and personal liberations. The section concerning the journey to Jerusalem examines how Jesus interacts with three sets of interlocutors, building on what went before and anticipating the climax in Jerusalem. Here the narrative establishes the theoretical basis for Jesus' praxis. The Jerusalem crisis will bring the gospel narrative to a close, but not without transitioning to the next book, Acts. The Jerusalem events look both to the end of Jesus's active ministry and the continuation of his movement reaching out to the ends of the earth.

I. THE ANAWIM

Luke's Gospel begins with a Prologue, consisting of four verses of formal diction. But immediately following that, the tone of the Gospel changes dramatically. The style of the rest of the first two chapters evokes the cadences and vocabulary of the Greek Old Testament, the Septuagint. Sharon Ringe has insightfully noted the probable effect this had on Luke's reader of that time. She finds a parallel today: " . . . for many people who were brought up on earlier English translations of the Bible such as the King James Version the rhythms of Elizabethan English connect them to the entire biblical story."[1] In both cases, time and distance confer an archaic patina upon the text. For the God-fearing reader coming to Luke's Gospel, a reader whose connection with the Jewish community is by way of the synagogue, the Septuagint would offer an emotional link to that tradition. For reasons like these, the first chapters of the Gospel can be considered analogous to the overture of a musical production. It previews the themes and prepares the audience for what is to follow.

As Raymond Brown has shown, the first chapters are constructed in a parallel sequence between John the Baptist and Jesus.[2] Each takes up in turn the announcement of birth, the birth itself, and the circumcision of the child. Two events break this pattern. One is Mary's visit to Elizabeth (1:39–56) and the other is the youthful Jesus holding forth in the temple, requiring his parents' return to retrieve him (Luke 2:41–52). The speech of Elizabeth is one of deference (1:42–45). It signals a similar relationship between the narratives of John and Jesus. Brown frames this in terms of the superiority of the Gospel to the Old Testament, of Jesus to John. But we can also specify it further by the indications of the text itself, in the comparison noted in chapter 2 between the narrative world provided John (1:5) and that provided Jesus (2:1–2). The first relates to the Judean context, the second to the imperial world. One is the setting for the Gospel; the other is the setting for the double narrative of Luke–Acts.

In addition to the parallel construction of the narrative, other aspects draw our attention. Devout and humble villagers provide the cast of

---

1. Ringe, *Luke*, 25. Along with Sharon Ringe's commentary on Luke, the commentaries on Luke's Gospel and the Acts of the Apostles by both Luke Timothy Johnson and Joseph Fitzmyer have proved most valuable for describing the narrative of Luke's Gospel. Ringe produces the most successful narrative-determined reading I've seen. While Johnson's narrative reading does not ascribe to the postcolonial perspectives of empire studies, nor adopts the perspective of the God-fearer as reader, his application of classical studies to Luke and Acts is very useful. Fitzmyer (*Acts*) is firmly source- and form-critical, but comprehensive in his attributions.

2. Brown, *Birth*, 250–53.

characters, some of whom will continue into subsequent parts of the story, and some of whom will not. These require consideration. Second, the text is interrupted with canticles that perform their own task of anticipating the narrative to follow. Finally, we take a moment to look at that final episode that stands outside the pattern of parallels, the account of the twelve-year-old Jesus engaging with the teachers in the temple. This will allow us to meet the protagonist of Luke's account, Jesus of Nazareth.

The Villagers

Luke begins his Gospel with portraits of poor villagers. These are the Anawim, the poor of Yahweh, to whom Third Isaiah promised good news.[3] Their roster includes Zachary and Elizabeth, Simeon and Anna, and Joseph and Mary. A belated member of this group is Joseph of Arimathea, who arranged for the burial of Jesus and is described in similar terms. His unexpected inclusion in the group provides a narrative bracket to Luke's life of Jesus. Those who attended his birth are now responsible for his burial. The traits of the Anawim distinguish them from other character sets that we encounter in the Gospel.

First of all, they are *poor*, living humble lives in the villages of Galilee and Judea. We are shown their poverty in the scene of the post-birth purification of Mary. The regulations given in Leviticus specify an alternative offering available to those unable to afford a lamb. "If, however, she cannot afford a lamb, she may take two turtledoves or two pigeons, the one for a burnt offering and the other for a purification offering" (Lev 12:8). This situates the couple in the context of the poor of the land. Their circle of family and friends all presumably share the same circumstances.

Second, they are *pious*, described as *devout* or *righteous*. Zechariah and Elizabeth, are "righteous in the sight of God, observing all the Lord's commands and decrees blamelessly" (1:6). Simeon is characterized as "righteous and devout, waiting for the consolation of Israel" (2:25). Anna "never left the temple, but worshiped night and day with fasting and prayer" (2:38). And Joseph of Arimathea is described as "a member of the Council, a good and upright man" (23:50–51). This portrayal of "authentic" righteousness prepares us for Jesus' debates, which explore the theme of false

---

3. This follows the Hebrew term, *'anawim*: Blenkinsopp, *Isaiah 56–66*, 222–23. Luke's Greek favors the term *ptóchos* (poor, destitute), Luke 4:18; 6:20; 14:13, 21; etc. For Luke's readers, the likely categories were the *humiliores*, as opposed to the *honestiores*. See Garnsey and Saller, *Roman Empire*, 111, 115–18.

righteousness, characteristic of the Pharisees and *nomikoi*—lawyers, or "teachers of the law."

Third, these characters are *peripheral* to the centers of power and influence in their world. Their poverty is not only in lack of resources, but also as occupying a place that is at the edge, and not the center, of the movements of history. They are not in a position to coerce events in their favor or toward the fulfillment for which they hope. They share a posture of waiting upon the Lord for a future desired, long hoped for, and now within reach of fulfillment. Simeon is described as "waiting for the consolation of Israel" (2:25). Anna speaks about the child "to all who were looking forward to the redemption of Jerusalem" (2:38). Joseph of Arimathea is said to be "waiting for the kingdom of God." (23:50–51).

But the perspectives of center and periphery are inverted in Luke's story. The humble villagers are in the foreground of the narrative. But in the background we are aware of the workings of the empire. The story of Jesus' birth involves a census mandated by Caesar Augustus (2:1). Luke uses this to characterize the imperial world into which Jesus is born. The *Pax Romana* was the universal peace established by Augustus, enforced by imperial fiat and force. The census was a symbol of that enforced peace. A census would be a telling indicator of the imperial presence.[4]

Generally a census had a certain set of purposes—determining tax rolls, finding able bodies for military conscription, and work corvée for public projects. As such, in biblical tradition, census-taking does not enjoy a favorable reputation. The story of David's decision to take a census of Israel and Judah, told in 2 Samuel 24, resulted in a plague in the land. In Luke's account of the nativity of Jesus, the narrative's attitude concerning the census is shown in the way that the young family is required to make a difficult journey at a perilous time for a pregnant young mother. The family's difficulties and the young father's strategies for overcoming them are a staple of every Christmas season.

The Anawim waiting upon the Lord is now seen as fitting into the eschatological scheme of Luke. Now those promises are presented in the form of a group of pious people awaiting their fulfillment. It describes a people awaiting the Jubilee era promised by the Isaian tradition, eschatologically deferred to the latter days, but now nearing fulfillment. The dominant mood is one of anticipation for what is about to come true. In this, it foresees the announcement in Nazareth: "Today this scripture passage is fulfilled in your hearing" (4:21).

---

4. Josephus (*Ant.* 18.1) speaks of the census-taking following the change to the procurator system, 4 c.e.

The Canticles

Along with the language and the characterization, we find testimonies in this section in the form of "canticles." While not literally songs, they have the format of Old Testament canticles and psalms. In Luke they have the function of previewing themes of the coming narrative. Mary's *Magnificat* speaks to the reversals to come. Zechariah's *Benedictus* looks to the Messiah and to John as his Elijah. Simeon's *Nunc Dimittis* elaborates Isaiah 49:6 to present Luke's theme of a "light to the gentiles." The overall message of the chapters that contain the canticles is that the day promised by the Isaian tradition has in effect arrived, and the barriers erected by the alternative tradition of Ezra are about to be relaxed. However, that is yet to be worked out in the coming narrative. Finally, we are given a brief scene introducing the protagonist, Jesus of Nazareth, as a precocious young teacher to whom all attend. It is as a teacher, especially, that Jesus is portrayed in this narrative. It is through him that the new day will arrive.

As expressions of hope, Luke's canticles represent the dreams of the Anawim who wait on the Lord. These two—waiting and canticles—have a common purpose: they prepare us for the narrative to follow. In that task, the canticles develop different aspects of that waiting and that hope.

The Magnificat (Luke 1:46–55)

The first canticle is Mary's psalm, the Magnificat. It evokes the song of Hannah in 1 Samuel 2:1–10. Hannah's song celebrates the wonders worked by God. This is an appropriate precedent for the Magnificat, for Mary's song also celebrates God's wondrous works. Hannah puts her song of praise in the traditional context of the Creator God. However, it concludes with a verse that looks in another direction, as it praises the coming king, the anointed: "May [Yahweh] give strength to his king, and exalt the horn of his anointed!" (1 Sam 2:10). In praising the kingdom and God's victory over foes, Hannah anticipates themes as yet unrealized in the biblical narrative, as her son will anoint the first of the kings of Israel, Saul, and the second, David.

Mary's psalm of thanksgiving is equally anticipatory, but here too the theme of reversals takes us beyond the world of creation to the historical arena of politics. The poem has two centers of gravity, pivoting on the notion of the servant, though the vocabulary changes. The first is personal, and proclaims the lowliness of the handmaid (*doulos*) Mary; the other is communal and historical, and rejoices in the historical reversals coming for

Israel his servant (*ebed*). In fact, the overthrow of the mighty stands as a major theme of the poem, and not simply an appended note. In each part, a refrain recalling God's mercy brings the movement to a proper conclusion.

vv. 46b–49	concerning servant (*doulos*) Mary
v. 50	*refrain*: God's mercy
vv. 51–53	concerning servant (*ebed*) Israel
vv. 54–55	*refrain*: God's mercy

Reversals become an integral part of the message of Jesus, seen particularly in the beatitudes of Luke (6:20–26). But the vision, or threat, of social reversals underlie the drama in the full narrative of Luke-Acts. This is seen in the teaching on status, where those attending the meal are invited to go lower and the host is invited to reach outside for attendees: "For everyone who exalts himself will be humbled, but the one who humbles himself will be exalted" (Luke 14:11), and it is expressed again concerning riches (Luke 16:14–15; 19–31). It is implied in the call to repentance throughout. In Acts 17:6, Paul and Silas are described by the protesting Thessalonians as turning the world upside down (*anastatoó*).

The Benedictus (Luke 1:68–79)

The psalm pictures the future and John's place in it. The primary point made is that Jesus is the coming Messiah, and in line with that John is delegated to prepare the way for him. Zechariah's psalm also divides into two parts:

| vv. 68–75 | The role of Jesus, of the house of David |
| vv. 76–79 | The role of John, in the manner of Elijah |

The themes presented here are shared with the other Gospels. However, the designation of John as the new Elijah is muted elsewhere in Luke's Gospel, with the references found in Mark omitted. There the kingship of Jesus is more eschatological than Davidic, and the roles of Jesus as teacher and prophet are equally emphasized. In Luke's account, these roles mutually influence one another.

And yet, this psalm anticipates the distinct roles of John and Jesus as given in Luke's account. We have already seen the separate announcements of Luke 1:5 and 2:1–2, distinguishing their respective arenas of influence. And we have also noticed that distinction in the Gospel and Acts that would separate the baptism with water of John from the baptism of the Spirit with

Jesus. The first privileges repentance; the second full conversion. This is a continuous pattern in Luke's narrative, and the premise is previewed here.

Nunc Dimittis (Luke 2:29–32)

The third of the canticles, Simeon's psalm, the Nunc Dimittis (Luke 2:29–32), is much shorter. It is a single movement and can be considered an elaboration and restatement of the promise in Isaiah 49:6.

> It is too little, he says, for you to be my *servant*,
> to raise up the tribes of Jacob,
> and restore the *survivors of Israel*;
> I will make you a *light to the nations*,
> that my *salvation* may reach to the ends of the earth.

Simeon dramatically announces the fulfillment of Second Isaiah's promise, proclaiming that he can now die in peace, having seen the fulfillment that the Anawim are awaiting:

v. 29	"Sovereign Lord, as you have promised, you may now dismiss your *servant* in peace.
v. 30	For my eyes have seen your *salvation*,
v. 31	which you have prepared in the *sight of all nations*:
v. 32	a *light* for revelation to the gentiles, and the glory of *your people Israel*."

Here too the song anticipates the coming narrative. In his programmatic speech in Pisidian Antioch, Paul brings the narrative up to date—" . . . we now turn to the gentiles. For so the Lord has commanded us, 'I have made you a light to the gentiles, that you may be an instrument of salvation to the ends of the earth'" (Acts 13:46–47).

Gloria in Excelsis (Luke 2:13–14)

But there is a fourth canticle as well, though it is not developed in the same way as the others. And yet it is crucial. The birth of Jesus is described as occurring during a trip from Nazareth to Bethlehem for the purpose of meeting the demand of census enrollment. As noted earlier, it evokes the Pax Romana, and to make the point Luke connects the census to the authority of Augustus: "In those days a decree went out from Caesar Augustus that the whole world should be enrolled" (Luke 2:1).

But the story continues, to inform us that the occasion is marked by angels making a celestial announcement to shepherds in the fields nearby. The announcement stands in dramatic contrast to the imperial peace:

"Glory to God in the highest,
and on earth peace to those on whom his favor rests" (2:14).

It is as if the heavenly powers do not know that the Pax Romana is already in place. But of course, that is much of the point. This peace is not that of the empire. What the powers do not realize is that the events that will change history are happening among these villagers, and not among the elites. Here the shift in perspective of center and periphery rises to its most acute expression. As readers, we are privy to the authentic center of events, while the empire, with its Pax Romana, is off in the distance.

Through the portraits of the villagers and the canticles, the opening chapters of Luke operate like an overture to a musical drama, sounding coming themes by way of characterization and evocative canticles.

Jesus as Protagonist

However, there remains one more episode. The Overture concludes with a brief scenario introducing the main character, protagonist, of Luke's narrative, Jesus of Nazareth, as a precocious young teacher. It is as a master teacher, introduced to us here as a child prodigy commanding everyone's attention, that Jesus will be portrayed in this narrative.

It is in the portrayal of Jesus that the widened horizon of Luke's Gospel is most evident, especially in comparison with his source. Mark features a peasant Messiah, a healer who nonviolently challenges the Jerusalem powers. Mark paints his portrait of Jesus with language that evokes the different expressions of the resistance movements in Galilee and Judea in the times of the Roman occupation. Mark's Jesus is a prophet in the tradition of Jeremiah, challenging the misguided leaders at his own cost.

Luke's Jesus is also prophet, as Johnson notes.[5] But Luke's use of the prophetic theme leans toward prophetic word more than prophetic action. His adoption of the pattern of prophecy and fulfillment endorses the notion of the powerful word. It becomes part of the structural component of Luke's narrative as a literary device of programmatic episodes. Luke certainly presents Jesus as Messiah, but his view of Messiah is closer to the apocalyptic Son of Man than it is to the popular revolutionary Messiah. This eschatological

---

5. Johnson, *Prophetic Jesus*.

theme carries through, from the "eschatologized" Third Isaiah that is the proclamation of Nazareth to the climactic conflict in Jerusalem.

But primarily Luke's Jesus is a teaching prophet. And what is notable in this regard is another theme developed by Johnson, namely, that in addition to invoking the prophetic tradition of Judaism, Luke presents Jesus as teacher in the *Hellenistic* mode.[6] This combination allows Luke to characterize his protagonist as a blend of biblical prophecy with the Graeco-Roman tradition of famous teachers and philosophers.

Such a blend is most noticeable in the narrative of the Passion, in which Jesus' silence in the face of the taunts of those opposing him contrasts with the Hellenistic ideal. It is as a teacher that Jesus is finally apprehended and condemned. Johnson has shown how the trial of Jesus is deliberately drawn to contrast with famous Hellenist teachers, such as Socrates and Zeno. The trope that is being worked here is the teacher who suffers for his witness to the truth, a scenario that the God-fearer reader can identify easily. The difference, however, is that Jesus fails to retaliate in the expected manner.

Jesus as teacher is already signaled in the youthful Jesus whose precocious wisdom draws the attention of the elders in the temple—"all who heard him were astounded at his understanding and his answers" (Luke 2:47). The theme is developed fully on the road to Jerusalem as Jesus debates with the Pharisees and lawyers. Here the teaching is tested against the wisdom of the land, as the *nomikoi*, the "teachers of the law," debate with him. It is in his role as a renowned teacher that the crowds acclaim him, and seek opinions and decisions from him. When he arrives in Jerusalem, it is as a formidable teacher that he enters. The request of the Pharisees (the last we hear of them), "Teacher, rebuke your disciples" (Luke 19:39), carries obvious implications regarding his movement, especially as it will be shown to expand in the subsequent volume of Acts.

With the anticipation of the Anawim setting the tone and the presentation of the protagonist Jesus as teacher, Luke's story is ready to begin. Following his entrance into public life, the *praxis* of Jesus will be depicted in his Galilean ministry (3:1—9:50). This will be followed by the extended journey to Jerusalem (Luke 9:51—19:27), in which the *theory*, the explanation of this ministry, will be presented in debates with the opposition. Luke's Gospel narrative will then conclude in Jerusalem (19:28—24:53), at which time one part of the story will end and another begin.

---

6. E.g., Johnson, *Luke*, 366–67.

II. GALILEE (LUKE 3:1—9:50)
"TODAY THIS PASSAGE IS FULFILLED IN YOUR HEARING."

Continuing the witness of the exilic prophet Second Isaiah, post-exilic Third Isaiah invoked the Jubilee vision of Leviticus. The phrasing of the proclamation of release in Isaiah 61:1 invokes Leviticus 25:10, which calls for lands lost by farmers forced into indentured servitude to be restored to them.[7] Like Second Isaiah's metaphor of the *goel*, mentioned earlier, the "redeemer" tasked with securing the lost freedom, property, or heritage of an unfortunate kinsman, the theme of the Jubilee year finds a powerful analogy in the plight of the returning exiles to the land of Judah. But unlike the political specificity of the proclamations of Second Isaiah, which were anchored in the decree of Cyrus for the return, the visions of Third Isaiah were vague and unspecific, looking to a distant future, thwarted by the disappointments of the failed restorations of Zerubbabel, and displaced by the "realist" measures taken by Nehemiah and Ezra. The vision of Third Isaiah was "eschatologized" into a distant future, along with its expectation of a mission to the nations, a "light to the gentiles."

Into this conflicted heritage Luke places his narrative. He announces it with Jesus' appearance in the synagogue of Nazareth, reading Isaiah 61:1-2 before an assembly of villagers: "Today this scripture passage is fulfilled in your hearing" (Luke 4:21). The listeners are at first appreciative, but turn skeptical. And that skepticism turns deadly when they attempt to heave him from the top of a cliff. What seems to us an overreaction to the presumptions of a hometown achiever can be understood from the point of view of a beginning narrative as a preliminary understanding of the implications of his words. One Jewish tradition is being replaced with another—the defensive posture with the open welcome to the outsiders. But this implies what will happen in the following narrative. In order to make the tradition available to the larger world, certain identity markers that set Jews apart from that larger world will need to be removed for the admission of those outsiders. The Jewish tradition will give its gift to the world, and the price will be a threat to Judaism itself—or so it is feared. The angry villagers of Nazareth are a premonition of that.

It is in the second part of Luke's Gospel, the time in Galilee (3:1—9:50), that the promise of Jubilee is shown to be realized. The Spirit of the Lord begins to be operative in the social world of Galilee. Those in bondage, understood here to include death and disease as well as debt, are liberated.

---

7. *Jewish Study Bible*, 905.

The blind are given sight, although some refuse to see. Luke has contrived to have eleven of the healing stories take place in the Galilee section.[8] In contrast, only four occur in the next part of the Gospel, in the journey to Jerusalem, and three of these are elaborations of Galilean stories. All but one of the miracle stories are from the source narrative of Mark's Gospel. It is worth discovering what Luke is doing to achieve his effects.

Reworking the Mark Source

Early Ministry in Galilee (Luke 4:14—6:49)

One method for assessing Luke's narrative is to identify the moves he makes in his work of construction, particularly as he has adjusted his narrative source, Mark's Gospel. Once this is seen, the next move is to see how the result reads. What different effect do these changes produce on a reader?

In this Galilee section of his Gospel, Luke has followed Mark's lead, albeit with some major alterations. Three deserve some comment. The first and most apparent is his decision to eliminate two chapters, Mark 6:34—8:26. One can surmise reasons for this. He intended to add a substantial amount of text (around ten chapters) later, and needed to reduce some of the Markan text. Even more likely, this part of Mark showed Jesus moving beyond the territory of Galilee into foreign areas. That is a theme that Luke wants to save for the Acts of the Apostles.

A second major change is to divide the borrowed Markan narrative into two parts, separated by other material, namely, the Sermon on the Plain (6:17-49) and the particularly Lukan chapter following it (7:1—8:3). The result provides distinct periods in the ongoing narrative of the Galilean mission—an initial phase and a mature ministry based on Mark, and a transitional period between them.

In Luke 4:31—6:16, the author establishes an early phase of the Galilean ministry by using the opening events of Mark's Gospel, there constructed to suggest an initial week, from a Sabbath to a Sabbath, a synagogue to a synagogue (Mark 1:21-28; 3:1-6). In Luke, the ministry begins with a report of John the Baptist (3:1-20), written to anticipate the mission to the nations (3:4-6). The narrative of John concludes with his arrest (3:20), effectively bringing John's moment in the narrative to an end. That is followed by the introduction of Jesus as Son of God at the Baptism (3:22), as Son of

---

8. Luke has delayed the departure for Jerusalem until after the second Passion prediction, allowing most of the healing stories to be during the Galilee ministry. In Mark, the three Passion predictions structure the journey to Jerusalem. Not so in Luke.

Adam, Son of God (3:23, 38), and by the ascription by Satan (4:3). And with that, the mission of Jesus begins in the synagogue of Nazareth (4:16–30).

Another departure from Mark's schema in the early ministry is found in two instances in which Luke has elevated certain moments into paradigmatic events. One is the reading of the Isaiah scroll in the synagogue of Nazareth. It provides a programmatic episode for the entire double work, as seen earlier. Borrowed and elaborated from Mark 6:1–6, it puts in place the opposition that will build during the narrative. A second instance of lifting an event to programmatic status is the call of Peter in Luke 5:1–11. As Luke reworks this event, it presents the model of discipleship, grounded in repentance.

It merits pointing out that events in the initial Galilean ministry are treated as normative by Luke, as he will use versions of them, or language from them, for later development in the next major section of the Gospel as Jesus makes his way to Jerusalem. Incidents, of which we will later hear echoes, are Levi's banquet, the cleansing of the leper, the synagogue healing of the man with the withered hand. In these cases and others like them, the initial Galilean mission of Jesus is characterized as representing the essential features of his mission.

Mature Ministry in Galilee (Luke 8:4—9:50)

In addition to the early ministry of Jesus in Galilee, Luke has adapted Mark's narrative to present an image of Jesus' mature Galilean ministry in Luke 8:4–9:50. Luke has performed some major surgery on Mark's account to arrive at this. In the final chapters of Luke's Galilee section, his adaptation involves elimination of two of Mark's chapters (Mk 6:17-29; 6:45—8:26). Mark's reference to a mission by Jesus beyond Galilee is not pertinent to Luke at this point, since he has his own agenda for that in the Acts of the Apostles. However, in his version of the Galilee ministry, Luke has produced an image of the works of Jesus that serve as a summation of his ministry of Jubilee liberation. In rapid succession we hear of parables, a storm at sea, a possessed Gerasene, Jairus's daughter raised to life, the healing of a woman with a hemorrhage, the mission of the Twelve, the miracle of loaves, and the transfiguration. Meanwhile, questions concerning Jesus' identity are raised—with Herod, and then with Jesus asking the disciples and Peter answering. And with that, there is the beginning of an answer that builds toward the move to Jerusalem.

In this part, Luke takes the story beyond Mark's midpoint messianic acclamation of Peter all the way to after the second Passion prediction. This allows him to cluster the miraculous work of Jesus—eleven healings, two nature miracles—in the Galilee section of the story—leaving only four on the journey, three of which Luke introduces—two Sabbath healings (13:10–17; 14:2–6), and the ten lepers (17:11–19).

Beyond Mark

Teaching the Disciples (6:17–49)

Inserted between these two stretches of Mark-derived narrative, we find two distinct sections. In Luke 6:17–49, taken from the Q Document, we have Luke's Sermon on the Plain, following upon the naming of the Twelve. As with Matthew's Sermon on the Mount, this cluster of teachings establishes a program for discipleship. This will be more fully elaborated in later chapters of the Gospel and come to a kind of completion with the Acts of the Apostles. The groundwork is being laid here.

In addition, a comparison of Luke's beatitudes with those of Matthew shows an incisiveness in expression unparalleled in the other Gospel. Luke's more direct "Blessed are *you*" in contrast to Matthew's third-person "Blessed are *those*" is reinforced by Luke's set of woes to balance the blessings. The sharpness of Luke's version pictures a reversal of fortunes that has Jesus' teaching fulfilling the promise of Mary's Magnificat. Where before the arrogant give way to the lowly, the hungry are filled and the rich sent empty away, now in the beatitudes the poor and the hungry, the mournful and hated are blessed, while the rich and the satisfied, the comfortable and the well-regarded are the subject of woes.

Luke 7

But perhaps the most telling of Luke's adjustments in his Galilee section is in the seventh chapter. The chapter is comprised of four episodes: the healing of the centurion's slave (7:1–10), the raising to life of the widow's son (7:11–17), the messengers from John and the subsequent testimony (7:18–35), and the repentant woman (7:36–50). We could probably include with this set the summary account concerning the Galilean woman following Jesus (8:1–3). Each of these express special concerns of Luke.[9]

---

9. Of these, two are from the Q Document (the centurion's slave and the messengers from John), one is from Luke's particular source (the widow of Nain), and one seems to be a development of the Passion story of the woman anointing Jesus' head.

Luke's version of the Capernaum centurion has been discussed in detail earlier. His version makes a point of the centurion's God-fearing friendship with the Jewish community and his building of the synagogue. The raising of the widow's son is an Elijah story, which follows from the statement in Luke 4:25-27, where Jesus aligns himself with Elijah and Elisha, signaling a mission beyond the confines of the Jewish world. Though it will not be discussed here, this theme follows throughout Luke–Acts. The fourth story, of the repentant woman and the unrepentant Simon the Pharisee, has also been discussed earlier. It is here that the series of scenarios contrasting repentance with the avoidance of repentance begins, as shown in chapter two, above.

The third of the episodes in this chapter deserves closer attention in any discussion of Luke's narrative construction. The passage is parallel to Matthew 11:2-19, with few alterations. But those few are interesting. Why, for instance, does Luke not mention that John is sending a message from prison, as in Matthew? It would fit into his program announced at the Nazareth synagogue—"He has sent me to proclaim liberty to captives . . . to let the oppressed go free." But, of course, the answer is clear. Luke has already told us that John has been sent to prison (3:20). We are to remember that.

Luke also indulges in some repetition, not found in Matthew's account. John tells them what to ask Jesus, and then they tell Jesus what John told them to ask. Jesus' answer is proceeded by a report about what he has been doing, which he then proceeds to claim:

> At that time he cured many of their diseases, sufferings, and evil spirits;
> he also granted sight to many who were blind.
> And he said to them in reply, "Go and tell John what you have
> seen and heard:
> the blind regain their sight, the lame walk, lepers are cleansed,
> the deaf hear, the dead are raised,
> the poor have the good news proclaimed to them.
> And blessed is the one who takes no offense at me" (7:21-23).

At this point we are invited to recall the text from Isaiah 61:1-2 that was read in the Nazareth synagogue, as a program for the ministry of Jesus, now enacted in Galilee.

> "The Spirit of the Lord is upon me,
> because he has anointed me
> to bring glad tidings to the poor.
> He has sent me to proclaim liberty to captives
> and recovery of sight to the blind,
> to let the oppressed go free,

and to proclaim a year acceptable to the Lord" (Luke 4:18–19).

In this way, the preview of Jubilee liberation set forth in the Nazareth synagogue is reciprocated by a look back from chapter 7 of the Gospel. But it also looks forward to the next part of the narrative. In 7:29–30, a parenthetical remark on behalf of the narrator introduces us to the *nomikoi*, the scholars of the law, who will appear so prominently on the journey to Jerusalem. The situation that prompts the remark is the response of the people to John's baptism.

> All the people who listened, including the tax collectors,
> and who were baptized with the baptism of John,
> acknowledged the righteousness of God;
> but the Pharisees and scholars of the law [*nomikoi*],
> who were not baptized by him,
> rejected the plan of God for themselves.

The theme of opposition to Jesus among the Pharisees was introduced early on, with the healing of the paralytic. As Luke inherited this story from Mark, it identified the scribes entering the narrative as the first on-site opposition to Jesus and his work. Luke uses this opportunity to introduce us to the Pharisees, and they are joined by representatives from another group, literally, the "teachers of the law" (*nomodidáskaloi*). We will meet another representative of this group in Gamaliel (Acts 5:34). Apparently the *nomikoi* are a lesser version of the same profession, "students of the law," perhaps, or "lawyers." They will be Luke's addition to the gathering of opponents all along the way to Jerusalem.

III. THE ROAD TO JERUSALEM

The Galilee narrative of Luke ends when the narrator announces in 9:51—

> When the days for his being taken up were fulfilled,
> he resolutely determined to journey to Jerusalem . . . .

The journey to Jerusalem will occupy the next ten chapters, as Jesus finally enters the city and temple in 19:45. These ten chapters comprise the largest stretch of narrative in Luke's account. The fact that he has created it, and that almost all of it is unique to his work, prompts the consideration that it deserves particular attention in any attempt to divine his narrative purposes. In fact, this unique contribution to the gospel narrative can be seen as the key to Luke's adjustment of the gospel narrative, adapting Mark to Luke's purposes and his readers.

The road to Jerusalem is long and winding. However, the account that follows doesn't work so well as a geographic description. We are entering Samaria in 9:51, but find ourselves back at Chorazin and Bethsaida in 10:13. Similar discrepancies appear throughout the journey. As late as 17:11, the story of the ten lepers, Jesus and his retinue are still traveling "through Samaria and Galilee." Eight chapters into the journey, and we are still somehow in the neighborhood of Galilee. However, we have learned that Luke is usually up to something when he appears to be losing his way. In this case, the journey narrative of this Gospel can be seen as a *dialectic* journey, rather than a geographic one. The geographical markers are invoked as necessary for the argument. In a sense, the journey, with its many meals, is a traveling symposium, a peripatetic sequence working out the teaching of Jesus in the presence of his opponents.

The discussions along the way travel through different topics as well, pursuing a general though not rigid plan. In the beginning phases, as is proper, we hear calls to discipleship, along with warnings of the cost of following. Invitations to repentance, along with expressions of dismay at the resistance to repentance that they encounter, become prominent themes.

In the fourteenth chapter, halfway through the journey, matters of relative status become a central topic of concern, as Jesus is invited to dinner at the house of a Pharisee and remarks on the efforts to seek higher places at table. His saying, ". . . everyone who exalts himself will be humbled, but the one who humbles himself will be exalted" (14:11), echoes the reversals sounded in the Magnificat and the beatitudes of Luke. Advice to the host to reach beyond the familiar circle in order to "invite the poor, the crippled, the lame, the blind" is repeated by the parable of the great feast and even extended to those beyond the city gates.

In Luke 15, repentance becomes the theme. The contrast between repentance and the sense of not needing it is expressed in a memorable way in the parable of the prodigal son. By Luke 16, matters of wealth take center stage, contrasting two masters, God and mammon. Again the beatitudes find an echo, along with the culminating contrast of the Pharisee and the repentant sinner.

As Jerusalem looms at the end of the journey, the topic turns to the coming kingdom. Here the Lukan concept of the eschatological age, arrived but not complete, is presented to the Pharisees and the disciples. Promised by the unfulfilled hope of Third Isaiah, its arrival announced by Jesus at Nazareth, it is now contrasted to the Pharisaic vision of a distant realization. It is yet to be completed, but it is already present, as leaven, as work of the Spirit, as the Messiah coming in an unexpected form.

Praxis to Theory—The Road as the Site of Teaching

An essential aspect of this teaching of Jesus on the road is its connection to the activity in Galilee, in Luke 3–9. Galilee represents the praxis of Jesus; the teaching and debates on the road are the explication and defense of that praxis, i.e., its theory.

This is seen first of all in how Luke has arranged eleven of the healings in Galilee, and only four on the road, an arrangement he makes possible by delaying the move to Jerusalem until after the second Passion prediction. However, Luke also has contributed three of the four healings on the way, inheriting only the blind man of Jericho from Mark. But he has special work for these three, all of which link back to Galilee.

There are at least three ways in which Luke forges links between the activity of Galilee and the teaching on the road. First, he has transferred items that would ordinarily be set in the Galilee mission to the time on the road. Among these are some parables and teachings that have an inaugural sense to them (and which Matthew has accordingly placed in the Sermon on the Mount). This gives a sense of continuity for the teaching in Galilee, especially the Sermon on the Plain, now extended to the teaching section proper. Another would be the handwashing dispute of Mark 7, now introducing the teaching dispute with the Pharisees in Luke 11.

A second way in which the Galilee activity is extended into the road section is by way of repeating items from the Galilee narrative, but now in a new register. The leper story is reprised as the ten lepers, the withered hand is elaborated in the Sabbath stories of Luke 13 and 14, the protest of the scribes and Pharisees is revived to introduce the parables of Luke 15. The story of Simon the Pharisee and the repentant woman sets the stage for the series of Pharisee dinners on the road.

A third method Luke uses, the most direct, to indicate that the discussions on the road interpret the mission in Galilee, involves reviving situations given there. Once revived, Luke uses them to set up a teaching or dispute, thereby explicitly presenting the theoretic remarks on the road as explicating practices of Jesus in Galilee. There are two ways in which this is done. In some cases, a parallel scene is given, which then sets the occasion for further elucidation. An example is the man with dropsy, which sets up the meal lessons of Luke 14. (This is similar to Mark's road pattern—teaching following Passion prediction.) In other cases, a healing or exorcism is mentioned, obviously expecting us to remember the occasions when these things happened in the earlier chapters, and these then become of the setting for teaching. For instance, the objection of the scribes and Pharisees in Luke 15:1–2, reminiscent of the same scene in the house of Levi (5:30–32), sets up the parables of the lost sheep, lost coin, and prodigal son. Again, the teaching on the road explains the *praxis* in Galilee.

Three Discourse Threads

Themes of the call and cost of discipleship, the reversals of status and riches, the contrast of repentance and self-righteousness are crucial for interpreting the teaching on the journey. But perhaps more importantly for understanding Luke's purpose for this section of the Gospel are his carefully distinguished three threads of dialogue, three sets of interaction between Jesus and others. The three groups are the disciples, the Pharisees (with special reference to the lawyers, the *nomikoi*), and finally, the crowds.

Each of these threads is marked by naming Jesus' dialogue partner at the time. Each thread represents a different position vis-á-vis Jesus—they are friends, opponents, and onlookers. As friends and opponents, the contrasting conversations represent two sides of a dispute. In this way, they set out a program of teaching and debate, working to clarify the issues of the Way, the teaching of Jesus, to be ironed out on the way to Jerusalem.

JESUS TEACHES THE DISCIPLES

After sending out the seventy-two on mission, Jesus teaches the disciples in various areas: prayer (Luke 11), struggle (Luke 12), trust and watchfulness, in the spirit of the Sermon on the Plain (Luke 12), detachment from worldly goods (Luke 16), and the importance of forgiveness and humility (Luke 17). The lessons conclude with a clarification of the meaning of the kingdom (Luke 17), insisting on the presence of the kingdom of God now, but not fulfilled (until the time of the gentiles is passed).

JESUS DEBATES THE PHARISEES

The main moments in this narrative are these: The initial engagement occurs with the *nomikos* in Luke 10 (great commandment, good Samaritan); the dispute about hand washing rituals, and the consequent *woes* and entrenched opposition of the Pharisees and *nomikoi* (Luke 11); the matter of status, teaching reversals, and humility (Luke 14); the question of values, using the presenting issue of wealth and detachment (Luke 16); and the final parable of the Pharisee and the tax collector (Luke 18:1–14). It is through these that the question of righteousness versus repentance is worked out.

Jesus Engages the Crowds

In contrast to the previous two groups, the crowds, as onlookers and bystanders, represent the larger arena, the background against which the disputes are highlighted. As they increase in numbers in the course of the move toward Jerusalem, the crowds provide a sense of a larger movement. This thread in the narrative includes harsh words about resistance to repentance as well as the invitation to join the discipleship group (Luke 10; 12). Public events are aired in this context, including mention of Galileans killed by Pilate, the fall of a tower in Siloam (Luke 13), building a tower and declaring a war (Luke 14). The story of the ten lepers, highlighting the "foreigner" who gives thanks, appears in this context and resonates with other Samaritans who fit this context (Luke 9, 10). The crowds represent the outsiders, looking upon the action, asking help and advice from Jesus, but essentially external to the contest between the two committed groups of disciples and opponents of Jesus.

Interactions Among the Threads

While Luke is painstaking in keeping the strands of discourse separate, he also lets us know that they intersect. The Pharisees will hear what Jesus says to the disciples and make an objection. Or, the Pharisees will ask a question, but Jesus' answer shifts from them to the disciples. And so forth.

This mutual interaction and interference can be seen most impressively in the beginnings of each of the three discourse threads. These occur in Luke 10.

The Disciples and the Crowds

In the first twenty-two verses, Jesus sends the seventy-two disciples out on mission to prepare the way before him. There are two initial aspects to this event that need to be noticed. First of all, it is an example of the practice of repeating something from the Galilee section, now in a new register. It repeats the mission of the twelve apostles in Luke 9. On the other hand, it looks forward to the mission of the discipleship community in Acts. In addition to anticipating the narrative of Acts in the very nature of its mission character, there are textual features that reinforce the connection. Upon the return from their mission, the disciples report the fall of Satan, while Jesus, rejoicing in the Holy Spirit, praises God. This mention of the Holy Spirit and the demonic opposition anticipates the role of the Spirit in Acts, where we also discover that the pagan idols are aligned with the demonic spirits.

In this, we see the disciples reaching out to the uninvolved group of bystanders, seeking commitment from them. The crowd discussion thread features the demonic themes of the road, in the exorcism and exchange about Beelzebul in Luke 11, for instance. The uncommitted and formless "crowd" represents those outside the two parties of disciples and Pharisees, both of whom are strongly committed.

The Pharisees and the Crowds

The opposition group enters the road narrative in the form of a *nomikos*, a lawyer, in the discussion in Luke 10:25–37. It begins with the question posed to Jesus, "Teacher, what must I do to inherit eternal life?" At this point, Jesus himself introduces a theme that has not been explicit thus far—"What is written in the law? How do you read it?" Just as the narrator introduced the lawyer, Jesus introduces the theme of the law, indicating that the law itself is on trial. In this Gospel, the interlocutor, not Jesus, provides the answer, reciting the passage about the great commandment.

This in turn leads to the question, "And who is my neighbor?" The question is legitimate, being a matter of considerable dispute in Jewish circles at the time. The verse cited, Leviticus 19:18, specifies that the neighbor refers to members of "your own people," though later in the same chapter it expands this to the stranger who lives in the land (Lev 19:33–34). The Greek Bible favored by Luke's God-fearing readers limits this to the proselyte, or convert to Judaism. Answers current at the time range from the narrower views of Qumran, where only their own community members were admitted as neighbors, to more expansive views that include other Jews, or Jewish converts, or even non-Jewish foreigners living in their midst. The striking answer of Jesus in the parable of the good Samaritan, unlikely to go unnoticed by Luke's reader, is that the question of the identity of the neighbor includes those who are called *foreigners* in the story of the ten lepers (17:18). In moving beyond borders, to the foreign Samaritan, Jesus opens the circle to include the outsider, here in the road narrative represented by the crowds, as noted below.

The Disciples and the Pharisees

The third and last drama of Luke 10 is the account of the meal at the home of Martha and Mary. This is a famously disputed passage, in that it seems to undercut the emphasis on service seen elsewhere (e.g., Luke 12:42; Acts 6:1–6). However we are to understand the theological merit of the passage, its contribution to the narrative concerns the emphasis it gives to the *teaching* of Jesus. Here at the beginning of the road narrative, disciples are told that his teaching is the priority. The context of the meal anticipates further meals along the way. Those meals, apart from this one, involve Pharisees hosting Jesus (e.g., 11:37, concerning false teaching; 14:1, concerning relative status). The meals will continue to be the site of teaching, contrasting the true teaching and the false, and operating as a species of convivium, or symposium. This is signaled in this initial story of Martha and Mary, where it begins with the friends.

Jesus and His Opponents: Luke's Dialectic

True Teaching and False

Two of the groups in the set are presented as relating to Jesus in contrasting ways. The disciples follow him and his teaching to the extent they are as yet able, and the Pharisees, now joined by the *nomikoi* stand in opposition. Negotiating the conflict described by these two groups is the main business of Luke's journey section.

As Mark Allan Powell has established, the religious leaders opposing Jesus are characterized by certain traits, but one is primary: "Self-righteousness is the leaders' root character trait from which other characteristics are derived."[10] But this term enjoys a range of meanings, and how Luke uses it is important. We customarily associate it with hypocrisy, and there is an overlap. The strict meaning of the term involves certain features—a claim to moral virtue, a firm degree of confidence in making that claim, and a sense of superiority in comparison to others. That this claim may not be grounded in reality brings us to the realm of hypocrisy.

But there is a fuller sense of self-righteousness that moves toward the theological, and that is what one might call *self-achieved righteousness*. This is in effect self-salvation, and refers to the sense of earning the good graces in which one finds oneself. This manner of righteousness sharply contrasts with that characterizing the Anawim in the first two chapters. The poor villagers are consistently said to be righteous and devout (1:6; 2:25, 38). However, they are also characterized as peripheral to the halls of power, unable to coerce events in their favor. They are in a condition of radical trust, waiting

---

10. Powell, "Religious Leaders . . .," *Journal of Biblical Studies*, 95.

upon the Lord. This righteousness is far from that self-righteousness that marks the opponents of Jesus.

Luke can be shown to be aware of the range of meanings involved here. We might present them in a list that ranges from the hypocritical to the theological:

1. Hypocrisy— pretending to virtue one does not possess:

   "The Lord said to him, 'Oh you Pharisees! Although you cleanse the outside of the cup and the dish, inside you are filled with plunder and evil'" (11:39; 12:1).

2. Piety as behavior confirming to oneself and dramatizing to others one's virtue:

   "Be on guard against the scribes, who like to go around in long robes and love greetings in marketplaces, seats of honor in synagogues, and places of honor at banquets (20:46).

3. A sense of superior virtue compared to others:

   "He then addressed this parable to those who were convinced of their own righteousness and despised everyone else" (18:9).

4. Confidence in one's virtue:

   "I tell you, the latter went home justified, not the former; for everyone who exalts himself will be humbled, and the one who humbles himself will be exalted" (18:14).

5. The theological meaning—self-salvation; a denial of the role of grace:

   "But because he wished to justify himself, he said to Jesus, 'And who is my neighbor?'" (Luke 10:29).

The range of meanings found here helps us understand how the movement of Luke's composition effects a transposition from *hypocrisy*, favored for instance by Matthew, to the more critical notion of *self-salvation* preferred by Luke. It is the latter that marks the teaching of the opponents, that identifies it as false in this Gospel.

A Contest of Views

But the dialectical exchanges on the road to Jerusalem do not simply characterize the teaching of the Pharisees and the *nomikoi* as false. They also place those teachings in a narrative that continually contrasts them to what

Jesus is teaching his disciples. After the introductions in chapter 10, in which a lawyer poses a question about the neighbor, the narrative takes up the dispute between Jesus and the Pharisees in earnest (Luke 11:37–54). We have just witnessed Jesus instructing his disciples on the proper manner of prayer (11:1–13). It is a lesson in trust: God will meet one's needs.

Now Jesus, invited to a dinner at a Pharisee's house, is observed failing to perform the customary rituals of hand-washing (11:38). It is a moment that stands in clear contradiction to the treatment of Jesus at the house of Simon the Pharisee in Luke 7, where Jesus was not extended the customs of hospitality. In the present instance, the criticism of Jesus by the Pharisees leads to a counter charge concerning the teaching and practices of those pitched against him. In a series of woes, Jesus accuses the Pharisees of performing many pious practices that do not represent a corresponding love of God (11:37–44). At this point, the *nomikoi* enter the exchange, arguing that Jesus' criticism affects them too. He agrees, comparing their teaching to those who killed the prophets (11:45–52).

Given this, the dramatic conflict is set. From now on they try to trap Jesus in his speech (53–54). This is telling, for Luke has moved a notice Mark uses to introduce the debates in the temple during the final week (Mark 12:13) and places it here at the early stages of the journey to Jerusalem. He signals that this narrative begins the testing early. The debates that follow begin here.

Those debates move through different themes in the course of the journey, applying its critical examination to other areas of cultural significance. In chapter 14 of the Gospel, at another dinner at a leading Pharisee's house, issues of status are raised, as guests vie for higher places at table. Jesus' advice echoes his teaching to the disciples following the status arguments of the Twelve (9:36–38): "The one who is least among all of you is the one who is the greatest" becomes "For everyone who exalts himself will be humbled, but the one who humbles himself will be exalted" (14:11). This in turn leads to the advice to the host that he move beyond the familiar circle of guests to invite "the poor, the crippled, the lame, the blind" (14:13). And this is echoed, and then expanded, in the parable of the great feast (14:15–24), as the invitation goes out not only to the streets of the town to invite "the poor and the crippled, the blind and the lame," but even beyond that to "the highways and hedgerows" (14:21, 23).

In *chapter 15*, in another meal setting, the topic turns to repentance, in the major treatment of this theme. The parables of the lost sheep and lost coin emphasize the rejoicing that repentance brings, and the prodigal son places that joy in contrast to the reluctance of those who feel no need to repent. The rejoicing of the father knows no bounds. The repentance of the lost son is total, as he reaches the fullness of self-realization as he comes to the end of his resources.

In *chapter 16*, the attention turns toward cultural values that compete with discipleship, presented under the heading of riches. Jesus has just instructed his disciples in the importance of honest stewardship, concluding with the insistence that it is impossible to serve two masters, God and mammon (16:1–13). Pharisees listening in deride his teaching. Jesus' response cuts to the heart of the matter:

> "You justify yourselves in the sight of others, but God knows your hearts;
> for what is of human esteem is an abomination in the sight of God" (16:15).

Here self-justification is contrasted with God's assessment, and those who exalt themselves, elsewhere contrasted to the humble ones, are challenged.

The parable of the rich man and Lazarus concludes the chapter (16:19–31) to cap this theme. In a story that baldly sets in opposition the rich and the poor, in order to invert them, as promised in the Magnificat and the Lukan beatitudes, the resistance to repentance is dramatized, now in terms of wealth. Again, repentance and self-achieved success are placed in opposition.

In *chapter 17*, as the journey nears its end, the topic of the kingdom of God gains attention. Prompted by a question from the Pharisees, Jesus addresses the eschatological expectations favored by the party of the Pharisees, with the idea that the kingdom is already present (17:20–21). The long-awaited day has arrived, as put on record in the proclamation at Nazareth, and it is now active in the Spirit-filled ministry of Jesus. But its completion in the fullness of time, the day of the Son of Man coming like the flashes of lightning, is some distance off (17:22–37). The meantime, as mentioned in the teaching given later in Jerusalem, will be the time of the gentiles, for bad and for good (21:24). The interim will bring an end to the city of Jerusalem, but it also launches the mission to the gentiles.

In *chapter 18*, the lessons about repentance and self-righteousness find a summary expression in the parable of the Pharisee and the tax collector, addressed "to those who were convinced of their own righteousness and despised everyone else" (18:9). The Pharisee in the parable is presented as the epitome of self-achieved righteousness. Not only does he live the proper life, but he goes beyond what is expected of the virtuous person. Furthermore, his prayer is a prayer of thanksgiving, attributing due credit to God for what he has been able to do.

We find here many of the features of the self-righteous. He is not hypocritical, in the sense that he presents himself pretending to virtue he does not have. For, after all, he is praying to God, who knows there is no room for subterfuge there. However, we do see other marks—complete confidence in his own virtue, a sense of superiority over others in that regard, and piety as a demonstration of virtue to oneself as well as others. And beyond, with the contrast of the repentant tax collector, his vision of righteousness is self-achieved.

In *chapter 19*, the Pharisees make one last appearance as Jesus enters Jerusalem. As the "multitude of his disciples" sing out praises on his entry into the city and temple, the Pharisees ask him to quiet them: "Some of the Pharisees in the crowd said to him, 'Teacher, rebuke your disciples.' He said in reply, 'I tell you, if they keep silent, the stones will cry out!'" (19:39–40). The Pharisees will not be part of the Jerusalem debates, for the climax of the Jesus' story will come in a struggle with another set of antagonists, the chief priests and scribes, the Sadducees, and the Jewish council, the Sanhedrin. And with the mention of stones, Luke's text sounds a new symbolic language to represent his teaching in Jerusalem.

The Crowds, and the Reader of Luke–Acts

Apart from the friends and opponents of Jesus—disciples and Pharisees—there is a third strand of interaction with Jesus, that of the crowds. These are the bystanders, observing the teachings and debates, but from outside the arena of contention. They have their own concerns. Someone, presumably impressed by Jesus' debates with the lawyers, asks him to resolve a dispute concerning his heritage (12:13). Another blesses him and the womb that bore him (11:27). And meanwhile, the crowds increase. It is not long before "so many people were crowding together that they were trampling one another underfoot" (12:1). Along the way, we hear that "great crowds were traveling with him" (14:25), and when we come to the final story on the journey, the encounter with the tax collector Zacchaeus, we learn that "he could not see him because of the crowd" (19:3).

But the crowds do more than provide a background for the procession-like march on Jerusalem, growing as the city nears. On the road to Jerusalem, as a dialectic more than a geographical journey, the crowds represent a crucial third position. They stand outside the debates concerning the meaning of Jesus' mission, waged between the two committed parties of disciples and Pharisees. In this sense, the onlookers to the debates represent those who are not party to the disputes, but have a stake in them.

It is in this regard that the dialogue strand featuring the crowds provides here in the Gospel narrative a surrogate for the later mission of Acts. As noted earlier, the mission of the seventy-two, inaugurating the journey, already prefigures the mission of Acts. Themes accompanying that mission are *Spirit* and *Satan*, intimating the Acts narrative. There the pagan idols of the gentile world are aligned with demonic spirits, as in the oracular spirit in Philippi, exorcized by Paul (Act 16:16–18). This foray into the larger world depicted in Acts is previewed here, as Jesus and his disciples move into the unrepentant towns and the curious, often enthusiastic, but uncommitted crowds. As has been noted, repeated references to *foreigners* in this part of the Gospel add support. The inhospitable Samaritans at the beginning (9:52–53) are countered by the good Samaritan, invoked to answer the question, "Who is my neighbor?" (10:29). Another Samaritan is found among the ten lepers, a story only in this Gospel, and is commended for being the "foreigner" who returns to give thanks.

Furthermore, the crowds, representing a separate strand in the discussions along the way, indicate a particular strategy of Luke in dealing with his gentile reader. An issue needing resolution is the place of the Gospel narrative for that reader. The traditional reading of Acts as attending to gentile concerns, while reserving the Gospel for Jewish concerns, separates the narrative into two, each with its own center of gravity. Thus, Jesus' engagement with his enemies in the Jewish establishment, Pharisees and *nomikoi* on the way to Jerusalem, the chief priests and Sanhedrin in the city itself, may be investigated, for instance, as a social struggle conducted within the framework of Jewish tensions. The Acts of the Apostles, on the other hand, tells a separate story, of the movement of the Spirit into the lands beyond Jerusalem and Judea, and the adjustments, concessions, and fresh emphases that such a movement required.

But Luke's gentile reader, represented by Theophilus, is a constant between the two, named in both (Luke 1:3; Acts 1:1). The Gospel narrative, and that of Acts, are presented for the benefit of the God-fearer, the gentile. For the Gospel, it is this road narrative, the journey to Jerusalem, that situates him. In effect, the God-fearing reader is inscribed in the text as the crowds, standing outside its debate about true and false teaching, but invited to take a position regarding it. The gentile reader observes the debates on the road, presented here for his benefit and given as a way of assessing its meaning.

In effect, the unique Lukan contribution to the gospel narrative, the ten-chapter journey to Jerusalem, is developed for the sake of this reader, to allow him an entry into the Jewish story of Jesus and the Jewish authorities. It inscribes him in the narrative and indicates how he, in his own circumstances, is challenged by its story.

In short, the Road to Jerusalem section of Luke's narrative is constructed to show Jesus interacting with three different dialogue partners—his disciples, his opponents, and the crowds. While essentially independent of one another, the three overlap, as shown in Luke 10, where they are individually introduced. Moreover, they listen in on one another. This allows a situation in which Jesus' instructions to his disciples can elaborate the lessons of his ministry in Galilee, and at the same time provide material for his disputes with the Pharisees and *nomikoi*. Meanwhile, debates with his opponents can work out the implications of his teaching in terms of self-achieved righteousness versus repentance. And finally, all of this is negotiated in view of the crowds, who stand apart from the debates, but for whom they have relevance. Insofar as the crowds represent a population outside the specific terms of the Gospel narrative, they anticipate the nations targeted in the outreach of the mission in Acts, and have particular relevance for the gentile reader of Luke.

IV. JERUSALEM

The fourth part of Luke's Gospel narrative takes place in Jerusalem, the destination of the long journey. Once again the tone changes, and, in support of that, a new cast of characters appears. The disciples remain, at least in the first part, at the Supper. While Luke omits the note that they all fled (Mark 14:50), the last we hear of them, apart from Peter, is at the arrest of Jesus.

The party of antagonists changes. Instead of the Pharisees, who leave the scene after their last words during the entry into the city (19:39), the chief priests, elders, and scribes (20:1) are introduced. They will be the class of leaders who manage the removal of Jesus in the final chapters of the Gospel. These are the ones who constitute the main body of the Sanhedrin, the Jewish council, which will provide the primary opposition to the council of apostles in Acts, as the conflict continues.

In another more subtle transition, the "crowds" (*ochlos*) along the road to Jerusalem are now largely replaced with the "people" (*laos*), a term that hasn't been seen in the account since Galilee. The "people" will prove to be a neutral gallery of observers, not actively participating in the antagonism of the opposition party. In this respect, they continue the onlooker role of the crowds along the road to the city.

The Kingdom Parable

As with other sections of his Gospel, Luke prepares the way for his reader with a programmatic piece. The discussion in the previous chapters has revolved around the coming of the kingdom of God. Already having assured the Pharisees that the kingdom is among them (17:21), Jesus, now turning to the crowd (19:3), speaks of how the coming of the kingdom is also immanent. In a teaching sometimes called the *parable of the pounds*, or *minas*, but which Luke Timothy Johnson calls the *parable of the kingdom* (19:11–27), Jesus anticipates the transactions that will occur in the coming Passion.[11]

The parable has the form of a story within a story, with the two stories further embedded in another story, the narrative of Luke's Gospel. At the center of all this, the parable about a nobleman who delegates servants with responsibilities is much like Matthew's parable of the talents, with some differences. While he is gone, the nobleman delegates operations to certain servants. But the reward given them on his return is not money, as in Matthew's parable of the talents, but rather delegated authority over cities. The slave who failed in his task is not punished, but removed from the list of the delegated. In Johnson's summation, "the possession motif is here a subsidiary to a political one."[12]

Luke's version is set within another story in which the nobleman's departure is for the purpose of obtaining a kingdom, although a delegation follows him to oppose his claim to kingship. Upon his return, he has them executed in front of him (Luke 19:12, 14, 27). With its echoes of Archelaus, the son of Herod the Great, this part of the parable evokes imperial policy, in particular, the Roman policy of granting kingship in eastern parts of the empire. When Archelaus sailed to Rome to appeal to Caesar for the crown, a delegation followed to oppose him. It is not recorded that he slaughtered them on his return. But his slaughter of opponents in the temple *before* his departure to Rome might be reflected here.

Noting that there is no delay in Luke's version of the parable, but implies immediate enactment, Johnson insists that it finds its meaning in the events about to unfold, and not in some distant future. He offers an attractive allegorical reading that presents the parable as the program for the Passion account, that has the nobleman as Jesus, the delegation of protestors as his opponents, and the servants given cities as the disciples of Jesus. The parable nicely foreshadows the two themes of the Passion. The delegation

---

11. Johnson (*Luke*, 292–94) makes a compelling argument that the parable participates in the kingdom discussion at the end of the journey and leads into a program for the Passion.

12. Ibid., 292.

of the servants prefigures that of the apostles at the Supper. The crisis of the nobleman facing his opponents is that of Jesus in his final hours, apparently defeated but ultimately triumphant.

However we are to take this, the portrait of the king, with its frank use of instrumental cruelty, reflects the kingship of Jesus with difficulty. On the one hand, the allegorical reading of a kingdom delegated to a vassal king, who then further delegates cities to his supporters seems to find support in Jesus' words at the Supper, "I confer a kingdom on you, just as my Father has conferred one on me" (22:29). But on the other hand, the political setting with its imperial naked ruthlessness evokes another strand of Luke's narrative, seen in the second temptation in the desert, when Satan shows Jesus the kingdoms of the world and makes an offer—"I shall give to you all this power and their glory; for it has been handed over to me, and I may give it to whomever I wish. All this will be yours, if you worship me" (4:6–7). For this reason it is difficult to accept on face value Johnson's allegorical reading which has the noblemen as Jesus, the delegation of protestors as his opponents, and the servants given cities as the disciples of Jesus.

But this tension between the allegorical reading that serves to set up the narrative for the coming Passion and the imperial reading of the ruthless king might be resolved in noting to whom the parable is addressed. This parable of nested narratives is in turn set within another—that of Luke's Gospel. The introduction tells us, ". . . he proceeded to tell a parable because he was near Jerusalem and they thought that the kingdom of God would appear there immediately" (19:11). Who is this "they"? The referent is ambiguous, but it would appear to be the "crowd" (19:3). Until now, only the disciples will have heard Jesus' predictions of what will happen to him in Jerusalem (9:22, 44; 18:31–33). In Luke's narrative, it is not yet time for this to be revealed to the crowds. That will come in the narrative. For now, what will happen is given in terms that everyone understands, the ways of absolute power.

Entry and Lament (Luke 19)

The time in Jerusalem unfolds in phases. The grand entry into the city and temple (Luke 19) precedes a time of extended teaching (Luke 20–21). The Passion account follows (Luke 22–23). The resurrection stories conclude the Gospel, with everyone remaining in the city (Luke 24).

Once they reach the city, Luke presents Jesus' entry as a grand, gradual procession, evoking for Luke's reader the *parousia*, or advent—the solemn arrival of an emperor or king to a subject city. An example vivid to the inhabitants of Jerusalem would have been the arrival of Alexander the Great, marching toward Egypt after having defeated Darius of Persia. Josephus reports how the high-priest Jaddus, loyal to Persia, at first resisted. But then, after Alexander's impressive conquest of Tyre and Sidon, thought better of it and mounted a splendid welcome.[13] In their book on Paul, Crossan and Reed provide a vivid description of such an event:

> A visitation from the emperor was a very special occasion for any given city and quite possibly a once-in-a-lifetime event. In times of war it was of course a threatening advent, . . . but under the *Pax Romana*, an imperial visitation would usually be a happy occasion. It demanded tremendous preparation for civic sacrifice, aristocratic festivity, and popular celebration, but especially formal greeting by elites and people at the submissively opened gates of the city.[14]

Luke deliberately marks moments and stages in Jesus' progress toward Jerusalem. After the encounter with the blind man, as Jesus is approaching Jericho (18:35), and then the encounter with Zacchaeus, as he is entering and passing through Jericho (19:1), Jesus and those with him enter Jerusalem in four distinct stages. We are told that he is upon the Mount of Olives (19:29); descends from the Mount of Olives (19:37; approaches the city (19:41); and enters the temple (19:45). Each of these marks a stage in the progress of entry, and at each stage a particular action is recounted.[15] First, procuring the colt, with the dialogue that accompanies this action, follows the pattern in the other Gospels. Next comes the procession with praise and rejoicing that evoke the angels' song to the shepherds:

> Blessed is the king
> who comes in the name of the Lord.
> Peace in heaven
> and glory in the highest.

In his answer to the Pharisees' rebuke at this praise, Jesus introduces the motif of "stones" that will overshadow the teaching in Jerusalem: "I tell you, if they keep silent, the stones will cry out!"

In a third scene, as he nears the city, Jesus pauses to lament over it, reprising the lament over Jerusalem in Luke 13:34-35. Again, we hear about stones, now in a vision of the fall of Jerusalem, with not one stone left upon

---

13. Josephus, *Jewish Antiquities*, 11.327-28.
14. Crossan and Reed, *In Search*, 168. See also the references in Carter, *Matthew*, n. 5, 599.
15. Curiously, Luke does not report Jesus' entry into the city itself.

another. The *parousia*, the occasion for rejoicing, is displaced by lament. The irony is bitter. The king who enters will be rejected, but that will mean the rejection of the city. The judgment on Jesus is a judgment on Jerusalem. Luke is looking ahead to his next volume, Acts, where the movement Jesus initiated moves beyond the city, which in the time of Luke's writing is no more.

The final and fourth scene occurs when Jesus enters the temple and drives out the merchants selling there. At this point, Luke makes a subtle but decisive alteration in his Mark source. In Mark's account, the temple action of Jesus, with the interpretation given it by his teaching, is the cause of the decision to move against him (Mark 11:18). In Mark, the teaching explains the action, and the action itself is what begins the countermove that will take him eventually to the cross. Luke, however, deftly separates the action from the teaching. And he has the latter, and not the action itself, be the cause of the mounting opposition against Jesus.

> Then Jesus entered the temple area and proceeded to drive out those who were selling things, saying to them, "It is written, 'My house shall be a house of prayer, but you have made it a den of thieves.'" And every day he was teaching in the temple area. The chief priests, the scribes, and the leaders of the people, meanwhile, were seeking to put him to death, but they could find no way to accomplish their purpose because all the people were hanging on his words (Luke 19:45–48).

We see here the world-renowned teacher bringing his message to the center of the Jewish world, where it finds a mixed reception. The crowds, whom we have discovered to be the audience, approves, but the authorities do not. The opposition to Jesus has changed personnel. The Pharisees drop out of the narrative. We now learn of "the chief priests, the scribes, and the leaders of the people." These comprise the Jewish council, the Sanhedrin, who will provide the primary opposition to the apostolic church in Acts. But we encounter them now as the authorities in Jerusalem, forming the new front of opposition to Jesus, with his teaching as the bone of contention.

The Stones of Jerusalem

While the opposition has shifted its attention from the temple cleansing to the teaching of Jesus, we learn that the teaching is in fact the lesson of the temple cleansing spelled out in words of judgment. The prophetic action reported by Mark now becomes the theme of an extended time of teaching, as projected by Luke's language of stones. The reader cannot fail to respond, if only subconsciously, to the recurring image of stones marking out Jesus' time of teaching in Jerusalem. They become a major rhetorical figure and characterize that teaching. As the Pharisees and the lawyers, the *nomikoi*, hand off the role of opposition party to the Jerusalem council, the theme moves from debates to judgment. The case has been argued, and now the decision is being drawn.

The events in Jerusalem largely follow the program that Mark has set for this story. However, there are significant departures from that precedent. Where in Mark the drama in Jerusalem comprises a single week (Mark 11:12, 20; 14:1; 15:1, 42; 16:1), Luke abandons this timeline to picture Jesus teaching over an indeterminate period of time. At the beginning, Luke simply notes "One day as he was teaching the people in the temple area and proclaiming the good news . . . " (Luke 20:1). The schedule is relaxed and indefinite, suggesting a continuous program. Notably, this is despite the fact that Luke would seem to have shortened the time, due to the transfer of the great commandment story, now used to set the tone for the debates on the road (Luke 10:25-28).

But he has some tricks up his sleeve. In addition to removing the timeline of Mark, Luke converts the farewell discourse of Jesus in chapter 13 of Mark to another purpose. Instead of a farewell, it is now a further elaboration of the teaching of Jesus. The event concludes without a sense of conclusion: "During the day, Jesus was teaching in the temple area, but at night he would leave and stay at the place called the Mount of Olives." No sense of immanent crisis is found here. Meanwhile, to make up for the part he repurposed, Luke introduces his own version of a farewell address at the Supper, where it also serves to pass on the mission to the apostles (22:24-30, 34-38).

Mark has only four instances of stones: the Gerasene exorcism (5:5), the parable of the tenants (12:10), the temple prediction (13:1-2), the tomb (16:3-4). It is the second and third of these that Luke builds upon to achieve his effect.[16] Mark's judgment of the temple, in 13:2, provides Luke with a refrain to use in the entry narrative as well (Luke 19:44; 21:6), framing the time of teaching in Jerusalem. This is reinforced in Luke 20:18, adding to the note of judgment in the parable of the vineyard tenants, as Jesus begins his formal period of teaching in the temple area. Meanwhile, subsidiary motifs fill out the trope. References to stoning the prophets (Luke 13:2; 20:6),

---

16. Other important sources are the Q Document, which provides Luke with the desert temptation (4:1-14), as well as special sources for the laments over Jerusalem. For the most part, however, the development is due to Luke himself.

stumbling stones (4:11; 21:6), and living stones (3:8; 19:40) add further dimensions to an already powerful set of images.

The effect Luke produces is notable. The laments over Jerusalem set the theme. The image of stoning the prophets introduces the motif. But these are stones for throwing, not blocks of stone for building. However, the continuation of the stoning motif proceeds at an indirect and suggestive level, in passages found only in Luke. After the temple action, the authorities react, but do not act for fear of the crowds, as in the other Gospels. Luke adds that they were afraid of being stoned by the people (20:6). And in another Lukan touch, when Jesus retires to pray at Gethsemane, he withdrew from the disciples "about a stone's throw," and knelt and prayed. The specter of throwing stones, here imagined for each side, sets the tone for the crisis that is coming.

However, the lament coming into Jerusalem shifts the image to the building blocks of stone that are now envisioned as coming down. As mentioned earlier, these frame the time of Jesus' teaching in Jerusalem. But now we can add another dimension. The image shifts its application in the course of the Jerusalem chapters. In Luke 21:6, the reference is the temple, as in Mark. Luke links it, however, to the "precious stones and votive offerings" in the temple, as the viewpoint now is from within, rather than from an observation point on the Mount of Olives. The "votive offerings" (*anathema*), are memorials by notable figures. *Anathema* literally means "what is set up," allowing some wordplay between this and the stones that are "thrown down."

But in the entry to Jerusalem, the same phrase, "there will not be left a stone upon another stone," is used for the lament over the city (19:44). The temple has not yet been reached. Luke expands the imagery to include judgment on Jerusalem. In the lengthy passage of Luke 21:5–38, the end of both temple and city are predicted, but distinguished. These in turn are clearly separated from the end time, when the eschatological era will be completed.[17]

In the meantime, between the eschatological announcement made at Nazareth ("Today this scripture passage is fulfilled in your hearing," 4:21) and the coming of the Son of Man with "signs in the sun, the moon, and the stars" is the intervening "times of the gentiles." This will include a dire future for Jerusalem, for "They will fall by the edge of the sword and be taken as captives to all the gentiles; and Jerusalem will be trampled underfoot by the gentiles until the times of the gentiles are fulfilled" (21:24). And yet, this is

---

17. LaVerdiere, *Luke*, 244–50, convincingly argues this division: Destruction of the temple, 21:5–19; destruction of Jerusalem, 21:20–28; end of time, 21:29–38. Luke carefully distinguishes between near and distant events (21:9, 12, 24).

the impetus to move beyond the city to the world beyond, in the mission to those same gentiles.

Another notable editorial adjustment by Luke needs to be mentioned. At the end of the parable of the vineyard tenants, a passage that introduces the debates in the temple area in all the Synoptic Gospels, Luke has introduced a further reference to stones. After the parable, Jesus cites a line from Psalm 117 (LXX): "The stone which the builders rejected has become the cornerstone." The import has shifted from the psalm, where it refers to Israel, to its new referent, Jesus himself. The figure of the stone is now no longer the temple or the city, but the protagonist of the drama. Luke adds another line:

> "Everyone who falls on that stone will be dashed to pieces; and
> it will crush anyone on whom it falls" (20:18).

The line has the antithetical form of a proverb, with its double and reciprocal vision of falling upon stone and being crushed by fallen stone. It sounds the theme of the stumbling stone and answers that with the image of destruction by collapse of the walls. In its reciprocity, this passage evokes the tension of mutual violence that marks this time of crisis. If this is also a reference to Isaiah 8:14,[18] it evokes the political crisis of Isaiah in the time of the Assyrian push toward conquest and the isolation of Isaiah in his opposition to the king. It is a word of assurance that they will survive if they "fear the Lord" rather than their oppressors. For Luke and his readers, it shows the power of the messianic threat, a power crucified but not cowed, killed but not contained.

And of course that reminds us that there is one more stone, that which would close the tomb of Jesus. But this stone has been rolled aside. It is not performing its work of closing the story of Jesus. It lies open, ready for the Spirit of Jesus to take the story into the next volume, the Acts of the Apostles.

The teaching of Jesus when he reaches Jerusalem centers on judgment and challenge. The debates along the road to Jerusalem presented the contrast of repentance and self-achieved righteousness. These are the terms of the conflict between Jesus and the prevailing ethos. Now he moves into the time of decision. The focus shifts from the debates with the Pharisees to the challenge to the authorities. The Pharisees hand over the opposition to the council. Jesus has been constantly moving toward Jerusalem. And what will happen there? Anticipation has been building. Lament has heightened it.

---

18. Johnson (*Luke*, 306–07) notes that the defining allusion in Luke 20:18 is Isaiah 8:14. See also Fitzmyer, *Luke*, 1286.

The challenge begins with Jesus' entry, and it prompts the council's opposition. In this sense, the hostility of the authorities is not unwarranted; it is stimulated by the judgment of Jesus on Jerusalem. But the judgment is mutual. The council will answer his challenge, but they will not win. The prophetic judgment on the city and temple in the long run will prove the prevailing truth. However, in the short run, they will judge and dispose of Jesus, with the help of the procurator. But this is just a passage, an *exodos* (Luke 9:31). The subsequent volume continues the story beyond the trial and execution of Jesus.

The "Hour": Luke's Passion Account

Luke introduces the events at the Last Supper with these words: "When the *hour* came, he took his place at table with the apostles" (22:14). In this, he changes the language of Mark, who speaks of "evening" having come. Particular Lukan touches include his own treatment of the garden scene, to which he contributes the title *Agony* (22:44), and the scene in which Peter and Jesus lock eyes after the denial (22:61). Major emphases include the addition of the scene with Herod, the delay of the council trial to the next morning, and the drama of the good thief.

In the previous chapter we noticed Luke's concern for sequentiality and chronological time, as would be proper to a writer with historical interests. In his use of the word *hour*, Luke frequently continues such interest. Many of the instances of his use of the word can be interpreted as meaning *chronos*, representing time in the sense of duration and sequence. However, in another set of instances the meaning he gives, as with the moment for the Supper, is closer to *kairos*, representing time as opportunity, as the right or critical moment.[19] These references are primarily clustered in chapters 12 and 22—along with a significant instant in 20:19. It is the difference between saying "that hour" as a scheduled time, and "*the* hour" as being a moment of particular significance. The first expresses a chronicler's interest. The second involves drama and the crisis of the narrative.

Luke reworks Mark extensively. Already in Mark's usage, the term is freighted with implication. In Mark's Passion account, the *hour* refers specifically to the arrest of Jesus (Mark 14:35, 37, 41), but with the understanding that this is the moment that Jesus is cast into the hands of his enemies, who are arranging for his death. In the three instances that Luke uses the term as *kairos*, concerning Jesus' Passion, to refer to his arrest, as in Mark's

---

19. As *chronos*: Luke 1:10; 2:38; 7:21; 13:31; 14:17; 22:59; 24:33; as *kairos*, Luke 12:12, 39, 40, 46; 20:19; 22:14, 53.

usage. In Luke 20:19, after the vineyard tenants parable, the authorities are shown to be interested in arresting Jesus, but the time is not ripe. However, in 22:53, the authorities achieve their aim, and Jesus responds, ". . . this is your hour, the time for the power of darkness."

The other instance has already been mentioned—the assigned time for the Supper (22:14). Luke has loaded this moment similarly, with the effect that the Supper takes its place alongside the trials and death as instances of the "hour." The Supper, with its assignments of delegation, lays the plans for continuing the movement beyond the death of Jesus. The arrest, as with Mark, is the "hour" in which Jesus is cast into the hands of his enemies, with the subsequent trials, humiliations, and crucifixion. As the parable of the kingdom foresaw (19:11–27), two primary actions are indicated: transfer of the work of Jesus and the Spirit over to the apostles (the Supper), and the crisis of Jesus' death, with its ironic judgment on those who bring it about (the cross).

The Supper of the Lord

Luke's account of the Lord's Supper places special emphasis on the commissioning and delegation of the apostles. Much of Luke's account follows the model he received from Mark. But his account also is distinctively his own in some important ways. Those requiring attention are the Supper narrative and the farewell speech that follows it.

The Two Cups

What sets Luke's Supper account apart from the others is that he tells a story of two cups shared by Jesus, rather than one. For anyone concerned to examine this account in relation to the Eucharist, the two cups are a problem. But if we ask about the function of the account in the larger narrative of Luke, we see other aspects. First of all, it should be noted that each mention of a cup is part of a balanced pattern. Second, we note that it follows the program announced earlier in the kingdom parable of 19:11–27. Delegation of the disciples is the theme of both the Supper and the speech that accompanies it.

The first cup pairs with the preceding remark of Jesus concerning the Supper—that he desires to eat this meal before he suffers. That last phrase aligns with the first cup, concerning which a similar thing is said. The second cup, paired with the saying about the bread, aligns with the declaration that it is given or shed "for you," indicating a memorial that more fully relates to the eucharistic meal.

The First Cup

14 When the hour came, he took his place at table with the apostles.	17 Then he took a cup,
15 He said to them, "I have eagerly desired to eat this Passover with you before I suffer,	gave thanks, and said, "Take this and share it among yourselves;
16 *for, I tell you,*	18 *for I tell you* [that] from this time on
I shall not eat it [again]	*I shall not drink* of the fruit of the vine
until there is fulfillment in *the kingdom of God.*"	*until the kingdom of God* comes."

The Other Cup

19 Then he took the bread	20 And likewise the cup
said the blessing, broke it,	after they had eaten,
and gave it to them, *saying,*	*saying,*
"This is my body,	"This cup is the new covenant in my blood,
which will be given for you;	which will be shed for you."
do this in memory of me."	

Surely Sharon Ringe is correct in her reading of this passage. In one sense, this is the last in the series of meals that Jesus has shared with his disciples—"the feeding of the five thousand (9:10–17); the meal when Jesus was anointed (7:36–50); the meal with Zacchaeus 19:1–10); the meal that was the setting for a healing, various teachings, and the parable of the great feast (14:1–24); and many others." In another sense, this meal looks ahead to the meals which characterize the faith community, beginning with Luke 24 and continuing into Acts. "As a meal that stands at the heart of the church's life, this Passover feast is reinterpreted in terms of covenant and remembrance focused through the approaching (and for the church, remembered) death of Jesus."[20] The first pairing concludes the narrative of

---

20. Ringe, *Luke*, 261.

the historical Jesus. The second looks forward to the life of the community of the risen Christ in the Spirit. The meals that occur so often in the Gospel come to completion here. The Easter meals of Luke 24 and the community of Acts proceed from here.

The Farewell Speech

The farewell speech of Jesus to his disciples occurs here at the Supper, as it does with much greater effect in John 13–17. Luke has transferred it to this location, from the farewell of the apocalyptic discourse in Mark 13, which he converted to other uses. Luke's Supper farewell is directly connected to the Supper, however, as it explains the sign of the meals and the cups.

The speech is in two parts. Each follows a prediction, in turn, of Judas's betrayal and Peter's denial, which Luke has arranged in a careful sequence. Following the announcement of Judas's betrayal, but without naming him, the first builds on the consternation that results. The argument among the Twelve as to which was the greatest leads to a comment on the true nature of authority in the kingdom of God. Jesus confers authority upon the Twelve. His discussion of authority responds to their arguing among themselves by identifying selfless service as the authentic characteristic of authority, demonstrated by his own example. He stands among them as one who serves at table.

Here for the first time Jesus speaks of his own kingdom, and it is in the context of delegating authority to the Twelve. The two cups close a past era and open a new one. In four key verses, the case is made:

> It is you who have stood by me in my trials;
> and I confer a kingdom on you, just as my Father has conferred one on me,
> that you may eat and drink at my table in my kingdom;
> and you will sit on thrones judging the twelve tribes of Israel (22:28–30).

The delegation anticipates the active place of the apostles later on. In this conferring upon his disciples the authority of the kingdom, we see again how the Supper of Jesus and his apostles looks ahead to Acts.

The second part of the speech follows on the prediction of Peter's denial. The language of crisis leads to a discussion of the apostles' role in the events occurring later that evening. It is here that the discussion of swords takes place. Again we have a passage that has generated conflicting interpretations, as some see here a warrant for Christian use of violence, while others see just the opposite. It is in this respect that a closer look at Luke's use of Isaiah, and how he reworks Mark's narrative, can be helpful.

Jesus as the Servant

In the Supper speech, Luke reconstructs the second and third Passion predictions as they appear in Mark. In Mark's account, the dispute among the disciples is connected to the second Passion prediction and provides the occasion for Jesus' words about the first being last and servant of all (Mark 9:33–35). Luke retains this in his own account of that incident (Luke 9:46–48), but he also brings it forward to the first part of the farewell speech at the Supper.

But more interesting is what he has done with Mark's third Passion prediction and its subsequent teaching (Mark 10:32–45). After James and John make a bid for the seats of honor in the coming kingdom, Jesus delivers a short teaching about service. According to Jesus, honor is unlike that of the gentiles, who lord it over one another. That is not the way for the disciples: The Son of Man came not to be served but to serve, and offer his life as a ransom for many.

While Luke retains the prediction (Luke 18:31–34), he omits the teaching that follows. Or so it would seem. On closer look, we see that the Markan teaching underlies Luke's farewell speech in both of its parts.

The first part echoes Mark 10:42–44 on the true nature of discipleship authority. It is not to be like that of the gentiles. However, Luke introduces a few changes. He softens Mark's picture of gentile authorities dominating by force (they "lord it over them"), and speaks of "benefactors" instead. There is literature on the role of benefactors in the Graeco-Roman system, and we remember that Theophilus is likely an example of such. Luke also shifts the language of Mark ("whoever wishes to be first among you will be the slave of all") to the image of one serving at table. There are overtones here reminiscent of the foot-washing of John. But Luke reports no action to accompany Jesus' words. In general, the Markan image of the servant who "gives his life as a ransom for many" is domesticated in the image of serving at tables, with its lesson of humility.

However, Luke doesn't leave it here. In the unnerving second part of the farewell, we have the exchange about swords. The passage appears to recommend that the disciples be armed. It begins with Jesus asking them about when they were sent out on mission in pairs. Notably, the instance he refers to is not the mission of the Twelve in Luke 9:1–6, but rather the mission of the seventy-two in Luke 10:1–12. As we have already seen, this mission anticipates the mission of Acts. At the farewell speech at the Supper we find an intensification of that mission. It follows upon the delegation already established, but now put in the crisis-oriented terms of *kairos*.

While some see here a justification for the Christian use of force, the view of most commentators that the sword is symbolic. That view is supported by Luke's text. The language of swords first appears symbolically, with the "sword" with which Simeon promises Jesus' mother she will be pierced (1:35). More directly pertinent is the scene of Jesus' arrest, when an actual sword is used. Not only does Jesus refuse to accept that move, but he heals the wound. The action of healing, as the practice of Jesus, directly confronts and opposes the work of the sword.

Most directly pertinent, however, is the lesson that Jesus draws here in the farewell speech from the discussion about swords—"For I tell you that this scripture must be fulfilled in me, namely, 'He was counted among the lawless [*ánomos*]" (22:37). The reference is to Isaiah 53:11—

> Therefore I will give him his portion among the many,
> and he shall divide the spoils with the mighty,
> Because he surrendered himself to death,
> was counted among the transgressors [*ánomois*, LXX],
> Bore the sins of many,
> and interceded for the transgressors.

Here is the verse with which Mark concludes his commentary on the third Passion prediction. It is about accepting suffering rather than inflicting it. Luke places this passage in the context of the discussion about swords. At one level of the narrative, he refers to the fact that they are about to be seen as outlaws ("counted among the lawless"). But at an underlying level, Luke makes reference to the Servant of the Lord, the suffering servant, who will make a later appearance in the Lukan theme of the suffering Messiah, as promised in the scriptures.

Trials, Cross, and Humiliation

Luke introduces many distinct features into his account of the Passion and death of Jesus. Most obvious is the appearance of Herod Antipas, said to be in Jerusalem at the time. When Pilate sends Jesus over to Herod, we have a scene reminiscent of the Gospel account of the Baptist's beheading (Mark 6:17–29), which was not recounted by Luke. Other Lukan touches include his depiction of the prayer in the garden, to which Luke contributes the description "agony" (Luke 22:44). In addition to the appearance of Herod, there are the women of Jerusalem and the good thief. But in the organizing of the action, Luke makes a significant change by delaying the trial of Jesus until the following morning. This allows him to elaborate the humiliating aspect of the hours to follow.

Crucifixion, as practiced by Rome, was seen as a deterrent that would dissuade even the most desperate or radical person from confrontation with the established authorities. In addition to its manifest cruelty in executing its targets, it specialized in an extreme degree of humiliation. The cross was a public feature, with the person dying in public view, naked and defeated. But in Luke's account, the humiliation begins early. With Mark, it begins after Jesus is condemned to death by Pilate. The soldiers mock him as a false king (Mark 15:16–20). But in Luke, it begins with the arrest of Jesus.

Since the trial is not to take place until morning, Jesus remains in the courtyard of the high priest overnight. In effect, the courtyard is a holding pen, where prisoners wait until the trials can begin. Meanwhile, Peter is there. Because Jesus is still outside, it is possible for Luke to set the stage for the moment when the cock crows, and Jesus and Peter lock eyes. Each knows that the other knows. But the wait till morning is also accompanied by taunts and humiliating performances, as they blindfold him and invite him to prophesy.

Once morning comes, the humiliation continues. One result of the appearance of Herod in the narrative is the opportunity to mock Jesus, dressing him in fine robes for effect, before he returned Jesus to Pilate. After Jesus is condemned and sent to the place called "the Skull," the taunting continues, first by the "rulers," then the soldiers. The mocking theme continues up to the thieves crucified on each side of Jesus, where the theme comes to a climax. In a dialogue between the two thieves, the first berates Jesus. But the second thief reproves the first with the words, "Have you no fear of God, for you are subject to the same condemnation? And indeed, we have been condemned justly, for the sentence we received corresponds to our crimes, but this man has done nothing criminal" (23:40–41).

Here the God-fearing reader is alerted to listen to the good thief's words. The thief continues, "Jesus, remember me when you come into your kingdom." And Jesus promises him a place in paradise.

Johnson places this theme in the context of the trials of famous teachers. We have seen that Jesus appears in Jerusalem as a teacher and is opposed for his teaching. Now that rejection of his teaching comes to a fulfillment at the hands of those who were intent on stopping him, but he had not come to the right "hour" (20:21). For the Hellenist reader, the issue was one of honor. The shaming of mockery needed a response. The assault on one's person and teaching required rebuttal. Socrates is shown bravely defending his position before the Athenian judges; Zeno defended himself against the tyrant Nearchus in a defense that involved biting.[21] In dramatic contrast to these confident and even aggressive responses, Jesus was silent. Mark would put us in mind of Jeremiah's response to his temple sermon (Mark 11:17; Jer 7:11; 26:12–15). But Luke has his gentile readers as well. Jesus' silence was incomprehensible to the Hellenist mind, even intolerable. Johnson cites the pagan critic of Christianity Celsus, "... who in his *True Word* (an extended attack on Christianity), criticized this very silence of Jesus (Origen, *Against Celsus* 2:35)."[22]

Striking in Luke's account is the neutral stance of the crowd. This is dramatized on the way of the cross. After the account of Simon of Cyrene forced to carry the cross for Jesus, we hear about a large crowd following Jesus. We are reminded of the crowds on the road to Jerusalem,[23] who were outside the action, but were observing and invited to enter into it. Here the crowd is separated from those who accuse.

Luke gives us another procession by presenting the way of the cross. None of the others have this; at best there is a mention of Simon of Cyrene in the other Gospels. And from among the people, many women who are mourning him are selected for our consideration. Perhaps these are professional mourners. Jesus instructs them to mourn for themselves, not him. The phrase *daughter of Jerusalem* is a common figure of speech to indicate Jerusalem itself. Here again we have the lament over Jerusalem in a continuation of Jesus' teaching in the city. The reversal again shows that the attack on Jesus is actually an attack on Jerusalem. The impact is reversed.

As mentioned, the scene of the crucifixion emphasizes the taunting of Jesus, leading up to the testimony of the good thief, who ends that line of the narrative. The thief, in upbraiding the other thief with the words, "Have you

---

21. *Apology of Socrates*, by the philosopher Plato (429–347 b.c.e.); *Apology of Socrates to the Jury* is Xenophon's literary contribution to the many apologia written to explain the trial of Socrates (399 b.c.e.) to the Athenian public. According to Diogenes Laertius, Zeno conspired to overthrow Nearchus the tyrant. Eventually, Zeno was arrested and tortured. According to Valerius Maximus, when he was tortured to reveal the name of his colleagues in conspiracy, Zeno refused to reveal their names, although he said he did have a secret that would be advantageous, for Nearchus to hear. When Nearchus leaned in to listen to the secret, Zeno bit his ear. He "did not let go until he lost his life and the tyrant lost that part of his body." According to Plutarch, Zeno attempted to kill the tyrant Demylus. After failing, he had, "with his own teeth bit off his tongue, he spit it in the tyrant's face." See Johnson, *Luke*, 366–67.

22. Johnson, *Luke*, 367.

23. Ibid., 372: Here, "the people" (*ho laos*) provide a contrast to those who have agitated for Jesus' death.

no fear of God . . . ?" alerts the God-fearing reader that the gospel invites the response of repentance.

Teacher, and Yet King

Luke presents Jesus as prophet and teacher (*prophet* from the biblical tradition, and *teacher* largely from the Hellenist world), in the process modifying the biblical image from confrontational action toward the direction of disruptive teaching. But Luke also presents Jesus as Messiah, king of God's kingdom. The first time this is made explicit is in the Supper discourse (22:29–30), but the theme of the kingdom had dominated the narrative since the latter chapters of the journey to Jerusalem. And in the parable of the kingdom (19:11–27), the journey came to an end with a look forward to the final days in Jerusalem. However, a dramatic difference separates Jesus' kingship from that of cultural expectations. And it is personified in his role as teacher, moving ideas of kingship away from the exercise of power and toward acts of persuasion, changing hearts and minds.

The messianic role of Jesus also dominates the Passion account of Luke, as the opponents of Jesus focus on claims to kingship as the argument that will move the Roman procurator to action (23:1–2). Deriding claims to kingship is the theme of the sustained mocking of Jesus. The good thief concludes his rebuke of the other thief with a plea for Jesus to include him in his kingdom. And the trial of Jesus before the council focuses exclusively on the messianic status of Jesus. Luke follows the narrative of Jesus' final days from Mark. But, unlike Mark's account where these charges are balanced with accusations of speaking against the temple (Mark 14:57–62), Luke has shifted the charges concerning the temple to the story of Stephen (Acts 6:13–14).

Resolving the Plot Conflict

Luke inherited his plot line from Mark. This includes the final moves of the narrative plot toward its resolution of conflict. Mark structures the concluding interactions between Jesus and his antagonists as a three-fold movement, their key moments being those of the temple cleansing, the garden arrest, and the crucifixion. Each is tagged with the term *lēstēs*, variously translated as "thief," or "robber," or "insurrectionist" (Mark 11:17; 14:48; 15:27). Each marks the conclusion of an initiative by one party or the other. The initiative of Jesus begins with his work in Galilee. Its focus shifts to Jerusalem and climaxes in the temple cleansing. The counter-reaction of the authorities begins there (Mark 11:18) and ultimately completes its move against Jesus in Gethsemane. Jesus refuses to retaliate in kind and is arrested, which then leads to his death on the cross—an *apparent* defeat only, as shown by the empty tomb.[24]

Luke makes each of these moments his own. Some of these instances we have seen. The first, the temple cleansing, is expanded in Luke's treatment into a time of teaching in the temple, leveling a judgment on the city and temple, imagined as a vision of falling stones. The judgment is the theme that coordinates the various teachings of Jesus in Jerusalem during those last days.

The second, the arrest of Jesus, develops as a contrast between the sword's wounding and the healer's repair of the wound. Already at the Supper, this contrast was indicated, as the sword, symbolizing Jesus' new status as an outlaw—a robber—is placed in direct opposition to his claim to be fulfilling the role of the suffering servant of Second Isaiah (Luke 22:37). But now, in healing the ear of the injured high priest's servant, Jesus demonstrates the true power of the kingdom of God.

At the crucifixion, the third moment receives fresh attention as well. A famous line, of admittedly disputed authenticity, reads: "Then Jesus said, 'Father, forgive them, they know not what they do'" (Luke 23:34).[25] Here we find a statement, often reduced to a footnote in Bibles, that still reflects Lukan sentiments, as seen in the similar pronouncement of Stephen, in the narrative already noted as a parallel narrative.[26] In this statement we can find the basic principle of nonviolent conflict resolution, the refusal to identify the opponents with the violence they afflict on others.[27]

The kingship of Jesus, then, contrasts sharply with the cultural expectations of such. It is the difference between the sword and the suffering servant, between injury and healing. In retrospect the reader can compare the image of kingship presented in the programmatic kingdom parable of Luke 19:11–27, with Archelaus as its archetype, and that of the Messiah hanging on the cross.

At the end, the good thief requests entry into the kingdom, and Jesus grants it. The centurion at the scene of the crucifixion does not announce Jesus is a Son of God, as in other Gospels. Rather, he joins a theme of

---

24. For a fuller description of this narrative structure, see Beck, *Nonviolent Story*, 119–29.

25. While this verse is missing in the many early manuscripts of Luke, scholars are loathe to abandon it entirely. It exhibits "self-evident tokens of its dominical origin" (Metzger, *Textual Commentary*, 180).

26. "Then he fell to his knees and cried out in a loud voice, 'Lord, do not hold this sin against them'; and when he said this, he fell asleep" (Acts 7:60).

27. Beck, *Jesus and His Enemies*, 170–71.

Luke's—that of righteousness. And in declaring Jesus "righteous," he aligns the crucified king and teacher with the Nazareth of his youth. And so it is appropriate that we come upon another such, Joseph of Arimathea, described in terms used earlier—a good and righteous man. He too is living in hope, "awaiting the kingdom of God." The women witnessing the event are those of Luke 8:1–3, now reappearing to note the place of burial, and retire to prepare ointments for the burial. "Then they rested on the Sabbath according to the commandment" (23:26).

The time in Jerusalem draws to an end. This Sabbath is a caesura, an interlude between two eras, two ages. There is a pause, and the story of Jesus of Nazareth comes to a stasis. After the Sabbath, a new story will begin. But for now, there is silence, and a time of rest.

Luke 24

In some ways, the last chapter of Luke counts as the first chapter of Acts of the Apostles. It takes us into a new realm, that of the kingdom of God in the Spirit. In other ways, it is the necessary prelude to Acts, just as it is the triumphant climax of Luke's Gospel. The three incidents that it relates—the empty tomb, the encounter on the road to Emmaus, and the appearance in the upper room—facilitate the transition. The first, the account of the empty tomb, follows the lead of Mark. Luke reworks it to remove some apparent awkwardness (going to the tomb without knowing how to accomplish what they plan to do, Mark 16:3), as well as to introduce another reference to the Passion predictions (Luke 24:7), in further support of the Supper farewell.

But the extraordinary contribution of Luke to the resurrection traditions occurs in the next story of the two disciples, Cleopas and a friend, traveling to Emmaus. On the one hand, it completes the Gospel narrative with its resurrection appearance of Jesus, now transfigured as had been foreseen.[28] On the other hand, it introduces themes of the post-resurrection story that will be told in Acts.

The Emmaus story is constructed in two phases—a liturgy of the word and a liturgy of the meal. In the first of these, Luke borrows a pattern he will use in Acts as the format of Peter's *kerygma* speeches. The pattern has a certain number of steps—Jesus of Nazareth was baptized by John, did works and wonders, was crucified, was raised by God, all according to the scriptures, and we are the witnesses. The pattern is credal, centering on the witness to the resurrection, supported by the affirmation of the death of Jesus (testifying to an authentic resurrection).

28. Luke 9:29, at the transfiguration, "the appearance of his face became different."

It is this that shapes the Emmaus story. When the stranger seems unfamiliar with "the things that have taken place there in these days," they proceed to tell him, following the pattern, recounting "the things that happened to Jesus the Nazarene, who was a prophet mighty in deed and word before God and all the people, how our chief priests and rulers both handed him over to a sentence of death and crucified him" (24:19-20). But when they arrive at the heart of the *kerygma*, they are stymied. Some women reported that the tomb was empty, and they saw angels. Some of us went and found the tomb as they said, but "him they did not see." What is missing from this is the experience of the resurrection on the part of these two. They are not yet equipped to be witnesses of the risen Christ. Rather, it is happening but they do not know it yet. At this point, Jesus begins to add one more item in the *kerygma* list—the witness of scripture. "Then beginning with Moses and all the prophets, he interpreted to them what referred to him in all the scriptures" (24:27).

It is when they arrive at the village to which they were going that the lacking experience is supplied, to complete the *kerygma*. Inviting him to stay with them, they shared a meal, and they recognized him in the breaking of the bread (24:35). The liturgy of the meal completes their experience, and they not only recognize him, and become authentic witnesses, but exclaim how their hearts were "burning while he spoke to us on the way and opened the scriptures to us" (24:32). Their resurrection experience is complete, and now that they are fully accredited witnesses according to the *kerygma* credentials, they return to Jerusalem to testify.

In the final scene of the Gospel, Luke shows the returning pair encountering another witnessing proclamation, that of the Jerusalem community of disciples. Their return ensures that the entire community, in dramatic contrast to the other Gospels, will remain in Jerusalem, available for the following narrative of Acts. Then they will begin in Jerusalem and move outward from the city.

This final scene covers a lot of ground for Luke. Jesus appears while they are exclaiming to one another. They are startled, and this prompts him to reassure them with demonstrations that he is not a ghost. Echoes of John's Gospel have him showing his wounds and inviting them to touch him, followed by an offer to eat a baked fish, as with the meal by the lakeside in John's last chapter—which he does.

At this point, the event takes a turn, as Jesus again opens their minds to receive the scriptures that relate to this event. The theme of repentance, which is so prominent in Luke's narrative, is added to the theme of resurrection, as it is in Peter's speeches in Acts. Finally, the account reports the ascension (Luke 24:50-53), which takes place on the same day, unlike the forty days delay of Acts. However, we are bringing this part of the story to a close, as we prepare to open the next volume.

In addition to the *kerygma* theme that supplies a structure to the Emmaus story, an important motif is that of the suffering Messiah, as foretold in the scriptures (24:26, 46). As commentators assure us, this is not found as such in the scriptures. But we see that here it is a summarizing concept to represent the meaning of the story of Jesus, crucified and risen, as Luke wants it known. But it is a perspective that is visible only from beyond the cross and resurrection. Beyond the time of the suffering Messiah is that of the risen Messiah and the Holy Spirit.

Conclusion

The story of Jesus told by Luke presents him as messianic royalty and a prophet, but his performance is primarily that of a renowned teacher, beginning early in his life. From the villagers in the early chapters to Joseph of Arimathea and the women at the burial, his story is framed by portraits of righteous and humble people, pictured waiting upon God for the salvation of Israel. Between these evocative bookends unfolds a story of Jesus, one filled with the Spirit, inaugurating his mission from his home synagogue at Nazareth. There he invokes an alternative theme of their tradition, that of the latter chapters of Isaiah, promising a light to the gentiles, and a Jubilee day of deliverance. For seven chapters he is pictured bringing light and life to the villages of Galilee. But at a certain point he turns his face toward Jerusalem, the center of the Judean world, to which he will then bring his message.

In an extended journey to the city, Jesus teaches about his mission as demonstrated in Galilee. The praxis of Galilee becomes the theme of his teaching, in which he interacts with three parties of interlocutors. With the disciples he emphasizes the need for repentance and trust in God. With the Pharisees and *nomikoi* he debates the meaning of authentic righteousness in repentance, as contrasted with the self-achieved righteousness of those who misuse the law for that purpose. For the God-fearing gentile reader, this contest between Jewish factions is a lesson in proper response to the call of Jesus. That reader finds a place in the narrative among the crowds, the third party of interlocutors.

Upon reaching the city, Jesus brings his message to the leadership, leaving the Pharisees behind. In Jerusalem his teaching raises dangerously hostile opposition. Luke frames the judgment on the city and the temple with images of fallen stones. The prophetic meaning of the temple cleansing is elaborated in his teaching in the temple, a protracted period in Luke's account. In the "hour" that concludes the life of Jesus, themes of crisis and delegation predominate. The disciples are commissioned with responsibilities in the kingdom during the Supper, as Jesus moves toward his trial and death. These moments are marked by a crescendo of humiliation, increasing toward the testimony of the good thief, and then the centurion who witnesses to the righteousness of Jesus. The Gospel narrative concludes with the appearance of the risen Christ, bringing suffering into glory, and preparing for the next part of Luke's story, the Acts of the Apostles.

CHAPTER FIVE

Reading the Acts of the Apostles
"God Shows No Partiality"

ALTHOUGH LUKE–ACTS IS A single narrative, it comes to us in the shape of two books. And this is not merely coincidental. Both the unity and the doubling contribute to the meaning of the work. Luke–Acts is increasingly recognized as a coherent project, planned from the beginning.

But the claim being made of the double work goes beyond asserting that the two books are a single project. It also says that the two form a single narrative.[1] Certain elements imply continuity of plot. A clue planted at the beginning of a narrative is intended to contribute to the final working out of the story. The baptism of John (Luke 3:3) is an initial step that is then discovered in Acts to be only a beginning of something much fuller (Acts 19:1–7). The theme of the mission to the gentiles thus is found in the traditions about John, both in his preaching (Luke 3:4–6) and his testimony to the difference between his baptism (water) and that of Jesus (the Holy Spirit). Meanwhile, in a complementary way, features of the gospel narrative (in Mark) are deferred to Acts. The temple charges at Jesus' trial, in Mark, are omitted in Luke's Gospel, but reappear in Stephen's witness in Acts 7. The death of Judas is incorporated in the incipient mission of the Eleven, soon to become the Twelve again. Simply put, the continuous narrative operates as a two-act drama. First, we hear the story of Jesus; then we hear how the movement that began with him spread out into the world.

---

1. E.g., Moessner and Tiede, "Two Books But One Story?" 1–4. Also, in the conclusion, "The four contributors to Part One all agree that the two prologues express narrative continuity by linking *two* volumes to produce *one* larger story of Israel's heritage," 358.

This continuous narrative is divided into two books, not simply sequentially, but by a shift in perspective. The book of Acts looks back at the Gospel as a completed text. The story is one that Luke has received. He and his readers are looking at it from the outside, as a text that is now closed. While it can be argued that Mark's Gospel is not a closed text—in the sense that the ending is left open to further revelations of the risen Christ—as far as Luke is concerned, it has been closed. One indication of this is his narrative use of the ascension event in Acts 1:3—he was "appearing to them during forty days and speaking about the kingdom of God." The resurrection appearances end, and the disciples wait for further instructions.

This perception of the Gospel as a completed work is seen in the manner in which it is referred to, in brief, as a text or object to be cited as a whole. At least two strategies are evident. One of these is the motif of the "suffering Messiah," said to be given "according to the scriptures" (Luke 24:26, 36; Acts 3:18; 17:3; 26:23). All of these instances of the term are post-resurrection and presume to explain the meaning of the death and resurrection. The other method of referring to the Gospel in its entirety is the *kerygma* credo that patterns the speeches of Peter in Acts (2:22–40; 3:12–26; 4:1–12; 5:30–32; 10:34–43). Seen already as structuring the Emmaus story in Luke 24, it has an earlier formulation in 1 Corinthians 15:3–9. In effect, this pattern, seen especially in its more complete forms, consists of a summary of the gospel narrative.[2] As such, it can serve as a symbol for that narrative. In each case—the motif of the suffering Messiah and the *kerygma* speeches of Peter—we have a shorthand reference to the narrative as initiated by Mark and handed on to others, including Luke.

And yet, while in one way it is closed, Luke is busy opening it up again. In fact, this re-opening of the story is essential to the meaning of Acts. It is in this sense that Acts, *as* a separate story, is *also* the narrative continued. And as Acts continues the narrative of Luke, it also situates it, in the sense that the Acts of the Apostles represents within the text the site from which the implied reader is reading. We saw something similar in the Gospel, in the "crowds" along the journey to Jerusalem. In the journey account of the

---

2. Again, the pattern of Peter's *kerygma* speeches give a summary of the main moments in the gospel narrative. In its fullest form, it includes these elements—
- a. Jesus of Nazareth
- b. was baptized by John
- c. did works and wonders
- d. was crucified
- e. was raised by God
- f. according to the scriptures
- g. we are witnesses of this event
- h. therefore, repent and be baptized

Gospel, characters within the narrative look at the conflict between Jesus and his opponents in the way an outside reader might—although Luke has brought that external reader into the narrative.

Something similar is happening in Acts. It provides the setting in which the gospel is remembered, preached, and enacted. In this sense, it also tells that story in terms of its implied reader for Luke, whom we have identified as the pious gentile, the God-fearer. We are intermittently reminded of this set of readers. In Acts 21, as Paul has returned to Jerusalem after his travels and is greeted by the church there, we read concerns about reports of his missionary work. We get a glimpse of a part of the church that is not at the center of this narrative: "Brother, you see how many thousands of believers there are from among the Jews, and they are all zealous observers of the law." As far as Luke is concerned, there is a large Jewish component among the community of believers, but they are not at the center of his story. The narrative of Acts has a particular focus, and we are occasionally reminded that it is not the whole story. There is also an untold story apart from the gentile church at the center of our attention, referred to obliquely when mentioning "how many ten thousands there are among the Jews who have believed" (Acts 21:20).

Ascension

In Acts, the ascension of Jesus supplies a temporal marker for Luke in a way that is not true of the ascension account in his Gospel. Luke articulates the post-resurrection moments by calendar days in a way that John, who gives us the same moments, does not. The death, resurrection, ascension, and consequent sending of the Spirit all occur in quick succession in John's Gospel. In Luke's, these are separated moments, notably forty days until the ascension and another ten until Pentecost. What this procedure does, in effect, is articulate a theme by way of narrative time. It is a literary construct to mark off periods of time as moments of theological significance. The resurrection of Jesus reaches completion in the return of the Son to the Father and the consequent sending forth of the Spirit.

This narrative practice also allows Luke to place emphasis on the ascension in ways no other evangelist does. It serves a number of purposes for him. As mentioned earlier, one of these is to signal the end of the time of resurrection appearances (Acts 1:3). And while he indicates this to be the case, Luke has no problem having Paul later experience an appearance of the risen Christ (though Paul himself speaks of it as out of due time in 1 Corinthians 15:9). It illustrates the use of the incident as a narrative strategy.

The ascension completes the time of Jesus (followed by a pause of ten days) before the beginning of the time of the Spirit.

But there are other implications as well, of preeminent importance for the narrative of Acts. Some have made the point that Luke's account of the ascension echoes the apotheosis of Augustus, ascending to his divinity.[3] Jesus is called *Lord* in the manner of the God of Israel.[4] And in this, we see an extension of Luke's eschatology into "apocalyptic" rule, as an alternative to the "lord" Caesar (Acts 25:26).

The eschatology of Luke began with the announcement at Nazareth, with the Spirit present in Jesus. At that time, the announcement that "Today this scripture passage is fulfilled in your hearing" established the beginning of the final time, when the message will be extended to the gentiles. But the time of the gentiles, now begun, is not to be shortened. With the ascension, the announcement is proclaimed that a new phase in that eschatological age has arrived. It comes into effect with the series of resurrection and ascension events, as announced by Peter: "'And it will be in the last days,' God says, 'I will pour out my Spirit on all flesh'" (Acts 2:17), and "Therefore let all the house of Israel know beyond a doubt, that God has made him both Lord and Christ—this Jesus whom you crucified!" (2:35-36). The Acts of the Apostles will unfold from here, with Jesus as Lord and the Spirit as motivating power. In its unfolding, the Lord and Spirit move into the world of the empire, confronting the lordship of Caesar.

I. PENTECOST: THE PROGRAMMATIC EVENT

Luke's characteristic method of employing episodes comes forward in a big way with the second chapter of Acts. The Pentecost event establishes the vision for the coming story. The event (Acts 2:1-13) is followed by an elaboration of its meaning by Peter and the apostles (2:14-41).

The Pentecost narrative is simply constructed. The event itself unfolds in two parts—the descent of the Spirit and the outpouring of languages.

---

3. See Bachmann, "Jerusalem and Rome," *Luke-Acts*, 74-78.

4. Rowe, *World Upside Down*, 111-12: "Luke's use of Joel here involves a christological extension of the use of *kyrios* in the OT. Where *kyrios* in the Joel text taken alone refers only to the God of Israel, in the context of Acts 2, *kyrios* refers both to the God of Israel and to Jesus, the only name by which there is salvation (see Acts 4:12). It is not the case, that is, that what we see in this text is a simple substitution of one *kyrios* for another—as if the *kyrios* of Joel 2:5 no longer applies to God. Instead, Luke's hermeneutical appropriation of the OT reflects a rather more complex theological move, one in which the prophecy of the text of Joel is expanded—not negated—to say that the Lord God's coming is actually and really fulfilled in the appearance of the Lord Jesus."

Images of wind and fire carry the narrative, with the former introducing the Spirit and the latter, separated into "tongues," anticipating the many languages, or tongues, that mark the event. Furthermore, the account of the response to the event builds a narrative from two building blocks—a list of nations and a refrain—"each one heard them speaking in his own language" (2:6, 8, 11). The nations listed are not specifically representative of the sites visited in Acts, and the populations named are not gentiles, but Jews and converts to Judaism. Luke does not explain how those of different languages discovered that others also heard the speech in their own language. Nor does he tell us how they discussed it between the different groups. We are not to inquire into these matters, but simply to understand that we are about to depart on a new dimension in the coming narrative of Acts.

As in previous cases, Luke builds his programmatic episodes by re-purposing accounts that appear in other contexts. In this case, the enthusiastic speech, or glossolalia, that seems to have been common among the early communities, is enlisted by Luke to provide the reader with a vision of the coming events. But he converts *glossolalia*, an enthusiastic overflow of speech unimpeded by constraints of grammar, to *xenoglossia*, the ability to speak an existent language one has never learned.

We know that in 1 Corinthians 12–14, Paul addresses the phenomenon of speaking in the Spirit and charged his audience with causing confusion if the gift of tongues is not accompanied by the gift of interpretation (1 Cor 14:13–19). This implies *glossolalia*. But Luke has something else in mind. He wants to set up the narrative of Acts with an image of moving out to real peoples, as represented by their real languages. It is Luke that has given us the notion that the biblical gift of tongues involves real languages.

Paul's concern about creating confusion is also flipped by Luke. In the Septuagint, the Greek Bible that provides Luke (and the gentile God-fearers) with access to the Old Testament, the story that we know as the Tower of Babel has another name—"the Tower of Confusion": "On this account its name was called *Confusion*, because there the Lord confounded the languages of all the earth, and thence the Lord scattered them upon the face of all the earth" (Gen 11:9). Luke echoes this with his account of the astonished assembly outside the upper room—"... the crowd gathered and was *in confusion*, because each one was hearing them speaking in his own language" (Acts 2:6). But the confusion was soon dispelled as the message became clear. And the march to the ends of the earth was about to begin.

Spirit

Pentecost introduces a new role for the Holy Spirit. In lieu of a consistent protagonist throughout the full extent of Acts' narrative, the Spirit adopts this position. In the Gospel, Jesus is the protagonist, a role made clear in the synagogue of Nazareth. In the earlier narrative the baptism of John with water is contrasted with Jesus' baptism of the Spirit. But now the Spirit of Jesus (Acts 16:7), is let loose into the community. The transfer from one drama to the other is accomplished.

The Spirit is characterized by certain actions. The works of the Spirit are *coming upon* or *descending upon, filling, revealing,* or *teaching*.[5] One is said to be "filled" with Spirit, which either overcomes or intensifies the actions of the one filled. Clearly it is an idiom. However, it also indicates a sense of personal transcendence, of being taken over by a greater power. But the image is a liquid one—a container is filled. In this sense of being heightened by a transcendent power, it contrasts with the unclean spirits who possess a person. Spirits take over persons. Just as the Holy Spirit "fills," the unclean spirit "possesses."

But it is this capacity to take claim of a person that allows the Spirit to assume a role in the action of the account. Insofar as the Spirit works through others who are the actual protagonists, it is the primary protagonist. But the Spirit is also something of a stage manager. In Luke's narrative the Holy Spirit directs the plot, sending persons in different directions for different purposes. The Spirit is said to direct the actions of principle characters in the drama. For example, it directs the selection of the seven deacons (Acts 6:3) and the five prophets and teachers, with special reference to Barnabas and Saul (13:2). The Spirit sends Philip to the Ethiopian (8:29). The Spirit directs Peter to Cornelius (10:19; 11:12) and confirms his mission there (10:44–45). The Spirit sends Paul and Barnabas on their mission (13:4). The "Spirit of Jesus" redirects that mission to Europe (16:7). The Spirit concludes that mission and sends Paul to Jerusalem (20:22), despite contrary messages from the Spirit (21:4). In other words, more than being a protagonist, the Spirit directs the action. However, insofar as the Spirit is "the Spirit of Jesus," it is the impulse behind the action of the protagonist, extended and extrapolated into the subsequent narrative of the Jesus movement.

---

5. In Acts, the full title, "Holy Spirit," appears forty times. In addition, the Spirit is referenced apart from the full title 13 times. Again, we have *receiving, filling, teaching* or *instructing* (including giving directions), *empowering,* and being *tested* or *opposed.* When the Spirit is seen as being received, the emphasis is on the experience as a gift, unwarranted. It is also a power, one that is envied by Simon Magus. The notion that one can be "filled" with the Spirit (ten instances in Acts) is interesting as an image.

II. NARRATIVE STRUCTURE

The Pentecost event provides Acts with a programmatic scene. But it does not stand alone in this regard. In addition, as Jesus is about to depart in the ascension, he commits the apostles to a mission, one that follows a succession of phases: "But you will receive power when the holy Spirit comes upon you, and you will be my witnesses in *Jerusalem*, throughout *Judea and Samaria*, and to *the ends of the earth*" (Acts 1:8). Each of these turns out to be a separate step in the journey outward into the world. And each is established in the text by four markers—a place name as given in the announcement, a list of persons, a commissioning rite, and a major speech—neatly dividing the following narrative into three distinct parts—Acts 1–5; 6–12; 13–28.

The list of persons describe different ministries within the community. They are, first, the eleven apostles (1:13); then, seven "Hellenists" (6:5); and, finally, five "prophets and teachers" (13:1). The rites of initiation include the casting of lots to select Matthias and return the roster of apostles to twelve in number (1:26), as well as the laying on of hands in the other two instances (6:6; 13:3). Most impressively, each of these stages is the occasion for a major speech, by Peter (2:14–36), Stephen (7:2–53), and Paul (13:26–41). These are the major speeches in the book. Among them they contain most of the scripture references in Acts. And each inaugurates one of the three movements, setting out a point of view to direct the reader in interpreting the action.

Finally, each is tagged with a reference to the territorial stage of the action, as given in the commission from Jesus—1:13, "Then they returned to Jerusalem from the mount called Olivet"; 8:1, "and all were scattered throughout the countryside of Judea and Samaria, except the apostles"; 13:47, "I have made you a light to the gentiles, that you may be an instrument of salvation to the ends of the earth."

Or, put more conveniently in a chart, we have this:

	Chapters 1–5	Chapters 6–12	Chapters 13–28
Places	1:12	8:1	13:47
Names	1:13	6:5	13:1
Rites	1:24–26	6:6	13:3
Speeches	2:14–36	7:2–53	13:26–41

This plan for Acts, elaborately given in the text, presents an image of centrifugal movement, a thrown stone creating ripples in a pond. It contrasts with the nearly obsessive image of linear movement in the Gospel in the long road to Jerusalem. It offers an image of reaching out into the empire; in this, it coordinates with other graduated series. A sociological sequence moves from Judean Jews or "Hebrews" to Diaspora Jews or "Hellenists" (6:1), to devout God-fearers (10:1), to "Greeks" (11:19-20). Similarly, the Pentecost event itself finds replications in a series leading out into the imperial world (2:4; 8:17; 10:44; 19:6). Clearly Luke's text makes a strong case for the outward movement of the Acts of the Apostles as representing the mission to the world.

And yet, when it comes to delineating the plot line of Acts, we find difficulties. While it serves to take us to the middle chapters of Acts, it offers little help beyond that. The mission of Paul is left as a large elaboration of the last step. Furthermore, the narrative concludes in Rome, a specific site, and not a generalized "ends of the earth." And so, while the pattern has some value in charting the movement from Jerusalem to Paul, its larger value is to present an image of the mission to the world. In fact, it serves more as a rhetorical statement of the purpose of Acts than a structure of the narrative.

But by attending to the narrative itself, we can arrive at a clearer sense of the plot line of the narrative. Here we can make use of the standard critical tools for determining narrative plots. This would include features of Luke's method we have already seen, such as programmatic episodes and shifting sets of characters as we move from one narrative section to the next narrative section. But in addition we can trace how those changing sets of characters result in different lines of engagement, as the narrative conflict evolves. With that, we can arrive at a more functional, and less thematic, structure for the book of Acts. This will guide the following description of the action. As discussed here, the unfolding drama after the opening scene will be these:

- Jerusalem (Acts 3-7)
- Judea and Samaria / Antioch (Acts 8-15)
- Ephesus (Acts 16-20)
- Jerusalem to Rome (Acts 21-28)

III. NARRATIVE OF ACTS

Jerusalem (Acts 2:42—7:50)

After the cosmic vision of Pentecost, opening to the wide world, the narrative narrows its focus to the city and the temple. The international throngs disappear, and we turn to the community headed by Peter and the apostles, as they deliver their witness to the people of Jerusalem. In the idealized images of the Pentecostal community, we have a parallel to the villagers of Luke 1–2, in their depiction of the righteous community. In three vignettes, the community is described as devoted to the teaching of the apostles, the common life, praying together in the temple and breaking bread in their homes (2:42–47; 4:32–35; 5:12–16). The second of these dioramas focuses on the practices of sharing goods and leads into the report of Barnabas, who reverses the deed of Judas by selling some property and donating the proceeds to the community (1:18; 2:36–37). He provides a contrast to the following account of Ananias and Sapphira, who were not as generous, and paid for it.

The narrative conflict is carried, in this part of the narrative, between the antagonistic parties of the Jewish Sanhedrin on the one side, and the apostles on the other. Dominating our attention in the Jerusalem part of the drama is this story of the Jewish council attempting to stop the nascent movement of Jesus-followers. Twice (4:5–22; 5:17–42) the apostles clash with the Sanhedrin. Called before "Annas the high priest, Caiaphas, John, Alexander, and all who were of the high-priestly class," Peter and John give an account of their movement, confronting the very leaders who had just previously arranged for the death of Jesus, Peter delivers a version of his *kerygma* speech (4:10–12). Warned to cease and desist, the apostles are then released.

But the apostles find themselves unable to comply, and before long they are again summoned by the Sanhedrin. And with that, we hear of the first miraculous release from jail: "But during the night, the angel of the Lord opened the doors of the prison, led them out, and said, 'Go and take your place in the temple area, and tell the people everything about this life'" (5:19–20). In response to the charge that the apostles have disobeyed the injunction against them, Peter pronounces his famous principle—"We must obey God rather than men" (5:29). And with that, once again, he recites his *kerygma* message (5:30–32).

Gamaliel

What follows is possibly the most famous incident in the Jerusalem section of Acts. Gamaliel, a Pharisee in the Sanhedrin, argues for the release of the apostles. His argument takes the form of weighing a set of alternatives. "For if this endeavor or this activity is of human origin, it will destroy itself. But if it comes from God, you will not be able to destroy them; you may even find yourselves fighting against God" (5:38-39). While this speech, and the Sanhedrin's decision endorsing it, is often interpreted as the author's way of showing that even the Jewish council finds itself endorsing the divine impulse behind the Jesus movement, there would seem to be more going on here.[6]

Ananias and Sapphira

But for that, we need to return to one of the more difficult and confusing passages in this part of Acts—the story of Ananias and Sapphira. This story, coming between the first and second summons of the apostles before the Jewish leaders, serves as an introduction to the Gamaliel story. They stand in contrast. Itself introduced by the report of the generous nature of Barnabas, the story of the couple, Ananias and Sapphira, demonstrates the contrasting impulses that inhabit the sharing community. Like Barnabas, they too sold a piece of property but only pretended to give the full purchase price to the community, retaining a portion for themselves. Peter, somehow learning about this, confronts Ananias with his deception, naming it a lie to the Holy Spirit. Ananias falls down dead, and some young men wrap him up and bury him. And great fear comes upon the community (5:1-6).

In the manner of folktales, a genre which seems to have affected this story, Ananias's wife Sapphira is unaware of his fate, and neither is she told about it. Coming in some three hours later, the pattern repeats itself with her. She lies about the gift, she falls down dead, the young men come and bury her. And fear consumes the community (5:7-11). Notably, while Peter is the one who calls to account, neither he nor any of the disciples exact the sentence of death, but rather God himself. Nonetheless, the sudden and punitive death of certain community members disturbs the idyllic nature of the early community, as we often prefer to view it.

But we have already seen that strife and conflict is a part of these early chapters, and the story of the unfortunate couple is a part of that. The account of Ananias and Sapphire is essential to the working out of this part of the narrative. What is occurring is a transfer of authority, at least in the view of the narrator. We can include, among the attributes of authority, the *power of correction*. Without this, any claim to authority would seem to be barren. But in the two stories of the couple, on the one hand, and Gamaliel,

---

6. Note Johnson, *Acts*, 102: "Remarkably, Gamaliel's little speech is often interpreted as entirely benign, and even as evidence for Luke's positive appreciation of the Pharisees. So to understand it is to miss entirely the signals the author himself has given us."

on the other, we see two expressions of this power of correction. In the two choices that Gamaliel presents to the council, he is saying, in effect, that if God is behind this movement, we cannot stop it, and if God is not, it will die of itself. Either way, the Sanhedrin has nothing to do in this matter. And if it cannot decide in matters like this, what then can it decide? What then is its role?

In contrast, Peter and the apostles possess the power of correction, as seen in the story of Ananias and Sapphira. They correct, and God endorses their decision. In other words, this part of the narrative shows the authority of the Sanhedrin being transferred to the Apostolic Council, at least in the view of the narrator.

We are to understand that the Apostolic Council is a *permanent, standing council*, and not something that exists only when it is called into session. The transfer of authority is indicated in this power of correction, futile in the case of the Sanhedrin (according to Gamaliel), but shown to be effective with the Apostolic Council. God is working through the apostles, not the Sanhedrin. And so it is that, when persecution hits the community in Jerusalem, while the others leave in missions of witness, the apostles stay in the city (Acts 8:1). And they do this despite the fact that *apostolos* means "one sent forth on a mission."

Stephen

What prompted the persecution in Jerusalem, or at least coincided with it, according to Acts, was the martyrdom of Stephen. This "Hellenist" was among the seven listed in Acts 6:5, selected to provide for the Diaspora Jews among the Jerusalem community. His speech, as noted earlier, is one of the three major speeches that mark out progressive stretches of the mission in Acts.

Stephen's speech largely consists of a review of sacred history. However, it focuses on Abraham and Moses. With Moses, Stephen brings his story to the founding of the tabernacle in the wilderness. Recounting the travels in the desert that bring the Israelites to enter the land promised them, Stephen segues quickly to the building of the temple by Solomon. He rejects that as against the wishes of God. Citing Amos 5:25–27 (LXX) and Isaiah 66:1 (LXX), Stephen echoes the views of those who opposed turning the tabernacle from tent into temple, from mobility to monument, represented in the narrative of 2 Samuel 7:5–7.[7]

---

7. And as memorably thematized by Brueggemann in *Prophetic Imagination*, Chap. Two, "Royal Consciousness: Countering Counterculture."

At this point in his speech, Stephen leaves off reviewing past events and, in an abrupt shift of reference from third-person to second, levels his accusations directly. "You stiff-necked people, uncircumcised in heart and ears, you always oppose the holy Spirit; you are just like your ancestors . . . They put to death those who foretold the coming of the righteous one, whose betrayers and murderers you have now become" (7:51).

What we see is unfinished business from the Gospel of Luke. Unlike his narrative source, Luke omitted the charges against Jesus at his trial that would include, in addition to messianic claims, defamation of the temple (Mark 14:58; 15:29). Instead, he transfers the burden of that claim to the present story of Stephen. And in so doing, he give us one more example of Jewish institutions and practices being marginalized by the narrative of Luke–Acts. Of course, when Luke is writing, the city and temple are long gone. His narrative anticipates their disappearance. Here we hear about the temple; later, in the larger narrative arc, we leave Jerusalem behind.

Judea and Samaria, and Antioch (Acts 8:1—15:35)

The narrative leaves Jerusalem behind at the beginning of Acts 8. As the setting changes, the parties in conflict—the Jewish Sanhedrin and the Apostolic Council—are replaced by others. At first we see Philip and Peter (still with us). And before long these are joined by Paul, who will be recruited by Barnabas. Their opposition is less defined now. But we begin to see the kind of opposition that will prevail during the mission encounters in the later parts of Acts. Simon Magus (8:9-13, 18-25) previews the encounter with popular or pagan religions, experienced by Paul in Lystra, Philippi, and Ephesus. Philip's instructions to the Ethiopian eunuch anticipates the move toward the God-fearers. But the primary action of this section involves Peter and Paul and concerns the removal of barriers presented by Jewish practices. With Peter it is the engagement with Cornelius and the revision of the food laws. With Paul and Barnabas it is circumcision that is put aside for the gentile converts.

We recall the initial, and programmatic, scene in the Nazareth synagogue, where Jesus reads from the Book of Isaiah, alarming the villagers of Nazareth. We noted in chapter three how one tradition is played off against another, reviving tensions of post-exilic Judaism. The vision of offering a light to the nations, proclaimed in the prophecies of Second Isaiah and perpetuated by Third Isaiah after the exiles' return to the land, was set aside in favor of a policy of accommodation to surviving as a colony of the Persian Empire. Without political independence and the identity it conferred on its citizens, finding itself in what seemed a hostile environment, the community feels the need for practices that distinguish its members. In the reformation of Ezra and Nehemiah, as we have seen, lines of community demarcation were drawn sharply. And the practices of circumcision, food laws, Sabbath worship, and marriage laws were enforced.

These became the identity markers of the Jewish community, and they came to be synonymous with being Jewish. But the vision of Second Isaiah remained on the books, and when Jesus read from the scroll of Isaiah and announced, "Today this scripture passage is fulfilled in your hearing," it was to say that the long-deferred dream of the light to the gentiles was about to be realized. The time had come. From within the Jewish tradition, a universalist strand that was open to the nations is about to be released, no longer buried beneath the prevailing stance of xenophobia, with its identity markers. It was that pronouncement in Nazareth, with its backstory, that lay behind the narratives of Acts, and in particular chapters 8–15. In all of this, Luke's concern is not so much with the central body of Jewish believers in the messiahship of Jesus, but rather with those gentiles who are hoping to join this community, or who have joined and wish to be affirmed in their place in it.

Acts presents the movement leaving Jerusalem as somewhat straightforward. First we observe Philip ministering in the nearby territories of Samaria (8:4–25) and Judea (8:26–40). Then we follow Peter's efforts at the very edge of the district, in the coastal towns of Lydda, Joppa, and Caesarea Maritima (8:32—11:18). Finally, we come to Syrian Antioch, which becomes the base of the missions of Paul (11:19–26). This fits well with the outward movement of the mission, as promulgated by the rhetoric of Acts. And in Antioch, the mission outward takes a further and decisive step:

> Now those who had been scattered by the persecution that arose because of Stephen went as far as Phoenicia, Cyprus, and Antioch, preaching the word to no one but Jews. There were some Cypriots and Cyrenians among them, however, who came to Antioch and began to speak to the Greeks as well, proclaiming the Lord Jesus (11:19-20).

However, the opening phrase of this passage places us back at the beginning of chapter 8 when the movement out from Jerusalem began, and we realize that this is an additional initiative, separate from that of Philip and Peter and concurrent with it. Instead of the territories around Jerusalem, it establishes a new center of operations in Antioch and will feature Barnabas and Paul.[8] In other words, two narratives intertwine, ostensibly part of the

---

8. Johnson, *Acts*, 203: "Luke clearly wants us to see these missionaries pushing

one movement out from Jerusalem, but best considered separately. Each presents a different challenge to the Jewish practices. First, we will look at the mission in Judea and Samaria, and the consequence for food laws. Then we will look at the mission from Antioch, and the debate over circumcision.

Judea and Samaria (Acts 8:1–40; 9:32—11:18; 12:1–24)

After the report of Philip moving out into the areas surrounding Jerusalem (Acts 8), and Peter having moved to the very edges of those territories (9:32–43), this narrative thread comes to the encounter between Peter and Cornelius. The extended account of their engagement is one of the main moments in Acts. Since this has already been discussed at some length in chapter one, only a few points related to the narrative movement need be made here.

First of all, in this encounter the story of Peter in this part of Acts makes its contribution to the overall project of Luke-Acts—testimony concerning the abrogation of food laws for gentile followers of Jesus. The revelation at Caesarea Maritima has been anticipated from the beginning. We have already noted the links of Peter's vision with the baptism of John, as well as with the Pentecost story. "The narrator has Peter take the reader back not only to Pentecost as the original of his behavior with Cornelius, but to an even more fundamental beginning for the fruition of Pentecost—to the beginning of the first volume."[9]

Furthermore, in addition to its connection with the baptism of the Spirit, the Cornelius event is also linked to the programmatic Nazareth episode by the word *acceptable* (*dektos*), which appears twice in the Nazareth story (Luke 4:19, 24). Not only are these the only other times in Luke-Acts that the term appears, but they are from the two texts that shape the Nazareth narrative—the scripture quotation and the proverb. In the passage quoted from Isaiah 61:1, in the present context announcing a new day of mission to the gentiles, Luke naturally follows the LXX translation, which translates "a year of favor" with "the *acceptable* year." And he reworks the proverb he derived from Mark 6:4 from "A prophet is not without honor except in his native place" to "no prophet is *acceptable* in his native place."

But while the story of Peter comes to its main moment, it does not end here. After a turn to the church at Antioch (11:19–30), it returns to Peter.

---

farther geographically than Peter and Philip had done. A connection to Cyprus was already established by reference to Barnabas' place of origin (4:36); it will (quite logically) by the place Barnabas and Saul go first on their mission (13:4) . . . "

9. Moessner, *Acts*, 103.

The account of events in Jerusalem is framed by a report from the other narrative strand concerning Paul (still called Saul) and Barnabas. The prophet Agabus predicts a famine, which prompts the Antioch church to send relief to Judea by way of Barnabas and Saul. The episode closes with the return of Barnabas and Saul (12:25).[10]

It is worth noting the formal properties of Luke's narrative at this point. Barnabas and Paul go to Jerusalem, and, at the end of chapter 12, return. We hear of nothing they did while there were there. However, it allows the narrative to shift its attention back to the city. In 11:19, the narrator has moved on to Antioch, describing events there. But there are still things to be related about Jerusalem, and so, with the two travelers from Antioch, the spotlight of narrative attention shifts back to Jerusalem. While we are there, we attend to the death of James, the arrest of Peter, and the death of Herod. We can presume that not all of these occurred during the period of Barnabas and Paul's relief mission. But that is not the point; we have been allowed to return our gaze to Jerusalem and what is happening there. Furthermore, the framing device of the relief mission reveals a similar mirror-like, or chiastic, pattern to the Jerusalem stories. Mention of Herod at the beginning and end (12:1–5, 18–24) frame two stories of Peter, one of escape from maximum security prison (12:6–11), and one about his inability to enter a locked house (12:12–17).

The events related include the deaths of James and of Herod. This is the third in a series of four Herods populating the world of Luke–Acts, beginning with Herod the Great (Luke 1:5), continuing with Herod the Tetrarch, present through much of the Gospel, but especially at the trial of Jesus (23:7–15), and now Herod Agrippa I, the grandson of Herod the Great. Before Acts is finished, we will meet his son, Herod Agrippa II (25:13). The looming presence of the Herods suggests that they represent a political atmosphere of persistent threat, as well as the local presence of the Roman Empire by way of its client kings.

The death of James, the brother of John, at the hands of Herod, suggests that the generation of original disciples is coming to an end. The story of Peter's incarceration fits in with this. We are in the waning narrative of Peter's story. The description of his arrest and imprisonment evokes the Passion of Jesus. The occasion for his arrest is explicitly identified as Passover (12:3).

---

10. Acts 12:25 presents a textual problem, with most translations taking the more difficult reading, in obedience to textual critical principles. However, all recognize the inappropriateness of that reading and try to amend it to fit the story. Here I will follow Johnson's adjustment (*Acts*, 216), redirecting the phrase *eis Ierousalem* so as to read, "After Barnabas and Saul completed their relief mission *in Jerusalem*, they returned, taking with them John, who is called Mark."

On that occasion, another "King Herod" had a role. And the language Luke uses revives those of the arrest of Jesus.[11] Here Luke is honoring Peter, as he does with Stephen and Paul, by enduring the cost of discipleship with a share in Jesus' own Passion. And where with Stephen it is the death that is compared, and with Paul it is the trials before king and governor, with Peter it is the arrest and imprisonment.

The story of the arrest and subsequent escape enlists good storytelling strategies to make the case that the most rigorous confinement cannot hold the message of liberation. Once Peter realizes that he is indeed free, but vulnerable, he goes to the house of the mother of "John who is called Mark," where he is famously left stranded on the street. Rhoda, the maid who answers the gate, is so overjoyed that she neglects to let him enter in her enthusiasm to tell the others. One cannot suppress the suspicion that Luke, or his source, is playing off the theme of the apostle with the keys to the kingdom. He can escape maximum security confinement, but he cannot enter the locked gate, for the authority of the keys adheres to the office and is not a personal possession.

Once Peter enters, he tells those inside to "report this to James and the brothers." This is clearly not James, the brother of John, who was murdered earlier in the chapter, but rather James, the "brother of the Lord" (Gal 1:19), whose leadership of the Apostolic Council Luke takes for granted.

At this point, the narrator says of Peter, "Then he left and went to another place" (12:17). And we hear no more. So we say farewell to Peter's participation in Luke's narrative. It is true that he will be involved in the Apostolic Council in Acts 15:6, but that will be to testify to what has happened in the chapters we have just read. The echoes of the Passion that color this vignette are suitable, for his own story in this narrative is over.

Antioch (Acts 9:1-31; 11:19; 13:1—14:28)

Interwoven with the story of Peter is that of Barnabas and Saul, to use the traditional Jewish name by which Paul is identified in these early chapters of Acts. Although this narrative thread properly centers on Antioch, it begins earlier. Barnabas, a Cypriot, is introduced already in chapter 4, where he is seen selling a field and donating the proceeds to the community.

Saul, in rather stark contrast, is first seen at the martyrdom of Stephen, where, it is said, those doing the stoning places their coats at the feet of Saul.

---

11. Johnson (*Acts*, 210) lists these: *laying on of hands* (Luke 9:44; 20:19; Acts 12:1); *arresting* (Luke 22:54; Acts 12:3); *delivering over* (Luke 23:25; 24:7; Acts 12:4); *leading forth* (Luke 22:1; Acts 12:2).

In line with other passages, in which properties are placed at the feet of the apostles (4:34; 5:2), including Barnabas (4:36), it is tempting to interpret this as suggesting Saul is already in a position of leadership. However, in 22:20 Saul says he was guarding the cloaks. Nonetheless, shortly thereafter we see Saul leading charges against the church—"But Saul began to destroy the church. Going from house to house, he dragged off both men and women and put them in prison" (8:3).

The story of Saul begins in earnest with the account in Acts 9 of his encounter with the risen Christ on the road to Damascus. The elaborate account has distinct parts. The event itself, the following baptism and instruction under Ananias in the city of Damascus, and the subsequent preaching of Saul in Damascus and eventually Jerusalem.

There is some consternation in whether to label this pivotal (for Acts) account as Saul's own resurrection experience, his call, or his conversion. But we might see the different parts of the account as speaking to each of these. The event itself, on the road, is clearly an appearance of the risen Christ, comparable to those of the other disciples earlier. We see this in the dialogue that ensues. The baptism that follows is his call, and, in his subsequent preaching of the Way, we see his conversion. All of this is of a piece, of course, but the different aspects are spelled out. It is in the last part of the conversion story that we see Barnabas entering the picture again, as he seeks out Saul, and brings him to the apostles (9:27). After this, Saul returns to his hometown of Tarsus. Once again the narrative announces a time of peace and growth of the church (9:31).

From this point on, we see Barnabas and Saul acting as a team and, when the Antioch community begins, involving men from Cyprus, as well as Phoenicia and Antioch. Upon learning that the Antioch community was welcoming Greeks as well as Jews, the Jerusalem church delegates the Cypriot Barnabas to oversee what was unfolding. Approving of what he finds, he once again recruits Paul from his home in Tarsus, and from now on the two of them are identified with the Antioch church.

The relief mission to Jerusalem, discussed earlier, brings them to Jerusalem and back (11:30; 12:25). The connection with Jerusalem keeps the Antioch project in communication with the larger church and will set a precedent for the later council meeting of Acts 15.

However, the main cooperative effort of Barnabas and Saul comes in the mission to Asia Minor—Pisidia and Pergamum—in chapters 13 and 14. At the beginning, Saul is named among the five "prophets and teachers" filling out the program of Acts 1:8, taking the message "to the ends of the earth." Although Barnabas is not mentioned as one of these, immediately the Holy Spirit instructs the Antioch community to set apart both Barnabas and Saul for the work about to be performed (13:1).

The mission in Acts 13–14 is a prototype of what will come later in Paul's mission. Almost immediately, Saul's name in the narrative is changed to Paul, presumably as his public name in non-Jewish settings, and this remains his name from now on. He encounters a benevolent proconsul named Sergius Paulus, but this is not stated as the source of the name change.[12] Reported events include an encounter with a Jewish sorcerer (13:8–11) and an unwelcome result of a healing in Lystra, when the pair are taken for Roman gods (14:1–18). Paul is stoned and left for dead (14:19–20), presaging difficulties to come.

But perhaps the primary event in this part of the story, and one getting the most space, is the major speech Paul delivers in Pisidian Antioch, completing the series of speeches begun with Peter, and continued with Stephen. It concludes with the significant quote from Isaiah 49:6—"I have made you a light for the gentiles, that you may bring salvation to the ends of the earth" (13:37). With that, the three-part mission announced in Acts 1:8 comes to completion, in the words of the departing Jesus—"... you will be my witnesses in Jerusalem, and in all Judea and Samaria, and to the ends of the earth." It would appear that this image of the expanding mission of Acts, described earlier as rhetorical rather than structural, might serve to describe the movement from the beginning of the book until the Council of Jerusalem in Acts 15. But some thirteen chapters are yet to unfold.

The partnership of Barnabas and Paul will bring them to Jerusalem for the council meeting of Acts 15, but it will not last much after that. A disagreement about Barnabas's proposal that John Mark continue with them leads to the parting of their ways. Barnabas and John Mark head for Cyprus, and depart from the narrative of Acts.

Council of Jerusalem (15:1–30a)

Throughout the narrative of Judea, Samaria, and Antioch, strife has met the missionaries at every turn. From misdirected message, as with Philip's encounter with Simon Magus or the interpretation of Paul and Barnabas as Greek gods at Lystra, to outright violence in persecution, as with James and Peter, this narrative has not been without conflict. However, there is

---

12. But consider Kahl, "Acts of the Apostles: Pro(to)-Imperial Script and Hidden Transcript," *Shadow of Empire*, 144: "In Greek this name *Paulos* is identical to that of the governor. It is hardly a coincidence that the most sophisticated writer in the New Testament mentions the change of name precisely at the moment when Saul makes his first high-ranking Roman convert."

an undercurrent of something more, something implied in the missions of Peter and Paul that comes to the surface in Acts 15 and the Council of Jerusalem. Whereas in the early chapters of Acts, the narrative conflict played out between the Sanhedrin and the apostolic community, now the tension comes from within that community itself.

Earlier, following the baptism of Cornelius and his household, we saw Peter was compelled by "those of the circumcised" in the community to explain himself: "You entered the house of uncircumcised people and ate with them" (11:3). And now, we discover a certain circumcision party within the movement aggressively advocating circumcision for gentile converts (15:1). And when Paul and Barnabas arrive at Jerusalem, they encounter the charge. "But some from the party of the Pharisees who had become believers stood up and said, 'It is necessary to circumcise them and direct them to observe the Mosaic law'" (15:5). At this point, the very issues that preoccupy Luke's project emerge in the foreground of the narrative, calling for a decision.

The Council of Jerusalem, as we have seen, is a standing "apostolic" council (8:1), under the leadership of James (12:17). Now it is being called into session for a particular pressing problem. The occasion is the missionary activity of Barnabas and Saul in Asia Minor. Although up to this time no indication has been given that circumcision has been in issue in the mission, an early warning sign was given in the first appearance of Antioch in the account, where it was said that an innovative practice observed there was openness to "Greeks."[13]

At this point, the two interwoven strands of the narrative following from the departure from Jerusalem—the Judea and Samaria strand associated with Peter, and the Antioch strand associated with Paul and Barnabas—are brought to a reckoning. Peter, returning to the narrative for a final word, testifies first (15:7–11). He alludes to his earlier witness, which we are to understand concerns an incident with Cornelius, that "the gentiles would hear the word of the gospel and believe." And that God "made no distinction between us and them," and therefore, he concludes, "Why, then, are you now putting God to the test by placing on the shoulders of the disciples a yoke that neither our ancestors nor we have been able to bear?" In other words, he applies to the issue of gentile circumcision his earlier realization that whoever "fears God" and is righteous, is "acceptable" to him (10:35). Following Peter's speech, Paul and Barnabas speak of their own experiences, without Luke elaborating about it at this point (15:12). And with that, both threads of the narrative text of Acts 8–14 are brought to a conclusion.

---

13. Acts 11:20—literally, "Hellenists," but presumably not the same as those in 6:1, who are diaspora Jews already an established part of the community of Jesus followers.

The decision itself allows four exceptions to a general rule. The general rule is to allow a broad degree of freedom, in particular from both circumcision and food laws. That the latter is also included, though not a part of the discussion, is seen in the four exceptions: "avoid pollution from idols, unlawful marriage, the meat of strangled animals, and blood" (15:19, 29). While this list has been exhaustively considered, perhaps the best understanding of the motivation behind it is to enjoin mixed Jewish-gentile communities to honor the sensibilities of those among them of Jewish background.

The decision of the council, delivered by James is stated twice. First, the decision is described (15:13–21), and then it is repeated in a letter to be sent along with Barnabas and Paul (15:23–29).[14] These have different purposes. The decision brings the previous narrative to a conclusion; the letter provides the following narrative with a charter. In an earlier phase of his life, Paul was authorized by a letter from the high priest to carry out the purging of the Jesus movement from Judaism (9:2). Now he has another letter, this time from leaders of the very movement that he persecuted, issued as an authorization for his mission among the gentiles. We see later that it is again invoked when Paul returns from his missions and is once again confronted with charges by the circumcision party in the community (21:20–21, 25).

And with that, the narrative of Acts turns a corner. The early accounts of departure from Jerusalem, described in stages—Jerusalem, Judea and Samaria, the ends of the earth—have brought us to the Council of Jerusalem and its pivotal decision. Now, the narrative turns to Paul, his mission, and eventually his official trials and departure for Rome.

Ephesus (15:36—21:26)

In the next four chapters we hear about Paul's mission—possibly the best known of the Acts narrative. The narrative begins with another change in the cast of characters. After the council has delivered its verdict, issued its letter, and adjourned, Paul and Barnabas have a falling out. Paul objects to Barnabas's wish to have John Mark join them. Their disagreement is intense, and Barnabas goes back to Cyprus with John Mark. Paul links up with Silas (15:40) and travels through "Syria and Cilicia," which is to say, overland toward the churches that were established in the earlier mission. At Lystra,

14. Source critics suspect that in his account of the Jerusalem council Luke has conflated two historical events (e.g, Fitzmyer, *Acts*, 544). One of these would involve a decision to absolve Gentiles from dietary laws. The other would concern circumcision as not required for Gentile converts. As we have seen repeatedly, conflation and/or repurposing of events are characteristic of Luke's handling of the narrative. Here it serves to bring together the issues surfacing during the Gentile mission till now.

he is joined by Timothy (16:1), whom Paul has circumcised, for, though his mother was Jewish, "they all knew that his father was a Greek."

With that, they set their sights on Asia, the province at the western edge of the peninsula, with Ephesus as its capital. In fact, Ephesus is the elusive center of the entire Pauline mission,[15] as their initial impulse is thwarted and they are diverted to Macedonia and Achaia.

Itinerary

The travels of Paul and his companions provide the narrative substructure of the next four chapters. Set in this itinerary are a number of notable incidents. We will first sketch the itinerary and then consider some of the more pertinent incidents.

Diverted from their destination by "the Spirit of Jesus" (16:7), they turn to Greek territories, following Paul's vision in which a Macedonian man pleads with him to come to his people. The narrative of Paul's mission moves from Troas (16:8-10), where Paul has the vision, back to Troas (20:4-6), where he raises an unlucky Eutychus[16] back to life. (After having fallen asleep listening to Paul speak, he fell from a window.) The tour concludes with a farewell to the elders of Ephesus (20:17-36).

The itinerary can be described simply. Crossing to Philippi, Paul and his company travel the main Roman roads east to Thessalonica and then south to Beroea, Athens, and Corinth, founding churches as they go (16:11—18:17). At Corinth, Paul is arrested and spends a year and a half in that city. During that time, he meets Aquila and Priscilla, Jewish Christians from Rome who, because of the persecution of the Jews by Claudius, left the city and put the Roman church in the hands of the gentile Christians. Together the couple and Paul sail to Ephesus (18:18-19), and he finally reaches the objective set out in 16:6.

Once in Ephesus, Paul leaves the narrative temporarily (18:21-23), traveling to Jerusalem and Antioch, while we witness Apollos coming to Ephesus from Alexandria, where he encounters the pair from Rome (18:24-28). Before Paul arrives back in Ephesus, Priscilla and Aquila have returned to Rome and Apollos has moved on to Corinth. Upon his return, Paul remains in Ephesus for a couple of years (19:10) for an extended time of teaching and proselytizing. Then, wishing to return to Jerusalem, apparently to convey the results of a collection for the Jerusalem community (although

---

15. In Luke's account of Paul's mission, Ephesus and Asia are cited as roughly equivalent (16:6; 19:10, 22, 26, 27; 20:16, 18).

16. *Eutychus* means "Good Fortune," or perhaps in a more popular idiom, "Lucky."

this is not made explicit), he first travels back to Corinth, perhaps putting out brushfires (20:1–3), perhaps arranging for the unmentioned collection for Jerusalem (20:4).[17] Upon his return, in a major farewell speech to the Ephesians, Paul takes leave of Ephesus without entering the city.

The mission of Paul concludes with a procession-like account of his island-hopping journey to Jerusalem. He makes landfall at Caesarea, staying at the house of Philip, and from there he travels up to Jerusalem where the final events will unfold.

Clashes and Other Incidents Along the Way

Interrupting the travel account of Paul and his companions are a series of incidents occurring at different locations. Generally, these involve clashes with inhabitants or even authorities. With the incident at Lystra (14:8–20) as a preliminary example, the mission of Paul, Silas, and Timothy offers a rich array of events in Philippi, Thessalonica, Athens, Corinth, and Ephesus. For purposes of reference, a brief description of each of these incidents, including the earlier one of Lystra, will be useful.

Lystra (14:8–20)

When Paul and Barnabas are in this town, Paul heals a man crippled from birth. In response, the townspeople hail Paul and Barnabas as gods come to earth, Hermes and Zeus, respectively. The priest of Zeus gets involved. Paul protests, appealing to the God of creation. Jews from Antioch and Iconium arrive and incite the people against Paul, whom they stone. After being left for dead, he gets up and leaves the city.

Philippi (16:16–40)

After first being welcomed by Lydia, Paul and Silas later encounter a female slave with the spirit of divination.[18] For many days she had been announc-

---

17. Of course, Paul in his letters speaks of the collection for Jerusalem (1 Cor 16:14, 2 Cor 8:1—9:15, Rom 15:14–32). In Acts 11:27–30 we learned of a delegation bringing aid to Jerusalem. Here, Acts 19:4 says that "Sopater son of Pyrrhus from Berea, and Aristarchus and Secundus from Thessalonica, and Gaius from Derbe, and Timothy, and Tychicus and Trophimus from Asia, were accompanying him." These accompany him to Jerusalem, where Trophimus is the occasion for an altercation (21:29). It is likely that these named are representatives of the communities delivering the aid to Jerusalem.

18. NAB, note: "Literally 'a spirit of Python'; Python was the name of the serpent

ing, "These people are slaves of the Most High God, who proclaim to you a way of salvation." Paul exorcizes her spirit, which antagonizes her owners, who take them before the magistrates, accused of being Jews disturbing their city. Beaten with rods, they are thrown into prison, after which a tremor shakes the earth. Despite the opportunity, Paul and Silas do not escape, and the jailer, fearful they had, is reassured and befriended, and eventually converted. When the orders come for the pair to be released, Paul objects that they have beaten a Roman citizen. Alarmed, the authorities ensure their departure from the city.

Thessalonica (17:1–9)

Paul has considerable success in the synagogue, preaching that Jesus is the Messiah. Jews and God-fearing gentiles are persuaded. But some stridently antagonist Jews mount an opposition, hiring a mob. Not finding Paul at the house of Jason, as they expected, they instead haul Jason and others before the magistrates with a specific charge: "These people who have been turning the world upside down[19] have now come here . . . They all act in opposition to the decrees of Caesar and claim instead that there is another king, Jesus" (17:6–7). The city magistrates take a payment from Jason and release them.

Athens (17:16–34)

Having left Timothy and Silas behind, Paul again begins his visit by preaching in the synagogue, where he meets a willing group of Jews and God-fearing gentiles. However, observing the many idols in the city, he takes the opportunity to preach the one God, debating in the synagogue and the public square with Epicurean and Stoics, in this city famous for its philosophers. Taken to the Areopagus, the council of Athens, he defends himself, citing the memorial to an Unknown God, which allows him to preach the God who is "Lord of heaven and earth." This passage includes some of the more incisive charges against idol worship to be found in Acts.

In the council of Athens, we can find a third council. Along with the two we have seen—the Sanhedrin (council of the Jews) and the Apostolic Council, we now have a representative council of gentile pagans. Scholars

---

or dragon that guarded the Delphic oracle at the foot of Mt. Parnassus and the word eventually came to be used for a spirit of divination."

19. In Greek, *anastatoó*, "create a disturbance," "upset," or literally "turn upside down." While the expression no doubt was a fixed idiom, the literal meaning also served Luke's purposes.

have long detected here echoes of the trial of Socrates. This evokes the similar echoes in the trials of Jesus in Luke's account. When Paul's remarks move from the one God to the specific historical event of Jesus and his resurrection from the dead, he loses much of his audience, while others request further discussion at another time.

Corinth (18:1–17)

Once Paul arrives in Corinth, he stays there for a year and a half (18:11). During that time, a number of events are recounted. He meets Priscilla and Aquila, coming from Rome because of the persecution of the Jews, and works together with them. Once again preaching in the synagogue, he is repulsed, and in response shakes out his garments and responds: "Your blood be on your heads! I am clear of responsibility. From now on I will go to the gentiles." With that, he leaves the synagogue and goes next door to the house of a God-fearer, Titus Justus. However, he also enjoys success with the synagogue leader, Crispus, his household, and many others who join with Paul.

An important event during this period is Paul's encounter with Gallio, proconsul of Achaia. When some Jews bring Paul before the proconsul, he refuses to make a judgment, noting, " . . . since it is a question of arguments over doctrine and titles and your own law, see to it yourselves. I do not wish to be a judge of such matters" (17:15). Gallio's refusal to enter into intra-Jewish debates, with its attendant implication that no Roman law is breached here by Paul, needs further comment, and will be given it in discussing the next part of this narrative.

Ephesus (19:1–40)

Paul stays in Ephesus some two years (19:8, 10). Once again, he begins his work in the synagogue, but after a while shifts his venue to the lecture hall of Tyrannus (19:9). During his time there, he becomes noted for healings and expelling evil spirits.

However, the incident that gets the most coverage in Ephesus is the riot of the silversmiths. A certain Demetrius, who has a small business selling silver images of the goddess Artemis was able to rally his fellow craftsmen against Paul, since, "not only in Ephesus but throughout most of the province of Asia this Paul has persuaded and misled a great number of people by saying that gods made by hands are not gods at all" (19:26). Arguing that the prominence of Ephesus as a religious center of the mother goddess, they are able to incite a riot. The disciples will not let Paul address the crowd, and some prominent locals, "Asiarchs," also protect Paul. A certain Jew named Alexander attempts an explanation, but is shouted down. Finally, the town clerk manages to calm things down, pointing out that no crime has been committed, and that, in his opinion, "The men you brought here are not temple robbers, nor have they insulted our goddess" (19:37). With that, Paul leaves for Macedonia (20:1).

It is in the context of these episodes that the *narrative conflict* surfaces in the account of Paul's mission. In some cases, the antagonists are *Jews* (Lystra, 14:19; Thessalonica, 17:1, 5; Corinth, 18:12; Ephesus, 19:33; 20:3). Both are instrumental to Luke's project and worth taking up one at a time. In other cases the adversaries are *pagan gentiles*, who typically are concerned about the economic impact of Paul's mission (Philippi, 16:19; Athens, 17:18–19; Ephesus, 19:24).

The dispute with the *Jewish adversaries* leads to a gradual disengagement with the synagogues. This we saw earlier, where, in the first chapter concerning the implied reader of Luke's work, we charted the series of notices that built toward a rupture. Beginning with the disturbance in Thessalonica that prompted Paul to leave the synagogue and go next door to the house of Titus Justus, we find a series of stock phrases that show Paul "discussing in the synagogue," that finally results in a shift to a neutral venue—the lecture hall of Tyrannus. As charted in chapter one:

17:2	discussing in the synagogue—Thessalonica (Titus Justus)
17:17	discussing in the synagogue—Athens
18:4	discussing in the synagogue—Corinth
18:19	discussing in the synagogue—Ephesus
19:8	discussing in the synagogue—Ephesus (on a later date), to . . .
19:9	discussing in the lecture hall of Tyrannus—Ephesus

In this series, we see the movement away from the typical teaching arena of Paul become less and less viable, until he makes the break in Ephesus, articulated in two adjacent verses.

In addition to the conflicts with the Jews, Paul also has confrontations with the *gentile pagans*. In the clashes with local inhabitants in Lystra, Philippi, Athens, and Ephesus, two themes predominate.[20] One is economic. In Philippi and Ephesus the impact of Paul's preaching is interpreted by the locals as detrimental to the local economy (16:19–20; 19:25–27). But underlying this is a deeper conflict concerning images of God, seen in Lystra, Athens, and Ephesus. At Lystra, prior to the present mission of Paul, the

---

20. The following is indebted to Rowe, *World Upside Down*, chap. 2, 17–51.

terms are set. When Paul and Barnabas are mistaken for Hermes and Zeus, Paul's protest takes the form of an appeal to the one God (14:15). If humans are made in the image of God, follows the implied argument, that does not mean that gods are made in the image of humans.[21] That is to reverse the process.

But both of these themes impinge on the cultural life of the cities involved. The Roman imperial social structure was of a piece, in that the economics and the gods were integral to the common life. An attack on any of these was an attack on the culture system as a whole. In this sense, the mission of Paul is presented as a threat to the empire as well, though not in the form of a direct assault on the political powers.

However, the political dimension is not excluded from the disruption either. It is in Thessalonica, where the outcry was that this movement of Christians was turning the world upside down, that the political dimension of Paul's threat finds expression. The charge, again, is that "These people who have been turning the world upside down . . . act in opposition to the decrees of Caesar and claim instead that there is another king, Jesus" (17:6–7). As Gallio shortly will imply in Corinth, and as the series of Roman authorities will insist in the final chapters of Acts, Paul is not in violation of Roman law. But that is not the nature of the threat. It is not direct, it is subversive, undermining the cultural and legal fabric of the imperial system. The lordship of Jesus is not one that mounts a rival empire, but one that operates at another level. The narrative of Acts begins with the ascension of Jesus to take his throne at the right hand of God. This eschatological reign competes with the apotheosis of Caesar, but it also claims a prior authority, over and above that of the empire. That is, it does not directly confront imperial power, but rather, the hegemony of empire is bracketed, made provisional, in the light of the eschatological reign of God.[22]

Returning to Jerusalem

After Paul bids farewell to the elders of Ephesus, he travels through the Mediterranean stopping at the islands of Kos and Rhodes and the port city of Patara. Passing Cyprus, they sail to Syria, landing at Tyre. From there he goes to Ptolemaic and then Caesarea, staying with Philip. Once again he encounters the prophet Agabus, who had predicted the famine earlier. This time Luke anticipates the arrest of Paul: "Coming over to us, he took Paul's

---

21. Rowe, *World Upside Down*, 38.

22. See, for instance, Bachmann, "Jerusalem and Rome in Luke–Acts . . . ," *Luke–Acts and Empire*, 74–83.

belt, tied his own hands and feet with it and said, "The Holy Spirit says, 'In this way the Jewish leaders in Jerusalem will bind the owner of this belt and will hand him over to the gentiles'" (21:11).

When Paul finally arrives at Jerusalem, he is greeted by the brothers and is challenged by a report that among the Jewish members of their group a rumor is circulating that Paul has been releasing the Jewish members as well as the gentiles from circumcision and other traditional customs. We, and the God-fearing reader, are reminded that this narrative primarily concerns the gentiles in the movement, as we glimpse another division of the movement with "thousands of believers," namely, the members of Jewish origin (21:20). Once again the letter issued by the Jerusalem council is mentioned, reminding us that this is the mandate under which Paul has been operating since Acts 15. Given the doubts expressed by the skeptics, Paul is advised to demonstrate his orthodoxy by purification rites in the temple. And that will spark the controversy that sends us into the next part of the story of Acts.[23]

And with that, the narrative of Paul's mission of establishing and maintaining churches comes to a conclusion. The Jerusalem community and the Apostolic Council disappear from the account, as attention shifts to other parties and other conflicts. Unheard from since the early chapters, the Jewish opponents of Paul, his former allies, reappear to provide the next party of opposition.

Jerusalem to Rome (Acts 21:14—28:31)

As we've seen at each stage of the narrative of Acts, the change is signaled by a new set of *dramatis personae*. And with the change in the cast of characters, we also have a shift in the terms of conflict. Ever since the narrative thread left Jerusalem in Acts 8, the antagonists consisted of opposed members *within* the Jesus movement. And since the council of Acts 15, the animating dispute was about requiring circumcision of gentile converts. But with the return of Paul to Jerusalem, the circumcision question receives its last mention (21:21). The Apostolic Council has directed the mission until now, issuing their letter to facilitate the new conditions for the gentile believers. But now the letter is referenced once more, and that part of the action comes to an end.

---

23. The letter from the Apostolic Council is mentioned again. While it reads as if Paul was unaware of it, despite his involvement in its formulation (Acts 15:23–29), it serves to remind the reader (Johnson, *Acts*, 376) of its existence and its role as mandate for the mission to the gentiles.

At this juncture the Sanhedrin, left behind since the early chapters, returns to provide opposition (Acts 22:30; 23:1, 6, 15, 20, 28; 24:20). A zealous party of Jews pursue Paul with particular animus. But now, with the change in personnel, the terms of conflict also change. We return to that which dominated the initial chapters of Acts. The charges of violating the temple and the law, framed in identical language, returns. Once leveled against Stephen, it is now repeated regarding Paul:

- "This man [Stephen] never stops saying things against this holy place and the law" (6:13).
- "This is the man [Paul] who is teaching everyone everywhere against the people and the law and this place" (21:27).

We are reminded that in the beginning Paul himself was a leading figure in this fervent defense of Judaism against perceived aberrations such as the Jesus movement. When Tertullus charges that the movement is a "sect," he is reminding us of the reason Paul was so zealous in persecuting the church in the first place. Paul was trying to purge Judaism of sects. But now he is on the other side, and this by itself is infuriating. The question presents itself as to whether this is not part of their antagonism toward Paul.

But there is another shift in direction. In the early chapters, the narrative conflict was waged between the two councils, the Sanhedrin and the Apostolic Council. When the charges were directed at Stephen, that action precipitated a movement out from Jerusalem into the Judea and Samaria, to the proverbial ends of the earth. That narrative has now come to an end. The similar charges against Paul move the narrative in another direction. Now another implication of the conflict is explored—the Roman world. Whereas earlier the narrative thread went from Stephen out to the mission into the world, now the narrative and the mission turn toward the Roman authorities. Then, to the synagogues; now, to the Roman courts.

These final chapters have a momentum of their own. But they involve a number of potentially confusing events, with repetitions and apparent duplications. A short account of the events in the closing narrative can be helpful.

Lysias and Felix

The trials of Paul occur in two phases, first under Felix, then two years later under Festus. The first phase begins with Paul's arrest in the temple in the final days of his purification rite. Believing that he has brought a Gentile into the area reserved for Jews, protestors threaten a riot, and this requires the intervention of the tribune Claudius Lysias, commander of Roman forces in Jerusalem. Paul is removed for his own safety, but not before he is allowed to address the crowd. As he describes his conversion, we hear the second account of his encounter on the road to Damascus. The response to the speech is hostile. Claudius Lysias takes Paul inside for questioning in order to get at the truth of a situation he does not understand. For a second time, Paul invokes his Roman citizenship, a tactical move that shapes the rest of the narrative of Acts.

Still trying to understand what is behind the disruption, the tribune arranges for a meeting between Paul and the Sanhedrin. Paul gives his second speech and divides his opponents by speaking of the resurrection from the dead, a doctrine favored by the Pharisees but disputed by the Sadducees. In the discord that results, Claudius Lysias is once again required to remove Paul from the scene. Learning of a threat on Paul's life, the tribune decides to transfer Paul to the Roman base of operations at Caesarea Maritima, a journey accomplished under heavy guard to avoid an intended ambush. It is there that Paul's first trial occurs.

Marcus Antonius Felix was governor of Judea from 52 to 60 c.e. His decision to allow Paul to face his accusers brings the attorney Tertullus, representing the high priest and elders of Jerusalem, into the story. He presents the charges against Paul: "We found this man to be a pest; he creates dissension among Jews all over the world and is a ringleader of the sect of the Nazoreans. He even tried to desecrate our temple, but we arrested him" (24:5–6). In his defense, Paul rejects the term *sect*, and speaks of "the Way" instead. At this, Felix halts the trial. Felix and his Jewish wife Drusilla are aware of the movement and want to hear more. Paul is kept in prison, with a considerable degree of freedom and complete access of his friends (24:10–23). Felix stalls, hoping that Paul's friends will pay for his freedom.

Festus and Agrippa II

A pause occurs in the trials of Paul, as matters come to a standstill, which ends only when Felix is replaced by his successor, Portius Festus (24:24–27). Festus moves quickly to take control of matters. Visiting Jerusalem he learns of Paul from his opponents. With that, the second phase of Paul's trials begins. Bringing some of Paul's accusers from Jerusalem to Caesarea, Festus sets up another hearing. They make their charges; Paul defends himself. Festus proposes a trial in Jerusalem, but Paul, recognizing that he is in mortal danger in that city, appeals to Caesar instead, exercising an ancient right of Roman citizens. Festus accepts this: "You have appealed to Caesar. To Caesar you will go" (25:12).

At this juncture, King Herod Agrippa II enters the picture, with his sister, Bernice.[24] They have come to pay their respects to the new governor. Festus takes advantage of the moment to inquire about Paul and the charges against him that Festus did not quite understand (25:13–22). Paul is brought before them and delivers his last big speech in Acts, including a third rendition of his encounter on the road to Damascus.

And in so doing, he brings certain themes of the narrative to a final expression. He is being sent to the Gentiles "to open their eyes that they may turn from darkness to light and from the power of Satan to God, so that they may obtain forgiveness of sins and an inheritance among those who have been consecrated by faith in me" (26:18). And instead of mentioning his own blindness, as in the earlier descriptions, he now affirms that he is to open other eyes. In a reprise of his words at Pisidian Antioch (Acts 13:46–47, Isaiah 49:6), he proclaims, "the Messiah must suffer and that, as the first to rise from the dead, he would proclaim light both to our people and to the Gentiles" (Acts 26:23). With that, Festus interrupts and brings the session to a close. Both he and Agrippa agree that Paul is innocent, but since he has appealed to Caesar, they have no choice but to send him to Rome.

On to Rome

The final two chapters narrate Paul's trip to Rome. Another centurion, Julius, enters the narrative as his escort. As they are late in the season, they encounter a storm and wash up on the shore of the island of Malta. There they winter over and catch the next Alexandrian ship to Italy. The storm and shipwreck place a caesura, a gap, in the narrative. All that has happened up till now is on the previous side of the wreck, and afterward a new day begins on Malta, then in Rome.

When Paul arrives at the city, members of the Christian community come to greet him. As the book of Acts closes, we hear some final words from Paul. After three days, he calls together the Jewish leaders of the city— the Roman correlative of the Sanhedrin in Jerusalem—explaining what has happened and why he is there. Upon speaking to them of Jesus, some

---

24. Johnson, *Acts*, 425: "Herod Agrippa II was the son of Herod Agrippa I, whose death was recounted in Acs 12:33 . . . and as a client of the Romans was loyal to them throughout the period of the Jewish War . . . Bernice was his sister, also the daughter of Agrippa I . . . Although she was apparently herself devout—to the extent of herself performing a Nazarite vow . . . she was also part of the Roman circle, in fact becoming for a time the companion of the conqueror Titus," 667–936.

believe, others do not. His last words stand as a final statement concerning his shift from a Jewish to a Gentile mission. Quoting Isaiah 6:9–10, warning that the prophet will encounter closed eyes and ears, he concludes with another oblique allusion to the light to the Gentiles of Isaiah 49:6—"Let it be known to you that this salvation of God has been sent to the Gentiles; they will listen."

Acts famously ends with ambiguity. For two years Paul remains in his lodgings, where he receives visitors. He continues to proclaim the kingdom of God and the Lord Jesus Christ "without hindrance." On the one hand, he is confined; on the other hand, he continues in his mission.

There are other questions this ending raises. Perhaps the most popular of these is Luke's failure to tell us about Paul's death. After all, Luke is writing long after these events and could easily have related those final days, about which we are so curious. And then there is the matter of the appeal to Caesar. That is what brought Paul to Rome. Why is it not mentioned once he arrives there? And what happened to Priscilla and Aquila, his dear friends in Rome? Why is there no mention of making contact again? Certainly, these omissions show us that Luke's narrative is not about Paul, but about the movement of which Paul is most recently the face. That narrative has reached its conclusion.

The Innocence of Paul

Throughout these finals chapters, repeated testimony affirms the innocence of Paul regarding violation of Roman law. This thread began earlier, with Gallio, but it moves to a completion in this part of the account, as Lysias, Felix, and Festus all speak concerning his case, representing the Roman perspective. Although the new controversy is the imputed violation of the law and the temple, the terms of the conflict with Roman authority were set with Gallio at Corinth (18:12–17). At that time, the members of the local synagogue were concerned about Paul's testifying that Jesus was the Messiah. However, the charge that they bring to the proconsul of Achaia is broader than that. "This man is persuading people to worship God contrary to the law" (18:13).

If we accept the view that Luke expects his readers to understand that the Jews of Corinth realize that the Roman procurator would not decide on Jewish legal matters, but only those that affect public order, then the word *law* (*nomos*) becomes a site of calculated wordplay.[25] Already in Luke 10:26, when the word is introduced as a term of contention, it is a site of ambigu-

---

25. Rowe, 59–60.

ity. In that passage, "The law, how do you read it?" becomes "And who is [our] neighbor?" And here too, the complaint leaves room for interpretation. Which laws are charged with violation by Paul—Jewish or Roman? The case can be made for either interpretation, since Roman law required allegiance to Roman gods, with an exception made for Jews. But if Paul is moving away from those conditions by admitting Gentiles (18:6), as if they were Jews but not having converted to Judaism, then Roman law is being flaunted as well.[26]

Gallio, however, decides that it is purely a Jewish quibble and does not concern matters of crime or fraud. And therefore he does not make a decision. Nonetheless, there have been ample demonstrations that a particular concern of Roman authorities, that of maintaining public order, is also at risk in the collision between Paul and his Jewish opponents. Already in Thessalonica there was a mob scene (17:5-6), and before long a riot in Ephesus (19:23-40). And now in the final chapters there is no scarcity of public disruptions.

But now that we are back in Jerusalem, the theme plays out with a sense of inevitability. First with Lysias, then Felix, and then Festus, and finally Agrippa, the Romans cannot help but be involved. Because of the riot, the tribune Lysias has no alternative but to intervene. The claim to Roman citizenship on Paul's part embeds the case in Roman circles and dictates commuting his case to Caesarea. The trial with Tertullus and Felix stalls momentum for a while. But with Festus taking up the case anew, followed by Paul's appeal to Caesar, the case moves inevitably toward Rome. What is made clear throughout is that the Romans do not understand what the problem is that so embroils the Jewish community. From their perspective, Paul is not guilty of treason or any crime.

The Narrative Conclusion of Acts of the Apostles

Two features of the closing chapters of Acts stimulate unending commentary. One is the indeterminate ending. The other is the pro-Roman character of the last eight chapters.

The ending of the book, with Paul lingering in the prison, but with no further information given, is reminiscent of a similarly problematic ending of Mark's Gospel. There too we have a non-conclusion; some early Christian scribes felt that to be untenable and added shorter and longer endings. It can be argued that Mark was leaving the ending open on purpose, looking to the unfolding of events in the world in which he lived. It is this ending that Luke

---

26. .See, for instance, Kahl, *Galatians Re-imagined*, 220–22.

closed with his Gospel, but opened again with Acts. This topic, in context, will be the subject of the following chapter.

The other feature of Acts' final chapters relates to the Lukan motif of the "centurions." Specifically, it is the favorable treatment of Roman officers and, even more notably, the increasing respect tendered Paul by the Romans, especially in contrast to his treatment by the Jews. Traditionally this has been interpreted as Luke's pro-Roman, pro-empire stance, and has generated the apologetic theories of the entire work that would see it as either reassuring Christians they have nothing to fear from the empire or reassuring the empire that it has nothing to fear from the Christian church.

But these perspectives fail to remember Theophilus and the implied reader of Luke's work, the God-fearing Gentile who is attracted to the Jesus movement. This reader, who has joined or is considering joining, provides a specific perspective on the work. Once Luke-Acts is admitted to the canon and its readership becomes more general, this specificity is lost, and apologetic theories concerning the church as a whole become prevalent.

But when we consider the Gentile reader that Luke has indicated is his, we arrive at a different understanding. Here the postcolonial perspectives of empire studies provide a guide. By its very nature, post-colonialism looks at imperialism from the side of the colonized, those whose nation, culture, and politics have been taken over by another nation, an alien culture, and a politics of suppression. The other Synoptics, Mark and Matthew, can be shown to have adopted, and seriously modified, Jewish resistance to the empire, taking post-colonialism straight up.

However, Luke reverses this perspective, adopting the viewpoint of the empire doing the colonizing. Among the colonizers are some who are sympathetic to the conquered people they now live among. Sometimes this kind of behavior is condescendingly referred to as "going native." In the case of Luke's God-fearers, we find Gentiles who not only are sympathetic to the local culture, but who are attracted to the one God of Judaism. And furthermore, they find the preaching of Jesus as Messiah persuasive. But for them, the tradition needs to be translated—not simply language to language, but also culture to culture. From the point of view of the God-fearing reader, the narrative of Acts offers such a translation.

From the time of the departure from Jerusalem, in Acts 8:1, we have seen two major moves—one to the synagogues, with Peter and then Paul, and another to the Roman courts in the final chapters. The first of these serves to remove Jewish barriers to conversion, specifically, those concerning common meals and circumcision. It would not do, for instance, for the centurion who has vowed loyalty to the empire by its gods to demonstrate through circumcision fidelity to another deity.

But if the first narrative of dispersion in Acts deals with Jewish practices, the second and last narrative concerns the imperial judgments. It is here that we see the honor and stature of Paul increasing as the narrative continues. Luke has developed a dramatic difference between the trials of Paul and those of Jesus. He establishes a correlation by describing the two scenes, one ending the Gospel, one ending Acts, with similar features.

The parallels are pronounced. Luke has developed each scene by describing a procession-like advance toward the city of Jerusalem. As Jesus moves toward the city, after the long journey to Jerusalem, the stages of entry are uniquely marked by Luke, as he arrives in Jericho, then the Mount of Olives, then descending the Mount, approaching the city, entering the temple (Luke 19). With Paul, Luke describes his journey from Asia as he moves from island to island, port to port (Acts 21). In a notable departure from the other Gospels, Luke reports that the trial of Jesus before Pilate is interrupted by a secondary trial before Herod Antipas, who happens to be in town at the time (Luke 23:6–16). This allows another correspondence between the two narratives insofar as each reports a hearing before both king and governor—Pilate and Herod in the Gospel, Festus and Agrippa in Acts. Luke elaborates the basic differences with incidental details to link the two accounts. Both Jesus and Paul aligned with revolutionaries—Jesus with Barabbas (Luke 23:18–19) and Paul with "the Egyptian" (Acts 21:38–39). Both are struck by minions of the high priest (Luke 22:63; Acts 23:2–5). These narrative strategies establish a parallel between the two events, one bringing the narrative of Jesus to a conclusion, the other doing the same for Paul.

However, a sharp difference separates the two accounts. Jesus moves toward his trial and death in a crescendo of humiliation, increasing until it reaches the testimony of the good thief, and then finally countered by the centurion who witnesses to the innocence (*dikaios*) of Jesus. In contrast, Paul increasingly grows in honor and stature. In many regards, the two are like a photograph and its negative. Jesus' death contrasts with Paul's deliverance. Jesus is not declared guilty, and in fact is declared innocent by the centurion at the foot of the cross. And yet he dies. Paul is also declared innocent, and yet is treated as if guilty, still in prison at the end of the narrative.

However, the primary difference is on the scale of shame and honor. Luke presents Jesus' death as a prototypical example of shame and humiliation. This is made more dramatic by Luke's previous presentation of Jesus as a major teacher of life-giving wisdom. Paul, in contrast, while undergoing experiences that Luke strives to present as parallel, continues to increase in the opposite direction, amassing honor.

The honor-shame cultural pattern shaped the ancient Graeco-Roman world. Honor has been defined as "a claim to worth that is publicly acknowledged."[27] Thus it has two aspects. In addition to the person's own claims, others also have a constitutive role in assigning honor. Without that social dimension, one claiming honor is actually dishonored. These aspects are active in Luke's comparison. And yet, there are complications, for the public acknowledgement is divided in each case. Although the authorities manage to have Jesus crucified, the crowds are notably reluctant to agree with them in Luke's account. And though Paul is accused by the Sanhedrin, he does not receive the condemnation by the Roman authorities—although in both cases, Jesus and Paul, it is the Roman authority that paradoxically condemns them.

Thus, while honor and shame are conspicuous features of the two accounts of the Gospel and Acts in the working out of their narrative conclusions, the cultural role of affirmation enters to affect the reading. Insofar as the crowds in the crucifixion of Jesus do not participate in the mocking, and in fact do not share in the approval of the action, they share the believing reader's sympathy with Jesus and disapproval of the abuse that he is receiving.[28] His honor then is not diminished but instead is enhanced, and the mockery is turned back upon those who would abuse him. A similar pattern is seen with Paul, although it plays out differently, with signals of honor that conform to the expectation of the Gentile reader.

Again, the Implied Reader

While the honor attributed to Paul provides a contrast with the treatment of Jesus, we can also understand this phenomenon in terms of *addressing the reader*. This God-fearer, coming from a culture which values honor claims very highly, is presented with a portrait of Paul as a person of great honor. During his trials his adjudicators increase in nobility to match his own growing stature. The centurion passes him on to the tribune, Lysias, who sends him to the governor, Felix, with a formal letter. Felix cedes his place to Festus, who brings in the king, to whom Paul makes his final appeal. In the terms with which he is familiar, the Gentile reader is shown a portrait of Paul that is appealing.

---

27. Plevnik, "Honor/Shame," *Handbook*, 106.

28. The same can be said of the teacher heroes of the Graeco-Roman tradition. The many accounts of the trial of Socrates assume a sympathy on the part of the reader, and consequently dishonor on the heads of those who take him to trial.

To put this another way, the two parts of the post-Jerusalem narrative of Acts—that to the synagogues (Acts 8–20) and that to the Romans courts (Acts 21–28)—invite the reader in contrasting ways. The first part can claim as its epigram Peter's dictum, that "in every nation the one who fears him and who does what is right is *acceptable* to him" (Acts 10:35). Which is to say, the Jewish tradition is opened to the foreigner, as a light to the Gentiles. But conversely, the second and last part of the post-Jerusalem narrative demonstrates this invitation from the other side. The Jewish tradition, as Paul presents it, fulfilled in Jesus Messiah, is *available* to the Gentile, as a fulfillment also of the Gentile's aspiration toward the highest values, as condensed in the honor-shame system. The Jewish tradition welcomes the Gentile in; the Gentile finds the invitation compelling.

Looking back on the overall narrative plot line of Acts, we see a narrative that begins with a six-chapter portrait of the post-resurrection community in Jerusalem. Then the stoning of Stephen, followed by the departure from Jerusalem in Acts 8:1, generates the mission into the wider world. Luke arranges to have multiple threads of narrative move from here. First, in 8:1—15:21, we are told of the move beyond Jerusalem to *Judea and Samaria*, featuring Philip and Peter. Meanwhile, we also hear the story of the *Antioch* community, with emphasis on Barnabas and Saul, as a separate initiative. But we discover that this is concurrent with the mission to Judea and Samaria, since we are referred back to the persecution as its origin (Acts 11:19). These come to a moment of decision in the Council of Jerusalem (Acts 15), and generate in turn the mission of Paul (Acts 16–20). Finally, we discover that these events can all be placed under the heading of mission to the *synagogues*, as now we turn to the *Roman courts*. But again, in the charges against Paul, replicating those against Stephen, we see that this continues another narrative strand begun in the persecution of Acts 8:1. In effect, all of the movements of Acts radiate out from the story of Stephen and his judgment on the temple.

IV. LUKE-ACTS, EMPIRE, AND THE GOD-FEARING READER

The double perspective of Acts—the synagogue and the Roman court—helps us to gain an overview of the entire project of Luke. Here as well we see a narrative with two sides. On the one hand, the entire double work, and not only Acts, in its mission to the synagogues, is devoted to presenting a portrait of Judaism that is open to the Gentiles. On the other hand, as reflected in the mission of Acts to the Roman court, the reader as God-fearer provides a perspective on the entire narrative that involves not only an invitation, but also a challenge.

The first of these, the openness to the Gentiles, has been shown to have governed Luke's narrative project from the beginning. It is shown in the announcement of John the Baptist as a voice in the desert crying out so that "all flesh shall see the salvation of God" (Luke 3:5–6). It is seen in John's baptism of repentance, leading to a baptism of the Spirit (Luke 3:16). But most importantly it informs the scene in the Nazareth synagogue, where Jesus invokes the post-exilic traditions of Second and Third Isaiah, over against the contrary prevailing tradition of Ezra and Nehemiah. His pronouncement, "Today this scripture passage is fulfilled in your hearing" (Luke 4:21), inaugurates the beginning of the eschatological era associated with the Isaian tradition, which Luke identifies as the sustained time of the Gentiles. It is a tradition that will invite them into the community of the one God's salvation *as Gentiles*, and not as converts to Judaism. It means an expression of faith community that moves beyond the identify markers that safeguard the Jewish community, which it turn was commissioned to safeguard the revelation of the one God.

In service of that light shining into the Gentile darkness (Luke 2:31–32; Acts 13:47; 26:23), Luke's narrative rather systematically brackets as provisional those identity markers, those Jewish practices that are also enjoined on converts to Judaism. In the Gospel, the release from bondage that is announced in the Nazareth synagogue are addressed in turn. These include release from death and disease, but also in a renewed understanding of the *Sabbath*, as worshiping God in serving human needs. Luke not only includes Mark's account of the withered hand, but on the journey to Jerusalem amplifies this with two more instances—a crippled woman (Luke 13:10–17) and a man with dropsy (14:1–6).

The journey to Jerusalem begins with a question about the *law* (Luke 10:26), reinterpreted by the parable of the Good Samaritan, and then picked up again in the final chapters of Acts to be taken in a new direction. In the Supper account of Luke, we see Jesus' conferring an *authority* on the apostles that begins to take shape in the first chapters of Acts, as the Sanhedrin is replaced, in this narrative's viewpoint, with the council of apostles. Shortly after this, Stephen pronounces a judgment on the *temple*, which occasions the mission outward from Jerusalem. This same set of tensions is revived with the story of Paul in his trials, now directed toward the Gentile setting.

And of course the major moments along these lines in Acts are represented by Peter, with the abrogation of *food laws* for Gentiles, and Paul, removing the requirement of *circumcision*. In the mission of Paul through Macedonia and Achaia, we see a gradual move away from the *synagogue* to the public arena. And in the final chapters (as well as the book of Acts as a whole) we witness the move from *Jerusalem* to Rome.

In all of these, we see one aspect of Luke's project, namely, accommodation of the Jewish tradition for the benefit of the Gentiles, yet presented as part of the promise contained within the Jewish tradition itself. The promise of a light to the Gentiles is part of the Jewish tradition, deferred to an eschatological hope. But now that hope is in the process of being realized.

But this accommodation, this release from identity markers, is not the entire story of Luke–Acts. In addition to the release from restrictions, we also find here a new set of demands, as reflected in the question presented to Jesus on the road to Jerusalem (Luke 13:22–30). When asked if only a few were to be saved, he answered, "Strive to enter through the narrow door." Against the notion of only the few, the many: "people will come from the east and the west and from the north and the south and will recline at table in the kingdom of God. Against the inclusion by membership among the elect, the narrow door of repentance is presented.

In the call to repentance issued by the Baptist to the Judeans we find a message of Luke's narrative to his readers. And that message involves a review of the values imparted by the Graeco-Roman culture that is the God-fearer's heritage. The very honor-shame value system that structures the culture of the empire is called into question by the teaching of Jesus. The death of Jesus demonstrates those alternative values. The resurrection of Jesus validates them. In this way, the correlation of the Passion of Jesus with the trials of Paul allow the former to inform the latter. The Roman centurion at the cross, who declares Jesus innocent (*dikaios*, righteous) anticipates the judgments of the Roman courts of Acts concerning Paul. His righteousness is his share in that of Jesus.

But that righteousness is presented to us first of all in the villagers of Luke's infancy narrative. It is there that we not only find Simeon's vision of a light to the Gentiles, but also Mary's Magnificat announcement of reversals—rulers thrown down, lowly lifted up, the hungry filled with good things, the rich sent empty away—that is echoed in Luke's beatitudes (6:20–26) and parables (16:19–31; 18:9–14). And it is the message of the programmatic declaration in the Nazareth synagogue, with its glad tidings to the poor and freedom to the oppressed (4:18). This scriptural quotation, which can be said to establish the theme currently referred to as "preferential option for the poor,"[29] revises dramatically the Roman value structure. This challenge is dramatized in the stories of Paul's mission. The economic

---

29. Blenkinsopp, *Isaiah 56–66*, 223. The passage under discussion is Isa 61:1, the same that is quoted in the Nazareth synagogue by Jesus, in Luke 4:18.

turmoil in Philippi and Ephesus, the confrontation between the cultural religious patterns and the message of Paul in Lystra, Athens, and Ephesus, all demonstrate a cultural upheaval attending the arrival of the Jesus movement. It is one that is supported by an allegiance to an alternative kingship of the risen and ascended Lord, a movement that the Thessalonians describe as "turning the world upside down" (Acts 17:6).

It is Luke who gives us the phrase, "the kingdom of God is among you" (Luke 17:21). And Luke who warns against the leaven of the Pharisees, which is hypocrisy (Luke 12:1), but who also affirms that the kingdom itself is like leaven (13:20–21), which works quietly, even subversively. And so it is that we find Paul, at the end of the long double narrative, in Rome, imprisoned. He is confined, but preaching and teaching "without hindrance." Or, to put it another way, he is proclaiming the kingdom of God, and the Lord Jesus Christ, even while a prisoner of the Roman Empire.

One way to appreciate the dimensions of the cultural reversal implied by Luke's project is again to appeal to the protests of one dismayed by it, the German philosopher Friedrich Nietzsche. Nietzsche lamented the disappearance of the classes of Graeco-Roman society—the few *honestiores* and the many *humiliores*.[30] For him there were the strong masters, "the noble, the powerful, the superior, and the high-minded," and then there were the weak slaves, "low, low-minded, and plebeian." But in the Western world that had been reversed in a "transvaluation of values." He blamed Christianity, with its roots in Judaism, of being "hostile to life," inverting nature. In the conclusion to his manifesto, "The Anti-Christ," he brings his case to strident expression: "I call Christianity the one great curse, the one great innermost corruption, the one great instance for revenge, for which no means is poisonous, stealth, subterranean, *small* enough—I call it the one immortal blemish of mankind."[31]

While Nietzsche is primarily railing against the forms of Christianity of his time, he allows us to get a glimpse of the severity of the impact that Mary's vision in the Magnificat would promise, and Luke's project in his longer narrative would deliver—

> "He has thrown down the rulers from their thrones
> but lifted up the lowly.
> The hungry he has filled with good things;
> the rich he has sent away empty" (Luke 1:52–53).

---

30. As noted in chapter two, above, referencing Garnsey and Saller, *Roman Empire*, 116–17.

31. Nietzsche, *Portable Nietzsche*, 656. See also above, 39–40.

CHAPTER SIX

From Edge to Center

THE GOSPEL NARRATIVE AS first established by Mark moves from the provinces to the capital, from Galilee to Jerusalem. In so doing, it brings a message from the marginalized to the authorities who make the decisions that control lives. The pattern is determinative for more than the geographical shape of the story. It becomes the narrative arc inherited by the other Gospels that use Mark as a narrative source, including Luke. It also describes the character of the appeal made by the protagonist, Jesus of Nazareth, as he attends to the afflicted, and then brings their plight to the attention to the authorities. The movement from edge to center is in fact descriptive of many aspects of the gospel story.

I. FROM THE IMPERIAL PROVINCES TO THE CENTER

Liberation Theology

This narrative arc amplifies the voices of the ignored and disregarded. Liberation theology, as developed in Latin America, is a theological corollary to this narrative, reminding readers that the gospel favored those at the margins. We have seen this concern for the Anawim in the writings of Second and Third Isaiah, which are pivotal for Luke. Here in the clarifications of the exile experience, presenting a new hope in ways unanticipated before, the prophets offer a vision of the renewed community, one born of suffering and discovered in the possibilities and perspectives that come from time spent in the margins. The exiled and diaspora communities lived in the provinces, looking toward Jerusalem. The Book of Isaiah too sends a message from the edge to the center. Those who returned had diverse visions of renewal, and it is in the tension among those traditions that Luke located his the narrative, both his Gospel and his Acts of the Apostles.

Often the shift of Christianity from marginal presence to establishment has been attributed to the conversion of Constantine, and there is no doubt that this is an important watershed. But many have asserted that the movement began with Luke and argue that the journey to the center in this Gospel simply carries the story to Rome, where it becomes available to Roman hegemony. But to what extent is the groundwork for an imperial reading of the gospel provided by Luke's text? Has Luke, in making the gospel available to the empire, had the inverse effect of making the empire the authoritative reader of the gospel? That is a large part of the question generating this book.

Postcolonial Criticism

In the world of biblical studies, the metaphor of "voices from the margin" has come to be associated with postcolonial writings.[1] Postcolonial criticism emerged from the colonies of western imperialism of the past four centuries, as articulate critics from the colonized peoples began to describe the experience of conquest from the side of the conquered. The primary impulse behind this set of critical writings is the manifest injustice of imperial imposition of political control and cultural dominance on a subject nation. Imperialism has been succinctly described as one country controlling another country. It is this imbalance of power, and the violation of justice, generally hidden from or ignored by the colonizer, that finds expression in the voice from the margins.

In recent years, the conceptual world of postcolonial criticism entered biblical studies under the rubric of "empire studies." It is this set of insights that has informed the reading of Luke ventured in this book. The reversal of imagination that shifted the readers' perspective of the text from the center to the margins was prompted by the realization that the Bible itself was a literary product of a colonized people. The Hebrew scriptures were gathered, composed, and shaped under a series of empires—Assyrian, Babylonian, and Persian. The Greek Empire, with its powerful and persuasive cultural impact, continued and in some ways increased the influence, seen especially in the Septuagint translation and the Greek-language apocryphal books, testifying to the cultural pressure, especially in the Diaspora. And, of course, the New Testament was written in the shadow of the Roman Empire, with

---

1. See, for instance, Sugirtharajah, *Voices*.

its commitment to Hellenist culture, endorsed and supported by an unsurpassed political and military system.

Empire studies teach us to read the texts of the New Testament with the eyes of the marginalized.[2] They provide a shift in perspective, a place to stand outside the center, that allows us to see things that had not previously been noticed. Just as the sun sees no shadows, when we read the Gospels from the center of the imperium, we fail to perceive the plight of the marginal and unacclaimed. One result of this new attention has been fresh awareness of the past uses of the Bible and biblical interpretation in support of western imperialism. New questions have been asked. To what extent was the Bible used as an instrument of controlling other peoples, other cultures? In this regard, the more explicit themes of postcolonial literature become more helpful and prominent.

The shift in perspective effected by postcolonial criticism impacted the world of biblical studies in another way. Empire studies adopted the perspectives of post-colonialism, and that perspective has revealed a world of the Bible not too different from our own in its uses of power, issues of complicity, the apparent futility of resistance, and yet the need for resistance. Suddenly, as if lifting a veil, the looming presence of the Roman Empire behind the readings became more visible. Heretofore unnoticed, partly because a subject people is circumspect about saying aloud matters that might earn reprisals, partly because we were reading from the side of the imperial societies.

And yet the documents of Luke seem to resist this kind of reading. When read as an apologetic to calm apprehensions of Roman authorities concerning Christianity, or conversely to assure Christians that they had little to fear from Rome, Luke was presented as sharing Roman values, assuring readers there was little difference to fear. This too is among the questions that generated this book.

However, there remains another dimension to these texts that escapes the concerns of the imperial culture, seen especially in the reversals proclaimed in the Magnificat and the Lucan beatitudes, and that is the challenge issued to the reader. So while conflict doesn't claim this writing in the same way it does with Mark and Matthew, in their opposition to imperial claims, a conflict still remains, on the level of those very imperial values. And where conflict is introduced, conflict resolution is required. For that, we will need to look further into Luke's handling of Mark's narrative resolution of conflict. Briefly stated, we see the narrative conflict and its resolution

---

2. Seminal works include Horsley, *Jesus and the Spiral;* Carter, *Matthew and Margins;* Kahl, *Galatians Re-imagined.*

redirected from horizontal axis of the plot line, as in Mark, to the vertical axis of the relation of text and reader.

Satyagraha

Postcolonial writing is not the only voice from the margins to be prompted by imperialism. The theoretical examination of the experience of colonization was earlier explored in the form of political action. British imperialism in India, for example, was the setting for the *nonviolent campaigns* of Mahatma Gandhi.[3] The various Satyagraha campaigns associated with the names *The Vykom Temple Road, The Ahmedabad Labor campaign,* and the legendary *Salt Satyagraha,* among others, show Gandhi's "experiments in truth" to be a response that finds power in apparent weakness. This was a response born out of a position of what seemed helplessness, but which Gandhi in his experiments discovered to be empowerment for confrontation and change. Once again we discover a movement from edge to center, but in this case in terms of action for change, rather than critical theory. And this too has a role in the gospel narrative.

II. GANDHI, MARK, AND THE GOSPEL NARRATIVE

With Gandhi we come to the matter of managing conflict—an aspect of Luke's narrative that differs dramatically from his source in Mark. Briefly characterized, Mark's account is a drama of resistance against those authorities in Jerusalem who represent the imperial presence. But Mark's drama contrasts with the forms of resistance current in his day in that he shows a nonviolent Jesus who resists without causing harm and who is nonviolent while continuing to resist. Yet, the implication of Mark's narrative is one of resisting imperial domination.

But Luke's set of concerns has required a different ending. Instead of mounting a protest against the empire, his resolution of narrative conflict involves a move out into the empire. Instead of resistance as a confrontation, he promotes a conversion in belief and lifestyle. But this leaves us without a clear sense of Luke's resolution of conflict. If we are to understand Luke's adaptation of Mark, we need to see how Luke has reconfigured Mark's narrative to fit his different needs.

With respect to understanding narrative conflict in the Gospel of Mark, Gene Sharp's comprehensive analysis of the praxis of Gandhi has proven

---

3. Bondurant, "Creative Conflict," 120–34.

a fruitful source.[4] Sharp's study is undergirded by a particular theoretics of social power, perceived not as moving from the top down, but rather from the bottom up. In Sharp's view of nonviolent campaigns, the power of authorities derives from the willing consent of the governed. When that consent is withdrawn, as it is in nonviolent action, that authority dissolves. Obedience no longer works smoothly and reflexively. When consent is not granted, dominant groups resort to force to achieve their aims.[5] Here force is seen as an instrumental expansion of individual strength, in contrast to social power.[6]

With this notion of social power as a foundation for nonviolent action, campaigns such as that of Gandhi can be divided into three theoretical phases that operate within a dialectic of resistance.

- The first move of the nonviolent "actionists" is *nonviolent confrontation*, undertaken with considerable discipline and deliberation in order to prevent a lapse into impulsive violence.

- This in turn evokes a *repressive reprisal* as a response by the confronted powers that resort to the methods of violent threat that have worked so well in the past.

- This threat is countered in turn by third move—*non-retaliation*—a disciplined refusal on the part of the nonviolent resisters to react in kind.[7]

One important aspect is that the non-retaliatory response of the nonviolent resisters is not to be confused with surrender. It may involve arrest, for instance, but without cooperation (as in "going limp"). Non-retaliation is not nonresistance. Moreover, it is to be distinguished from psychological theories of "passive resistance," which refers to a personality disorder that expresses hostility in an indirect and subversive manner.[8] In contrast to both, nonviolent action holds itself accountable. Nor, on similar grounds, is it to be confused with sabotage, in which the perpetrators fail to take

---

4. See Beck, *Nonviolent Story*, chapter 2; *Banished Messiah*, chapter 2; *Jesus and His Enemies*, chapter 2.

5. Arendt, *On Violence*, 4–5.

6. Sharp, *Power*, 25–31.

7. Sharp, *Dynamics*, chapters 9, 10, 11.

8. The American Psychiatric Association defines passive-aggressive personality disorder as a "pervasive pattern of negativistic attitudes and passive resistance to demands for adequate performance in social and occupational situations," https://www.psychologytoday.com/us/blog/communication-success/201405/how-recognize-and-handle-passive-aggressive-behavior.

responsibility, operating surreptitiously. Nonviolent resisters claim their action and accept the consequences.

Sharp's analysis helps us understand the conflict resolution in Mark's original gospel narrative as a drama of resistance. Not an example of non-resistance in which Jesus is shown simply passively accepting the punishment directed toward him, Mark's resolution presents a continued posture of resistance, though nonviolently. Nor is it a matter of momentary non-retaliation, as the instance of refusing retaliation is performed in the context of a larger pattern of action, which is defined as one of resistance.

Non-retaliation indeed is evident in the story of the garden arrest of Jesus. However, Mark puts that moment in that context of a larger pattern of resistance, of which it is the final step. The historically-weighted term *lēstēs*, meaning thief or revolutionary, concludes three moves in Mark's plot. These coincide with the analysis of Sharp concerning the dynamic properties of nonviolent resistance. The initiative of Jesus begins in the synagogue of Capernaum (1:21–28) and concludes with the temple cleansing (11:15–19). The response, with threats of "destroying" him, begins here and continues to the arrest in the Garden (14:48). This in turn is the beginning of the non-retaliatory counter response of Jesus, causing the disciples to flee, and leading to the cross, with the other "thieves" (15:27).

In effect, these three highlighted moments, each seen as the culmination of a narrative movement, shape Mark's storyline—*from synagogue to temple, from temple to garden, from garden to cross*. Jesus' nonviolent initiative begins in the synagogue of Capernaum, expelling unclean spirits (1:21–28) and concludes in the cleansing of the temple (11:15–19). The repressive response begins at the cleansing of the temple (11:18) and leads to the arrest in the garden (14:48). The non-retaliatory counter-response begins in the garden and concludes at the crucifixion between two *lēstēs*.

Like the territorial move from province to capital, nonviolent resistance also is a move from edge to center, but now in terms of power, moving from the people on whose part Jesus acts, to the Jewish establishment in Jerusalem which is tasked with representing the Roman authority. Furthermore, in its nonviolence this resistance demonstrates the difference of Jesus' movement from other popular movements of the time.

This much shows us the dynamics of Mark's narrative plot for his Gospel. It is this narrative that Luke borrows and adapts to his purposes. However, those purposes are quite different from others in Mark. The Gospel of Mark, succinct and narrow as it is (and implicitly directed toward liberation from imperial control), was the narrative of Jesus available to Luke. But for Luke's purposes, the story required deft and decisive surgery. And yet it had to remain essentially intact if it was to show Luke's message was rooted in the gospel as received.

Luke's first move is to replace Mark's pattern of nonviolent resistance with another. Luke does not share Mark's interest in nonviolent conflict resolution, at least not in the form described above. Unlike Matthew who adapted Mark's conflict-resolution pattern to his own ends, Luke would appear to abandon it entirely. We find no distinct delineation of the three moves: action, response, and counteraction. Instead, we encounter a somewhat relentless barrage of insults culminating in an acrimonious execution by the authorities, with particular reference to the Jewish elites.

And this in turn traces to another clear difference from Mark—that is, Luke's shift in perspective from a resistance against the imperial forces to an invitation to include them in the gospel story. Mark dramatized the action of Jesus as joining those who resisted, but he portrayed Jesus as rejecting the methods of violence, contrasting them with the movements of his day.

Included in this adjustment is the addition of a second book, continuing the narrative beyond the time of Jesus himself. The shape of the narrative is adjusted, but it still preserves the movement from edge to center in the Gospel, as Luke's story, with its long narrative on the road, moves inexorably toward its resolution in Jerusalem. But this, in turn, is placed within a larger frame by the Acts of the Apostles.

III. REREADING MARK, AND TAKING GANDHI FURTHER

Of course, neither Mark nor Luke had theories of nonviolent action at hand to inform his understanding of Jesus' action. However, insofar as these patterns are constitutive of nonviolent action, they help us see how the evangelists perceived Jesus as resisting nonviolently. The pattern is older than the analysis of it.

And with that assurance, we come to discover that Gene Sharp shows us how Mark's nonviolent drama also opens a way for Luke. We can get a sense of Luke breaking the fourth wall, as it were, translating the nonviolent confrontation of Mark's storyline into an invitation and challenge to the reader. In a later chapter of his book, Sharp addresses what he calls the three "mechanisms" of nonviolent action. His names for them are *Conversion, Accommodation,* and *Nonviolent Coercion.*[9] "Accommodation" is essentially a mixture of the other two operations. For our purposes, an explanation of the first and third is sufficient—conversion, and nonviolent coercion.

9. Sharp, *Dynamics*, 705–06.

At one extreme is "nonviolent coercion," in which the opponent grants the resisters' demands without accepting their point of view, acting more out of necessity than conviction. In Sharp's view, however, the more practical mechanisms of accommodation and nonviolent coercion are more likely to achieve the resisters' desired result. Here Sharp distinguishes between *violent* and *nonviolent* coercion. The difference lies in the intention, which is direct on one case, indirect or permitted in the other.[10] In this, Sharp is returning to his argument that power emerges from the consent of the governed. Withdrawal of that consent is coercive. It leaves the authority powerless, requiring it to shift its operations to forceful methods of repression, beyond consent. For Sharp, nonviolent coercion resides in this very withdrawal of consent.[11]

The argument sheds light on Reinhold Niebuhr's classic objection to gospel-based theories of nonviolent action. In Niebuhr's view, all forms of nonviolent resistance involve coercion, even those of Gandhi. His presenting example is the boycott. Its effectiveness derives from the hurt it afflicts on the seller who is boycotted, inducing him to change his practice. Sharp's category of coercive nonviolence falls under the description that Niebuhr criticizes, and to that extent does not reflect the ideal of gospel nonviolence.

In this way, an understanding of nonviolent coercion is useful in order to see what the Gospels do not recommend. And here we come to the other "mechanism" of nonviolent action. In the optimal case, nonviolent action inspires the opponent to adopt the resister's point of view voluntarily. Thus Sharp also describes another mechanism of nonviolent change, one which Gandhi preferred—*conversion*. Implied in the properly nonviolent confrontation is a regard for the person on the other side. This includes an implicit invitation to change from opposition to support. Conversion means that "the opponent, as the result of the actions of the nonviolent person or group comes around to a new point of view which embraces the ends of the nonviolent actor."[12] Gandhi sought to achieve change by means which

---

10. "Involved in the former [violent coercion] is the deliberate intention of inflicting physical injury or death; in the latter [nonviolent coercion], the coercion largely arises from noncooperation, a refusal of the nonviolent group to submit despite repression, and at times removal of the opponent's ability to inflict violence: "nonviolent coercion forces the opponent to accept the [nonviolent actionists]' demands even though he disagrees with them, has an unfavorable image of the [nonviolent group], and would continue resisting if he could" (*Dynamics*, 742).

11. Engler and Engler, *This Is an Uprising*, tells the story of the successes of nonviolent coercion in the political history of the late twentieth and early twenty-first centuries.

12. Sharp, *Dynamics*, 707.

did not "humiliate' the opponent, but rather sought to "uplift him."[13] Thus conversion stands as the preferable operation. "The Satyagrahi's object is to convert, not coerce the wrongdoer."

It is here, in the encounter with the opponent, that we find a connection with Luke's narrative. This transformed encounter has been described by Thomas Merton, Trappist monk and interpreter of Gandhi:

> Instead of trying to use the adversary as leverage for one's own effort to realize one's ends however ideal, nonviolence seeks only to enter into a dialogue with him in order to attain, together with him, the common good of man. Non-violence must be realistic and concrete. Like ordinary political action, it is no more than the "art of the possible."
>
> But precisely the advantage of non-violence is that it lays claim to a *more Christian and more humane notion of what is possible*. Where the powerful believe that only power is efficacious, the non-violent resister is persuaded of the superior efficacy of love, openness, peaceful negotiation and above all of truth.[14]

Conversions

Thus far we have encountered diverse ideas of conversion. Can we introduce some order into this concept for our reading of Luke?

Religious conversion has a history. For our purposes, it begins with proselytes converting to Judaism.[15] Specifically, the exilic experience of the universal God involving the nations as more than enemies of Israel to be overcome has implications for the theme of conversion, as Luke presents it. The engagement with foreigners as other than hostile, even as co-sufferers of imperial force, altered the notion of God's relation to the nations. This new engagement becomes the basis for the diaspora experience of the conversions of the nations.

Second-Isaiah's notion of "light to the exiles" expresses this—and Luke adopts this as an important constituent of his message. Already in this exilic

---

13 .Again, this is described as the optimal result of nonviolent action, and that for which Gandhi typically strove: "[My] non-cooperation is non-cooperation with evil, not with the evil-doer." Also: "My non-cooperation is with methods and systems, never with men," Gandhi, *Non-violence in Peace and War*, 65, quoted in Sharp, *Dynamics*, 707.

14. Merton, *Faith and Violence*, 19–20.

15. Blenkinsopp, *Judaism*, 25–27.

prophet a shift in Israel's relationship to the nations is conceived. With the prophet, this is a matter of expansion of witness, as in the second Servant Song:

> It is too little, he says, for you to be my servant,
> To raise up the tribes of Jacob,
> and restore the survivors of Israel;
> I will make you a light to the nations,
> that my salvation may reach to the ends of the earth (Isa 49:6).

Simply put, conversion seems to have been a rare phenomenon in the ancient world, due to the implications of rejecting one community and heritage for another. However, during the Babylonian Exile and the diaspora, the exposure of other nations to the Jewish belief in the one God seems to have generated a number of conversions, so that, from the time of the Babylonians to the Hellenists, the number of Jews increased up to tenfold.

Coming into New Testament times, under the Roman system, Judaism was a known phenomenon, officially given explicit safeguards and permissions. However, the identity markers that had been set up to frame the believing community were in tension with the impulse to convert from paganism. As we have seen, Paula Fredriksen speaks of *conversion* as involving a major displacement of self and community. For this reason, she discerns few conversions among the God-fearers of the New Testament era, and instead views them as pagans, essentially, including the God of Judaism among their collection of divine beings, but not forswearing idols.[16] In this sense, conversion is a rarity.

Luke's depiction of the Gentile adherence to the Lord God, through Jesus, involved removing the identity markers, but made other demands of considerable self-searching. The repentance and conversion scenarios of Luke–Acts show this. Here conversion to the one God is marked by a change of heart and direction, as seen in chapter two.

At the same time, New Testament conversion is a continuation and extension of something that enters history as a possibility with the earlier Gentile conversions to Judaism, insofar as it too involves a personal change that moves one beyond one's native heritage and congress of beliefs. The call to repentance, for the kingdom is at hand, is an appeal to personal conscience. Luke, as we have seen, distinguishes between the call to repentance, associated with John the Baptist and the act of conversion to a new public commitment, seen in the baptism of the Spirit. For Luke to extend the call to an act of conversion, to a distinct religious expression, is of a piece with

---

16. Fredriksen, *Jesus*, 130–31.

original conversions to Judaism. In both cases a voluntary act of commitment is required—a pattern that traces back to the experience of diaspora Judaism. Voluntary allegiance is the common determining factor.

But now we have another claim on the term, *conversion*, as enunciated in the response to an invitation given to an adversary in a situation of conflict. Insofar as the action invites consideration and voluntary change of heart and mind on the part of one's opponent, it can be identified properly as a conversion. The claim being made here is that this too applies to the gospel narrative, including Luke's version of it. The kind of conversion described by Gene Sharp invites the nonviolent acceptance of an opponent. The call to conversion implies an openness to the other that finds its extreme expression in openness to the enemy. To repeat Thomas Merton, "nonviolence seeks only to enter into a dialogue with him in order to attain, together with him, the common good."

Here, the term is applied to the form of nonviolent resolution of differences that describe the narrative plot of the gospel, as first designed by Mark. However, in Luke's hands, the term *conversion* describes more than action *within* the gospel narrative; it also applies to a reader *outside* the narrative. It invades the relationship between the text and one encountering the text. Within the framework of the implied reader, the text pictures a call to repent and convert that rises from the page to question the reader's own self-understanding. And this would even apply to the hostile reader, the one who had been considered an opponent, beyond redemption.

The Suffering Messiah

Confirming our sense of Luke's extension of the moment of non-retaliation into conversion, we have the Gandhian theme of *self-suffering*, which is described as a willingness on the part of the nonviolent actors "to endure sacrifices—such as poverty, injury, imprisonment and even death—in furtherance of their beliefs or cause." This, it is pointed out, "is likely to demonstrate the sincerity of the nonviolent activists."[17] Thus, "[s]acrifices incurred in violent conflict also demonstrate sincerity, as already discussed, but, it is argued, sympathy for the actionists is more likely when they are not also inflicting suffering on the opponent."[18] Thus, "change may be influenced by reason, argumentation and other intellectual efforts. It is doubtful, however, that conversion will be produced solely by intellectual effort. Conversion is

---

17. Sharp, *Dynamics*, 721.
18. Ibid., 721.

more likely to involve the opponent's emotions, beliefs, attitudes and moral system."[19]

Gandhi's notion of self-suffering contributes to our understanding of the place of non-retaliation in Mark's Gospel. After all, the refusal to respond to the arresting officers with the same violence that they brought to the occasion seems to end in defeat. Jesus rebukes the bearer of the sword that cut off the servant's ear. It is an explicit refusal to respond in kind. And so, the forces of repression seem to have their day with him. And yet Luke suggests already that this is not so. It is Luke who tells us that Jesus healed the man's ear. Here the power of healing is posed against that of injury. Unlike the sword, healing cannot be used to threaten.[20]

One way to retrieve the lost victory of the gospel is to interpret the cross in analogy to ritual sacrifice. That is an honored tradition. Jesus died for our sins. His death satisfied a need, repaying a debt that was owed to a wronged divinity. But in the context of a narrative coming to a dramatic conclusion, this interpretation is insufficient, since it reaches outside the narrative at hand in order to save it.

However, in the model of nonviolent conflict resolution, tested in social campaigns by Gandhi and as thematized by Sharp, we see a dynamic that turns out to be integral to the narrative itself. For Mark, it is seen in the non-retaliation that led to the cross, as a version of self-suffering that leads to conversion. Jesus accepts death rather than a coercive form of resistance. The gospel assures us that his death is not a defeat, but a victory. An unexpected future opens in the assurance of nonviolent action resolving conflict. The suffering and death of Jesus on the cross is not a defeat. In narrative terms, it evokes a sympathetic response from onlookers, and in Mark's Gospel, one in particular—a centurion.

Luke

Meanwhile, in Luke's account, the accusations brought against Jesus charge him with messianic ambitions, presented as promoted by Jesus' opponents with an eye to engaging the interests of the Roman procurator. The charges are threefold—"We found this man misleading our people; he opposes the payment of taxes to Caesar and maintains that he is the Messiah, a king" (Luke 23:3). Apart from this, the Gospel is rather reticent about attributing

---

19. Ibid., 707.

20. It is in light of Luke's narrative that we find Jesus' response at the Supper—"It is enough"—to be ironic (Luke 22:38).

the title *Messiah* to Jesus.²¹ Largely, it raises the question—Is Jesus the Messiah?

When we survey the text for references to the Messiah, we find that the book of Acts is more liberal with the title. Three clusters of reference are proper to the post-resurrection accounts, both in Luke 24 and especially in Acts. One set is found in the proclamation, especially by Paul, affirming that, yes, Jesus is the Messiah (Acts 9:22; 17:3; 18:5, 28; along with Philip, Acts 8:5, and as originating in the nascent community, Acts 5:42). This responds to the question raised by the Gospel.²²

In addition, there are two sets of passages of particular interest that appear only after the resurrection of Jesus. One of these is the *kerygma* pattern shaping Peter's speeches in Acts. In addition, a version of it gives shape to the Emmaus account in Luke 24:19-27. The kerygma pattern is almost a summary of the gospel narrative, in its fullest version. As we have seen, the proclamation has the form of an early creed, and its function is to profess belief in the occurrence of certain events, culminating in the raising of Christ. It serves Luke's narrative as a witness to the resurrection. Furthermore, as a summary of the gospel narrative, it can also be used by Luke as a concise symbol *for* that narrative, as an entire account viewed as an object in itself.

But this credal summary of the gospel gains in implication through its intersection with another cluster of references, that of the "suffering Messiah (Luke 24:26, 46; Acts 3:18; 17:3; 26:23). The claim being made is that the Messiah must suffer, as was promised in the scriptures.²³ All the refer-

---

21. Johnson, *Luke*, 151.

22. Generally, the term *Christós* sorts into four clusters in Luke-Acts. As a title preceded by an article ("the Messiah"), it is found in the Gospel, where it typically raises a question—Is Jesus the Messiah? A related set involves the title, but is affirmed of Jesus ("Jesus is the Messiah"). While this appears in the Gospel (9:20), it primarily provides the substance of Paul's preaching, "proclaiming Jesus as the Messiah" (Acts 9:22; 17:3; 18:5, 28, along with Philip, Acts 8:5, originating in the nascent community, Acts 5:42. Apart from these are two other sets found exclusively in *post-resurrection* contexts. One of these features *Christós* as a name for Jesus and appears almost exclusively in the kerygma proclamation, usually in the mouth of Peter (2:31, 36, 38; 3:20; 4:10; 10:36). The fourth and last is the post-resurrection proclamation of the suffering Messiah (Luke 24:26, 46; Acts 3:18; 17:3; 26:23).

23. It is commonly held that nowhere in the Scriptures does it promise that the Messiah should suffer. The Messiah is generally presented as a descendent of David, a king who presided over the fullest extent of the Judean territory. The expected Messiah is not so much one who must suffer, but rather one who can cause the enemy to suffer. One can reconstruct Luke's development of the theme by positing its grounding in the predictions of the Passion, along the road to Jerusalem (Luke 9:22, 44; 18:31-34). Here Jesus foretells his own suffering. But the claim that this is according to the scriptures is not supported. That Luke can use this motif as a summary of the gospel suggests that for him the Messiah achieves his mission through suffering, and not through conquest,

ences come after the resurrection. The first two are provided by the risen Christ himself, on the road to Emmaus, and then in the upper room. The others, scattered across the book of Acts, conclude with Paul's affirmation, "that the Messiah must suffer and that, as the first to rise from the dead, he would proclaim light both to our people and to the Gentiles." We find coming together there the themes of the Messiah's suffering and the mission to the Gentiles, significantly placed in Paul's penultimate proclamation, followed only by that in Rome (Acts 28:25–28).

As mentioned earlier, these two themes intersect. The most telling instance of this is in the Emmaus episode (Luke 24:19–32), where the *kerygma* contributes its form to shape the account. When asked by the unrecognized figure on the road what it is they discussed, the two disciples react with surprise, and then begin to recount the events of the past days. Their description follows the kerygmatic pattern. But when they come to the central affirmation that that Jesus "was raised by God," they cannot say this, and instead speak about the experiences of others. They are not yet candidates for personal witness. That comes shortly, at the breaking of the bread in the meal at the inn.

But it is not without interest that this episode also contains the first mention of the "suffering Messiah"—"And he said to them, 'Oh, how foolish you are! How slow of heart to believe all that the prophets spoke! Was it not necessary that the Messiah should suffer these things and enter into his glory?' Then beginning with Moses and all the prophets, he interpreted to them what referred to him in all the scriptures" (Luke 24:25–27). The two themes are aligned. Together they represent the gospel account for Luke, as given in a nutshell: The Messiah must suffer, for suffering is at the heart of the meaning of the Messiah for Luke, and so it has an integral role in his narrative of Jesus. To understand its significance, we need to take a brief detour through extra-biblical witnesses to the structure of Mark's narrative, in order to see what Luke has accomplished.

IV. CENTURIONS, AGAIN

Mark

Again, the road to Luke passes through Mark. It begins with Mark's centurion at the cross, who observes the crucifixion, and responds accordingly.

---

as in popular expectation.

> When the centurion who stood facing him saw how he breathed his last he said, "Truly this man was [the] Son of God!" (Mark 15:39)

In Mark's narrative program, the centurion stands in for the disciples. It is their role to respond to the revelation of Jesus' identity. At Mark 1:1, the program was announced to the reader as the beginning of the gospel of Jesus, both Messiah and God's Son. The ensuing narrative takes these claims up one at a time. At the end of the Galilee section, concluding the first half of the Gospel, Peter acts in the name of the apostles in proclaiming of Jesus, "You are the Messiah!" (Mark 8:29). So far, so good. But at the end of the second half of the Gospel, all the disciples have left the scene. They have abandoned this narrative—in the garden scene for most, but later in the high priest's courtyard for the more persistent Peter. So none of them are on site at the crucifixion. The task falls to the centurion as proxy to make the expected proclamation—"Truly this man was the Son of God" (Mark 15:39). To be clear, Mark is not depicting him as a disciple, but rather as one who stands in for the disciples, doing for the narrative what they should be doing but are literally in no position to do so. And yet, the response is an unexpectedly sympathetic response to the event just witnessed.

Then follows the burial scene. The centurion is again in the position of testifying—in this case witnessing to the death—and indirectly to the resurrection:

> Joseph of Arimathea, a prominent member of the council who was also himself looking forward to the kingdom of God, came acting courageously and went in to Pilate and asked for the body of Jesus. And Pilate was surprised that he was already dead, and summoning the centurion, asked him whether he had died already. And when he learned of it from the centurion, he granted the corpse to Joseph (Mark 15:43–45).

Strictly speaking, the centurion is reporting to his superior. In a larger sense, however, he becomes an actor in the text's *witness to the resurrection* of Jesus. He affirms the death that underlies the belief in resurrection. This in turn is the burden of the *kerygma* of Peter (and Paul) in Acts—that Jesus died and that he rose on the third day. This is the witness of the early community. Mark's centurion is a virtual disciple, standing in for those who have left.

Luke

It is in this centurion at the cross, proxy to the disciples in his witness, that Luke finds the narrative opportunity for his own soldiers and centurions. Where Mark opens the way, Luke occupies that place, with his centurions, his reader, and his narrative point-of-view. A single centurion makes his appearance in Mark. But Luke multiplies that figure many-fold in the course of his narrative.

We can begin with the centurion at the cross, who is present in Luke's death scene as in Mark's. In Luke's account he delivers a different message—not that Jesus is Son of God, but that he is "righteous": "Now when the centurion saw what had happened, he began to praise God, saying, 'Certainly this man was righteous!'" (23:47). Righteousness is a major theme of Jesus' teaching in the debates on the road to Jerusalem. In his response, the centurion shows an appreciation of the values Jesus proclaimed.

But as we have seen, centurions occupy a prominent place in the narrative of Luke. A centurion named Julius accompanies Paul to Rome (Acts 27:1, 3). And, of course, the most prominent, as we have seen, are the unnamed centurion of Capernaum in Luke 7 and the centurion Cornelius in Acts 10. Their positive portraits are supplemented with those of Roman soldiers. Some seek a change of life (Luke 3:14), not unlike others in the Gospel who repent. Some rescue and assist Paul (Acts 21:35; 23:23, 31). The series culminates in another centurion, Julius, custodian of Paul (Acts 27). Centurions are given a prominent and even favored place in Luke's overall narrative.

In a comprehensive study of the centurions in Luke–Acts, Alexander Kyrychenko notes how Luke "employs Roman military characters, and especially centurions, as representative figures for the targeted audience of the Christian mission to Gentiles."[24] His survey of the Graeco-Roman and Jewish literature touching on this topic, he concludes that the Roman army was the common image of the empire, with the centurion as a major representative figure. He ends his study with these words:

> The discussion of Luke–Acts has demonstrated that Luke employs the Roman military, and especially centurions, as prototypical figures for the Gentile believers in the Empire, who comprise the targeted audience of the Christian mission.[25]

As we saw in the first chapter, the two centurions of Luke 7:1–11 and Acts 10:1–49 are presented as representatives of the God-fearing reader

24. Kyrychenko, *Roman Army*, 189.
25. Ibid., 189.

of Luke's work. The "centurion" is a figure for the implied reader of Luke's double work. And in so doing, Luke disrupts the plot of Mark, the narrative of his source. And yet, he is seizing on an opportunity that Mark's narrative presents to him.

SUMMARY

First, Luke exploits Mark's invitation to *embrace the enemy*, in the person of the centurion, and makes that the linchpin for his mission to the Gentiles, taking it beyond partisan lines. In Mark, this is embodied in the centurion at the cross. Luke's centurion at the cross recognizes authentic righteousness, or the ethical value of Jesus' self-offering. But Luke introduces an array of centurions—the centurion of Capernaum (Luke 7), Cornelius (Acts 10), and Julius, custodian of Paul (Acts 27). These positive portraits are supplemented with Roman soldiers. Some seek a change of life (Luke 3:14), not unlike those in the Gospel who repent. Some save and assist Paul (Acts 21:35; 23:23, 31), culminating in the centurion Julius.

In focusing on one part of the pattern of nonviolent confrontation—non-retaliation—and taking it as an invitation to *conversion*, Luke accepts the invitation to love one's enemy, implied in Mark's narrative. He understands that refusing to respond to violence with reciprocal violence is a deliberate choice that follows from a conviction that the opponent should not be targeted for harm. It holds that one regards even one's opponents with the respect we accord our friends and associates—or, in other words, with love. Again, the overriding question is how to enter into conflict while not abandoning the mandate to love.

Second, in making the centurion a *God-fearer*, one who doesn't convert to Judaism but instead repents and is converted to the community of Christian disciples (Acts 11:26), Luke extends the nonviolent principle of openness to the opponent to the extent of making it a principle undergirding the mission to the Gentiles. Insofar as the God-fearer is emblem for the Gentile mission, to characterize him further as a centurion adds the dimension of embracing the enemy.

Again, we will recall Sharp's definition of conversion—"the opponent, as the result of the actions of the nonviolent person or group, comes around to a new point of view which embraces the ends of the nonviolent actor." As Luke works his narrative, this is indicated first by the call to *repentance*, shown being answered by the soldiers coming to John the Baptist (3:14). In the Gospel, it culminates in the centurion's response at the cross. These two passages frame a series of repentance scenarios, as shown in the previous chapter. In this regard, the gospel narrative is an invitation to conversion.

Third, in making the *God-fearer* a *reader* of the work, one who is invited to repent, Luke moves the narrative from a depiction of repentance to an address to the reader, a call for the reader to repent. And in so doing, he presents a case for the Graeco-Roman Gentile to reconsider his cultural heritage; the values that were simply a given now are put under the lens to require a deliberate choice—to continue living by these values or not. And as we have also seen, in addition to the implied reader as God-fearer, the inscribed reader, Theophilus, shares the title, *Most Excellent* (*kratistós*), with the Roman procurators Felix and Festus (Acts 24:3; 26:25). This suggests a prominent place in the Graeco-Roman world, and one that would not be easy to relinquish. (The alternative response would be to find a way to make use of the place one is given.)

If we retain as part of his awareness what we have described as the postcolonial perspective of the original gospel narrative of Mark, and if we do not [simply take Luke's narrative as a straightforward apologetic, we see the stance he adopts is a consequence of nonviolent demands. Luke regards the forces of the empire—in fact, the operative military forces of occupation in Judea, and oppression of the Jews in the time of Luke—as also claimants for the operations of nonviolent opposition. In his narrative, Luke has addressed his reader not as the opponent to be vanquished, but as the one-time adversary invited to conversion, here presented in the guise of the Roman centurion.

V. FROM EDGE TO CENTER: THE NARRATIVE ARC OF LUKE AND ACTS

Luke began his Gospel by contrasting two worlds—the Judean world in which the story of the Baptist is told (1:5) and the expanded imperial world of Jesus and what will subsequently be his movement (2:1–2). One invokes Herod the Great; the other, Caesar Augustus. This also describes the setting of the two books in Luke's double work. The Gospel unfolds in the Judean world (Luke 1:5; 6:17; 7:17; 23:5; Acts 10:37), and within the confines of this world, the narrative moves from Galilee to Jerusalem.

On the other hand, the story of Jesus that begins in the Gospel expands to the larger world ruled by Rome in the following account of the Acts of the Apostles by way of the movement that he began. The continuity is established by way of the Holy Spirit, identified also as the Spirit of Jesus (Acts 16:7). This narrative both includes the Gospel as the first "drama," as a distinct narrative in itself, and moves beyond it into a new narrative that embraces both books.

That first "drama" is grounded in Mark, which has given Luke's Gospel its determinative shape. Here we see the story beginning in the villages of Galilee, where Jesus is attending to the excluded and marginal, those who are peripheral to society and those who have been made peripheral, like the leper (Mark 1:40-45). The story of the leper is paradigmatic in the sense that Mark pitches his account in the ritual terms of the *Holy* and the *Unclean*, with the Holy Spirit contesting with the "unclean" spirits. In this vein, his healings typically involve overtones of confronting the unclean, in favor of the exercise of compassion. In this way, Mark's story of Jesus begins with those at the edge of the community. But when he makes his move toward Jerusalem, to culminate in the action in the temple, he brings the marginal with him in a virtual manner, declaring the temple "a house of prayer *for all peoples*" (Mark 11:17).

Beginning with Mark, the gospel story, then, shows a movement that ranges from the margins to the center. In the arc of this inaugural narrative, it takes the form of a move from the peripheral territory of Galilee, an outlier of Judea, returned relatively recently to the Judean fold by the Hasmoneans. It was seen as the hinterlands of Judea, and often considered condescendingly. The scene with Peter in the high priest's courtyard memorably identifies him as a Galilean, likely identified by his dialect (Mark 14:70). The gospel narrative begins in the villages of Galilee and moves to its climax in the city of Jerusalem, in fact, in its temple. In this way, the movement follows the pattern from edge to center in many ways—the marginal, the excluded, are brought into the community and declared so at the center. But the larger geographical symbol is the move from the provinces (Galilee) to the capital, Jerusalem.

Luke retains this shape in his own gospel account, even exploiting its possibilities by extending the journey to Jerusalem to ten chapters. The move from the edge to the center is retained, altered, and in some ways strengthened. During the course of the journey tension builds; anticipation of what will happen when Jesus arrives in the city is voiced among the crowd.

The movement from edge to center in the geography of Luke's gospel narrative, however, is also unlike Mark. Where Mark's concern is patently one of returning the excluded to the community, Luke's concern is to promulgate a lifesaving teaching. The praxis of Jesus, established in Galilee, is now being brought to the center in the form of the teaching of Jesus. There it is established, before the teacher himself is eliminated. While he is rejected by the authorities once he arrives as a teacher, spreading his message, his story doesn't end. He is executed, but his message continues. It becomes the basis for a movement, now moving out from Jerusalem to the outside world. One of the lessons of Acts is that the story does *not* end with the death of Jesus. Once the movement has reached Jerusalem, at the center of the Jewish society, it metamorphoses into something greater, moving out into the world beyond Jerusalem. Acts projects the message outward into the universe of the Roman Empire. The message has not been quelled, but released.

But Luke ends his narrative in Acts in what seems a peculiar manner. The general movement of Acts is that of a widening circle, moving out from Jerusalem, which contrasts with the concentrated shape of the Gospel, moving ineluctably toward Jerusalem in a straight line, as it were. But while Acts elaborates an image of a widening circle, it concludes with a journey to Rome, with Paul, who is under house arrest, but still evangelizing. The turn toward Rome seems to contradict the progress of the narrative. Except, of course, in Acts Luke has contrived to repeat the pattern, but on a larger scale. In this case the story begins in the remote provinces—specifically the province of Judea—and finds its way to the hub of the empire, the capital city of Rome and cultural home of Luke's reader. Again we encounter the geographical image of moving from the provinces to the capital, from the edge to the center.

The implication is that what has reached out from Jerusalem, with the Gospel, will now continue to reach out from Rome, but at an even grander scale. Just as the Gospel became the beginning of a new narrative, but continuous with the old, so will the story in Acts. But here that story is only intimated. It remains to be told.

POSTSCRIPT

Writer and Reader

WE BEGAN THIS BOOK by considering the implied reader, and this has been our guide to reading Luke–Acts throughout. But what about the *author*, the writer who stands at the other end of this act of communication? What can we know?

First of all, we do *not* know if the author was actually named *Luke*. As Fitzmyer points out, the work is anonymous, for nowhere in the writing does the author reveal his name.[1] Church tradition has assigned him the name *Luke*. Also, the work itself tells us that he was not an eyewitness himself, but depended on the witness of others. We know he was educated and was capable of writing sophisticated prose.

A strong tradition also holds that Luke was a Gentile. In addition, the evidence used above to identify the implied reader as a Gentile would seem to make that true of the implied author as well. Tyson concluded that the range of experience that was required of the reader to manage the work Luke produced would have to be that of a cultured Gentile, specifically a God-fearer.[2] However, it is possible that these characteristics could be found in a Hellenist Jew as well. Flavius Josephus comes to mind. Yet, there is a distinct difference between identifying the characteristics of an individual, the author, and that of a class of persons, the readers. The former allows for an exceptional example; the latter does not. In that case, a typical example, even if narrowly defined, is what we need.

If we take the approach outlined in this book seriously, then what we do know is that the author is inviting the Gentile into the tradition, into

---

1. For a comprehensive discussion of the author, see Fitzmyer, *Luke*, 35–59.
2. Tyson, *Images*, 34, 36–37.

the narrative. This posture of invitation is one that imagines an insider addressing an outsider. And while this doesn't settle the question of Luke's Jewishness or Gentile character, it does speak to the role of the author vis-à-vis the reader. The author presents himself as someone who is a position to welcome and advise the reader, who is in turn presented as someone who needs these helps. Beyond this it is difficult to make any firm determinations of the writer.

Yet, despite this elusiveness, there is one way in which the author is constantly present throughout these pages, and that is as constructor of the narrative. While the role of the implied reader has been highlighted in focusing our own reading of the text, we also paid continual attention to the work in which Luke is engaged as he builds a narrative from the materials at hand. We've attended not so much to the quality of his writing but to how he has shaped his account. His sources have interested us in how they have been redacted, precisely as they serve to shape a distinctive narrative. We are not as interested in how the finished product reads as we are in efforts taken to bring it to realization. In this regard, what has been described here as *reading* Luke and Acts can also be understood as *constructing* them.

In particular, it is Luke's treatment of his primary narrative source, Mark's Gospel, that demonstrates how Luke works his materials. We learn how he adopts certain set pieces, like the rejection at Nazareth or the question about the great commandment, and reworks them into programmatic episodes for his drama. We see how he boldly rearranges the sequence of events, such as presenting John's arrest before the account of Jesus' baptism, despite the difficulties that it might present to the reader, and how these rearrangements serve his project. In particular, we have seen how he has not only updated Mark's story for his own purposes, but also how he has played that Gospel against itself, reversing its point of view to accommodate a reader from the other side of Mark's dramatic conflict.

As for that *reader*, the portrait of the implied reader has been the guide to the approach taken in this book. It defines that person as a God-fearing Gentile of some social stature who is attracted to the news about Jesus of Nazareth. As a God-fearer, he is a friend of the synagogue, but not a Jew. He is standing outside the tradition that he admires and the narrative that he is attracted to. As Luke portrays him, he is a believer in the one God and no longer a pagan believer in idols. Luke is showing a way for this person to enter the Jewish tradition and its narrative through the promises of that tradition, now declared to be fulfilled in Jesus of Nazareth. The key is that the tradition itself shows the way in. An alternative thread of the exilic and post-exilic prophecies of the Book of Isaiah, proclaimed by Jesus himself as his precedent, opens the way for the Gentile. Thus, the God-fearer enters, invited by the tradition understood as being now in its fullness.

Furthermore, in the primary examples that Luke's Gospel employs to depict this God-fearer, he is a centurion, an officer in the Roman army. This is the same army that is responsible for the occupation and (by Luke's time) the destruction of Jerusalem and its temple. In this manner, the implied reader guides the interpretation of the text. Implied here is a perspective reversing the viewpoints of Mark and Matthew who tell the story of Jesus from the side of Jewish concerns. Postcolonial readings of these two Gospels indicate a shared opposition to the Roman occupation with its deleterious results, though these evangelists radically alter the violent opposition that was current in their day, favoring nonviolence and forgiveness as dominant qualities of the disciple. Luke goes further and adopts the viewpoint of the opposing party in a radical invitation to conversion, challenging that reader to a reevaluation of the cultural set of values that undergird membership in Graeco-Roman society. Themes of honor and shame, of wealth and destitution, of power and powerlessness are turned on their head, from the point of view of imperial culture.

What has not been discussed here to any extent, and in many ways simply finessed, is whether that God-fearer is already a member of the Christian community or interested in being one. Most likely, the implied reader is already a Christian.[3] This is implied in the prologue, as Theophilus is given assurance "that you may know the certainty concerning the things about which you were taught" (Luke 1:4). And we remember that the narrator of the Gospel speaks of Jesus as "the Lord"[4]— unique among the Gospels, where characters in the drama use that title, but not the narrator. It suggests that the author, reflected in the narrative voice in this case, belongs among the community of believers, just as it also suggests that the reader belongs here as well.

And yet Luke's narrative also voices a note of invitation, seen in the challenge to repentance that is repeated, especially in the Gospel. In that way it retains the character of invitation to commitments still unmade, as well as offering a word of assurance concerning those already in place. It invites one to consider the fuller implications of a decision already made. In this way, Luke's writing not only serves to offer his reader a "certainty concerning the things about which you were taught" (Luke 1:4), but also a

---

3. To use a title for members of the Jesus movement the use of which Luke reserves to those outside it—Acts 11:26; 26:28.

4. 7:13, 19; 10:1, 39, 41; 12:42; 13:15; 18:6.

challenge—to remain on a journey as its radical implications continue to be discovered.

Once Luke's text leaves the circumstances of its writing and enters the biblical canon, the reader is no longer the same as that implied in the text. Lacking the focus provided by the implied reader, the text opens itself to a universal readership, untethered by the particular circumstances of the God-fearer of Luke's day. Now lively questions become possible concerning its apologetic character mediating between Christian church and Roman Empire. Now, in a church largely composed of Gentiles, it becomes possible to interpret it as a repudiation of Judaism. Ironically, these readings are made possible by the universal point of view toward which Luke's project aims from the beginning. In its argument for converting the nations, it stands open to the possibility that those nations will bring to it their own agenda. Nonetheless, Luke–Acts still retains its critique of the accommodations of culture, whatever that culture may be.

Bibliography

Albertz, Rainer. "A History of Israelite Religion in the Old Testament Period." In *From the Exile to the Maccabees* II, 407–456. Louisville: Westminster John Knox, 1994.
Arendt, Hannah. *On Violence*. New York: Harcourt, Brace, and World, 1970.
Bachmann, Michael. "Jerusalem and Rome in Luke-Acts: Observations on the Structure and the Intended Message." In *Luke-Acts and Empire*, edited by David Rhoads, David Esterline, and Jae Won Lee. Princeton Theological Monograph Series 151. Eugene, OR: Pickwick, 2011.
Beck, Robert. *Banished Messiah*. Eugene, OR: Wipf & Stock, 2010.
———. *Jesus and His Enemies*. Maryknoll: Orbis, 2017.
———. *Nonviolent Story*. Eugene, OR: Wipf & Stock, 2008.
Berlin, Adele, and Marc Zvi Brettler, eds. *The Jewish Study Bible*; 2nd ed. New York: Oxford University Press, 2014.
Blenkinsopp, Joseph. *Ezra—Nehemiah*. Louisville: Westminster John Knox, 2015.
———. *Isaiah 56–66: A New Translation with Introduction and Commentary*. Anchor Bible 19b. New York: Doubleday, 2003.
———. *Judaism, the First Phase: The Place of Ezra and Nehemiah in the Origins of Judaism*. Grand Rapids: Eerdmans; 2009.
Bondurant, Joan V. "Creative Conflict and the Limits of Symbolic Violence." In *Conflict: Violence and Nonviolence*, edited by Joan Bondurant. Piscataway, NJ: Aldine Transaction, 2008.
Brink, Laurie. *Soldiers in Luke-Acts: Engaging, Contradicting, and Transcending the Stereotypes*. Tübingen: Mohr Siebrek Ek, 2014.
Brown, Raymond E. *The Birth of the Messiah*. New York: Doubleday, 1975.
Brueggemann, Walter. *The Prophetic Imagination*, 2nd ed. Philadelphia: Fortress, 2001.
Carter, Warren. *John and Empire: Initial Explorations*. London: T & T Clark, 2008.
———. *Matthew and the Margins: A Sociopolitical and Religious Reading*. Maryknoll: Orbis, 2001.
Conzelmann, Hans. *The Theology of Luke*. Philadelphia: Fortress, 1982.
Crossan, John Dominic, and Jonathan Reed. *In Search of Paul: How Jesus' Apostle Opposed Rome's Empire with God's Kingdom*. New York: HarperOne, 2005.
Dunn, James D. G. *The Epistle to the Galatians*. London: A & C Black, 1993.
Engler, Mark, and Paul Engler, *This Is an Uprising: How Nonviolent Revolt Is Shaping the Twenty-first Century*. New York: Nation Books, 2016.
Fanon, Franz. *The Wretched of the Earth*. New York: Grove, 1963.
Fitzmyer, Joseph. *The Acts of the Apostles*. Anchor Bible 31. New York: Doubleday, 1998.

———. *The Gospel According to Luke*. Anchor Bible 28. New York: Doubleday, 1981.
Flavius Josephus. "Jewish Antiquities." In *The New Complete Works of Josephus*, translated by William Whiston, 47–661. Grand Rapids: Kregel, 1999.
Fredriksen, Paula. *Jesus of Nazareth, King of the Jews: A Jewish Life and the Emergence of Christianity*. New York: Vintage, 2000.
———. *Paul: The Pagan's Apostle*. New Haven: Yale University Press. 2017.
Garnsey, Peter, and Richard Saller. *The Roman Empire: Economy, Society and Culture*. Berkeley: University of California Press, 1987.
Graetz, Heinrich. In *Ideas of Jewish History*, edited by Michael Meyer, 217–44. Detroit: Wayne State University Press, 1988.
———. "The Significance of Judaism for the Present and the Future." In *The Jewish Quarterly Review* 1:1. Philadelphia: University of Pennsylvania Press, 1888.
Greimas, A. J. *Sémantique structural*. Paris: Seuil, 1966.
Haenchën, Ernst. *The Acts of the Apostle: A Commentary*. Translated by Bernard Noble and Gerald Shinn. Philadelphia: Westminster, 1971.
Horsley, Richard. *Hearing the Whole Story: The Politics of Plot in Mark's Gospel*. Louisville: Westminster John Knox, 2001.
———. *Jesus and the Spiral of Violence*. Augsburg Fortress, 1993.
Howell, David B. "Circumcision: In Apocryphal and Rabbinical Literature." In *Jewish Encyclopedia*. New York: Funk and Wagnalls, 1906.
———. *Matthew's Inclusive Story: A Study in the Narrative Rhetoric of the First Gospel*. Sheffield: University of Sheffield Press, 1990.
Johnson, Luke Timothy. *The Acts of the Apostles*. Collegeville: Liturgical, 1992.
———. *The Gospel of Luke*. Collegeville: Liturgical, 1991.
———. *Prophetic Jesus, Prophetic Church*. Grand Rapids: Eerdmans, 2011.
Kahl, Brigitte. "Acts of the Apostles: Pro(to)-Imperial Script and Hidden Transcript." In *In the Shadow of Empire: Reclaiming the Bible as a History of Faithful Resistance*, edited by Richard Horsley, 137–56. Louisville: Westminster John Knox, 2007.
———. *Galatians Re-imagined: Reading with the Eyes of the Vanquished*. Minneapolis: Fortress, 2010.
Kiberd, Declan. *Inventing Ireland*. New York: Vintage, 1996.
Kyrychenko, Alexander. *The Roman Army and the Expansion of the Gospel: The Role of the Centurion in Luke–Acts*. Boston: De Gruyter, 2014.
LaVerdiere, Eugene. *Luke*. Collegeville: Liturgical, 1990.
Merton, Thomas. *Faith and Violence*. South Bend: University of Notre Dame Press, 1968.
Metzger, Bruce. A *Textual Commentary on the Greek New Testament*. Philadelphia: United Bible Societies, 1971.
Miller, Amanda C. *Rumors of Resistance: Status Reversals and Hidden Transcripts in the Gospel of Luke*. Philadelphia: Fortress, 2014.
Moessner, David P. "The Appeal and Power of Poetics (Luke 1:1–4)." In *Jesus and the Heritage of Israel* 1, edited by David P. Moessner, 84–123. Harrisburg: Trinity, 1999.
Moessner, David P., and David L. Tiede. "Two Books But One Story?" Introduction to *Jesus and the Heritage of Israel* 1, edited by David P. Moessner, 1–4. Harrisburg: Trinity, 1999.
Muñoz-Larrondo, Rubén. *A Postcolonial Reading of the Acts of the Apostles*. Bern: Lang, International Academic Publishers, 2011.

Myers, Ched. *Binding the Strongman: A Political Reading of Mark's Story of Jesus*. Maryknoll: Orbis, 1988.
Neyrey, Jerome. *Honor and Shame in the Gospel of Matthew*. Louisville: Westminster-John Knox, 1998.
Nietzsche, Friedrich. "The Anti-Christ." In *The Portable Nietzsche*. Translated by Walter Kaufmann. New York: Viking, 1799.
———. *Beyond Good and Evil*. Translated by Walter Kaufmann. New York: Viking, 1966.
———. *On the Genealogy of Morals*. Translated by Walter Kaufmann. New York: Vintage, 1967.
———. *The Portable Nietzsche*. Translated by Walter Kaufmann. New York: Viking Press, 1977.
Petterson, Christine. *Acts of Empire: The Acts of the Apostles and Imperial Ideology*. Sino-Christian Studies: Supplement 4. Chung Yuan: Chung Yuan Christian University, 2012.
Plato. "The Apology of Socrates to the Jury." *The Trial and Death of Socrates*. Translated by G.M.A. Grube. Indianapolis: Hackett, 2000.
Plevnik, Joseph. "Honor/Shame." In *Handbook of Biblical Social Values*, John J. Pilch and Bruce J. Malina, eds. Peabody: Hendrickson, 1998.
Powell, Mark Allen. "Religious Leaders in Luke: A Literary-Critical Study." *The Journal of Biblical Studies* 109:1 (1990).
Ringe, Sharon H. *Jesus, Liberation, and the Biblical Jubilee*. Philadelphia: Augsburg Fortress, 1985.
———. *Luke*. Louisville: Westminster John Knox, 1995.
Rowe, C. Kavin. *World Upside Down: Reading Acts in the Graeco-Roman Age*. Oxford University Press, 2010.
Scott, James. *Domination and the Arts of Resistance: Hidden Transcripts*. New Haven: Yale University Press, 1992.
Sharp, Gene. *The Politics of Nonviolent Action 1, Power and Struggle*. Boston: Extending Horizon, 1973.
———. *The Politics of Nonviolent Action 3, The Dynamics of Nonviolent Action*. Boston: Extending Horizon, 1973.
Sugirtharajah, R. S. *Postcolonial Criticism and Biblical Interpretation*. New York: Oxford University Press, 2002.
Sugirtharajah, R. S., ed. *Voices from the Margin: Interpreting the Bible in the Third World*, Revised ed. Maryknoll: Orbis, 2006.
Tannehill, Robert C. *The Narrative Unity of Luke–Acts I, The Gospel According to Luke: A Literary Interpretation*. Philadelphia: Fortress, 1989.
———. *The Narrative Unity of Luke–Acts II, The Acts of the Apostles: A Literary Interpretation*. Philadelphia: Fortress, 1990.
———. *The Shape of Luke's Story: Essays on Luke–Acts*. Eugene, OR: Cascade, 2005.
Tyson, Joseph B. *Images of Judaism in Luke–Acts*. Columbia: University of South Carolina Press, 1992.
Walton, Steve. "The State They Were In: Luke's View of the Roman Empire." *Rome in the Bible and the Early Church*, edited by Peter Oakes, 1–41. Grand Rapids: Baker Academic, 2002.
Wright, N. T. *The New Testament and the People of God*. Philadelphia: Fortress, 1992.
Yoder, Joshua. *Representatives of Roman Rule*. Berlin: De Gruyter, 2014.

Index

"abominations," cleansing the community of, 62
Abraham, 31
absolute power, 96
acceptability, to God, 13, 15
acceptable (*dektos*), 129
acceptance, 54, 65
accusations, brought against Jesus, 166
Acts of the Apostles. *See also* Luke-Acts
concluding with a journey to Rome, 174
as a continuation to the Gospel, 46
deserving distinct attention, 67
ending with ambiguity, 146
expanding to the larger world ruled by Rome, 172
functional structure for, 123
giving title of God-fearer to gentiles, 3
looking back at the Gospel as a completed text, 117
Luke extending the story to include, 48
narrative conclusions of, 147–51
narrative of, 123–51
narrative structure of, 122–23
overall narrative plot line of, 151
pagan idols aligned with demonic spirits, 87
placing Luke's Gospel within larger frame, 161
presenting the movement leaving Jerusalem, 128
projecting outward into the Roman Empire, 174
providing the setting for the gospel, 118
reading, 116–54
re-opening of the story essential to, 117
sections of, 122
as a single narrative in a double work, 46
situating the narrative of Luke, 117
telling a separate story beyond Jerusalem and Judea, 93
Theophilus at the beginning of, 2
affirmation, cultural role of, 150
Agabus, 48, 130, 141–42
Agrippa, 145
Albertz, Rainer, 33–34, 56, 58, 62
Alexander (the Jew), 140
Alexander the Great, arrival in Jerusalem, 97
Ananias and Sapphira, 124, 125–26
anathema, meaning "what is set up," 100
Anawim (the poor of Yahweh)
concern for in Isaiah, 155
Luke's canticles representing the dreams of, 72
righteousness of, 88–89
traits of, 70
waiting on God to deliver his people, 68
waiting upon the Lord, 71
The Anawim section of Luke, 68, 69–76

angels, celestial announcement to
     shepherds, 75
aniconic monotheism of Judaism, 5, 9
Anna, 70, 71
"anointing," of Jesus, 26
anomalies, in Luke's text, 41, 44–48
antagonists, to Paul, 140
The Anti-Christ (Nietzsche), 40, 154
anticipation, for what is about to
     come true, 71
Antioch, mission from, 128, 131–33
Antioch community, story of, 151
Apollos, 136
Apology of Socrates (Plato), 109n21
apostles. *See also* disciples
  clashing with the Sanhedrin, 124
  conferring the authority of the
     kingdom upon, 105
  mission of, 122
  staying in Jerusalem during persecution, 126
  transfer of the work of Jesus over
     to, 103
apostolic calls, scenarios involving, 30
Apostolic Council
  confirmation of on Cornelius, 15
  conflation of reports about two
     apostolic events, 50
  disappearing from the account, 142
  James' leadership of, 131
  letter to Paul, 142n23
  as a permanent, standing council,
     126
apotheosis of Augustus, 119
Aquila and Priscilla, 136, 139
Archelaus, 95
Areopagus, the council of Athens, 138
aristocratic orders, of Rome, 39
arrest of Jesus, 103, 108, 111
ascension
  of Jesus in Acts, 118–19
  Luke reporting, 113–14, 117
Asia, treated as equivalent with Ephesus, 136n15
"Asiarchs," protecting Paul, 140
Athens, incidents in, 138–39
Caesar Augustus
  apotheosis of, 119

authority of, 74
census mandated by, 71
invoking, 172
Jesus' birth in the time of, 42
"authentic identity," quest for, 61
"authentic" righteousness, 70–71
authenticity, 62
author of Luke-Acts, 175–77
authorities
  afraid of being stoned by the
     people, 100
  forming the new front of opposition to Jesus, 98
  hostility of not unwarranted, 102
authority
  Jesus conferring on the apostles,
     152
  Jesus recognized as having, 9–10
  in the Kingdom of God, 105
  transfer of to the Apostolic Council
     from the Sanhedrin, 125–26

Babylonian Exile, 55
baptism. *See also* John's baptism
  completed in the coming of the
     Spirit, 32
  of Cornelius and his household, 15
  of the Ethiopian eunuch, 13
  of the Holy Spirit, 32
  of Jesus told without mentioning
     John, 45
  of John in Acts as a beginning of
     something much fuller, 116
  Pharisees and the scholars of the
     law (*nomikoi*) not feeling the
     need for, 27
  as a public act, 32
  with water of John separate from
     the baptism of the Spirit with
     Jesus, 73–74
Barabbas, 149
Barnabas
  bringing Saul to the apostles, 132
  departing from the narrative of
     Acts, 133
  generous nature of, 125
  going to Jerusalem and returning,
     130, 130n10

introduction of, 131
mission to Asia Minor, 132
not requiring gentile converts to be circumcised, 65
recruited Paul, 127
selling some property and donating the proceeds to the community, 124
beatitudes, of Luke comparing with those of Matthew, 80
believer, God-fearer as, 3
Benedictus (Luke 1:68–79), picturing the future, 73–74
benefactors
  in the Graeco-Roman system, 106
  of synagogues, 6n10
Bernice, 145
Bible, as literary product of a colonized people, 156
biblical studies, in the conceptual world of postcolonial criticism, 156
births, of John and Jesus, 42
Blenkinsopp, Joseph, 34, 36, 58, 60
"Blessed are you," in Luke compared to Matthew's "Blessed are those," 80
blind, given sight, 78
blind man, encounter with, 97
Boaz, as *goel*, 57
bondage, 77–78
boundaries, constructed by Ezra and Nehemiah, 60
boycotts, effective, 162
Brink, Laurie, 38
British imperialism in India, 158
Brown, Raymond, 69
bystanders, observing the teachings and debates, 92

Caesarea Maritima, Paul transferred to, 144
call of Peter, 79
calling, scenarios of, 30–32
canticle of Mary, 40
canticles, in the Anawim section, 72–75

Capernaum centurion
  finding his difficulties solved by Jesus, 22
  Luke's vision of, 81
  story of, 9–11
  unnamed, 170
  wishing to be inside, 23
Capitolina, 6n10
Carpernaum synagogue, 43
Celsus, 109
census, 71, 74
centurion(s)
  affirming the death of Jesus, 169
  at the cross, 111–12, 170
  described as "God-fearing" three times, 15
  as a friend of the synagogue, 10
  healing of the slave of, 80
  Lukan motif of, 148
  as the most prominent God-fearers in Acts, 23
  as representatives of the God-fearing reader, 170–71
  standing in for the disciples in Mark's narrative, 169
  sympathetic response from in Mark's Gospel, 166
centurion of Capernaum. *See* Capernaum centurion
characters, changing sets of, 123
charges, leveled against Paul, 143
chief priests, elders, and scribes, managing the removal of Jesus, 94
child prodigy, Jesus as, 75
Christ, appearance of to Saul, 132
Christian community, greeting Paul in Rome, 145
Christianity, 154, 156
Christós, as a name for Jesus, 167n22
chronos, 102n19
circumcision
  Ezekiel's emphasis on, 60–61
  as an identity marker, 62
  put aside for the gentile converts, 127
  question of receiving its last mention, 142

circumcision *(continued)*
  removing the requirement of, 152
  as a serious difficulty for Roman citizens, 7
circumcision party, 134, 135
clan system, reworking of, 55
cleansing, language of, 60
Cleopas and a friend, traveling to Emmaus, 112
coercive nonviolence, 162
colonized peoples, 61
commentaries on Luke's Gospel and the Acts of the Apostles, comparison of, 69n1
commission from Jesus, 122
commitment, voluntary act of required, 165
community
  confessional signs of membership in, 34
  growth of the Jewish, 56
  in Jerusalem described as righteous, 124
  lines of demarcation, 128
  safeguards of, 63
  sudden and punitive death of members, 125
conflict
  entering into with love, 171
  resolution in Mark, 160
confrontation and change, empowerment for, 158
consent, withdrawal of, 162
conversion
  defined, 162
  diverse ideas of, 163–65
  invitation to, 171
  kinds of in Luke's work, 35
  meaning of in ancient times, 7
  not likely produced solely by intellectual effort, 165–66
  questions concerning, 32
Corinth, incidents in, 139
Centurion Cornelius, 22
  in Acts 10, 170
  bringing the gentile inside, 23
  language of "God-fearing" and, 13–15
  naming as one who "fears God," 53
council of Athens, 138–39
Council of Jerusalem, 133–35, 134, 151
credal pattern, centering on the witness to the resurrection, 112
credal summary, of the gospel, 167
creditor parable, addressed to Simon the Pharisee, 26
Crispus, 139
cross
  centurion's response at, 171
  interpreting in analogy to ritual sacrifice, 166
crowds
  anticipating nations targeted in the mission in Acts, 94
  in confusion at Pentecost, 120
  disciples interacting with, 86–87
  interacting with Pharisees, 87
  Jesus engaging, 86
  large, attending Jesus, 48
  neutral stance of, 109
  providing a surrogate for the later mission of Acts, 93
  replaced with the "people" (*laos*), 94
  representing those not strongly committed, 87
  size of increasing, 92
crucifixion, 108, 109, 111, 169
"the cry of the poor," in Exodus, 37
cultural self-discovery, struggle toward, 61
cultural upheaval, attending the arrival of the Jesus movement, 154
cultural values, 38, 91
cups, two shared by Jesus at the Lord's Supper, 103–5
Cyprus, mission to, 129n8
Cyrus of Persia, 52

daily discussions (*dialegomenos*), in the lecture hall of Tyrannus, 21n24
daughter of Jerusalem, indicating Jerusalem itself, 109
David, 71, 72

deacons, selection of, 121
dektos, acceptable, Luke's use of, 53
Demetrius, 139
demons, announcing the identity of Jesus, 18
Demylus, 109n21
dialectic journey, of Luke's Gospel, 83
dialectical exchanges, of Jesus with his opponents, 88–92
diaspora experience, of the conversions of the nations, 163
Diaspora Jews, Stephen selected to provide for, 126
dietary regulations, as an identity marker, 62
disciples. *See also* apostles
  interacting with the crowds, 86–87
  interacting with the Pharisees, 87–88
  Jesus teaching, 85
  reporting the fall of Satan, 86
discipleship, 83, 86, 106
"discussing in the synagogue," by Paul, 21
Dismas and Gestas, 29
distant realization, Pharisaic vision of, 83
domination, vision of opposition to, 33
Dorcas, 54
Drusilla, 144

early ministry in Galilee (Luke 4:14–6:49), 78–79
eavesdropping, as a feature of Luke's writing, 1
economic themes, of Paul's clashes with gentiles, 140
economic turmoil, in Philippi and Ephesus, 154
edge to center, as the narrative arc of Luke and Acts, 172–74
Edict of Cyrus, doing the work of God, 57
"the Egyptian," Paul aligned with, 149
Egyptian eunuch, 23
Elijah, 51, 54
Elisha, 51, 54, 55
Elizabeth, 69, 70
Emmaus story, 112, 113, 117, 168
empire studies, 156, 157
empty tomb, account of, 112
the ends of the earth, witnessing in, 122
enslavement or imprisonment, "release" from, 52
entry, into Jerusalem and temple, 96–98
Ephesus, Paul's mission to, 135–42
ephexes, "in order in a row, one after another," 46n5
episodes
  kept distinct by Luke, 47
  of Luke having themes, 42
  Luke rearranging, 43, 44
eschatological era, 34, 83, 152
eschatological expectations, favored by the Pharisees, 91
eschatological reign of Jesus, competing with the apotheosis of Caesar, 141
eschatological time of Third Isaiah, arrival of, 65
eschatology, of Luke, 8, 119
essentialism, risking distortion of, 61
ethical monotheism, 36, 63
Ethiopian eunuch, 11–13, 22, 54
Eutychus, 136, 136n16
events, Luke boldly rearranging, 176
excluded, reintroducing into the community, 52
exorcism, delaying at Capernaum, 43
Ezekiel, temple law of, 60, 63
Ezra, 34, 60–61, 128

faith community, 104, 152
faith in the one God, 63
Fanon, Franz, 61
farewell discourse of Jesus, 99, 105
"fear of the Lord," 3
Felix, Marcus Antonius, 3–4, 144, 172
female slave, with the spirit of divination in Philippi, 137–38, 137n18–38n18
Festus, Portius, 4, 144, 145, 172
"filled" with Spirit, 121

fire, separated into "tongues," 120
first cup, verses in Luke about, 104
Fitzmyer, Joseph, 50, 69n1, 175
five thousand, feeding of, 104
food laws, 61, 129, 152
force, 159
foreigners
   engagement with as other than hostile, 163
   exposure to Judaism leading to "voluntary adherence," 34
   inclusion in God's rule, 33
   repeated references to, 93
foreshadowing, of Luke, 48
framing device, of the relief mission, 130
Fredriksen, Paula, 5–6, 8, 164
freedom, from both circumcision and food laws, 135
fullness of time, as some distance off, 91

Galilee
   Jesus attending to the excluded and marginal, 173
   representing the praxis of Jesus, 84
Galilee mission, 68, 78
Galilee section of Luke (Luke 3:1–9:50)
   praxis of Jesus depicted in, 77–82
   presenting the mission of Jesus, 68
   repeating something from, 86
Gallio, 139, 147
Gamaliel, 124–25, 125n6
Gandhi, Mahatma, 158–59, 162–63
gentile(s)
   acceptance of in the story of Cornelius, 54
   attracted to the one God of Judaism, 148
   becoming part of the promise, 22
   coming to the final gathering as gentiles, 8
   conversion of including the military order, 38
   entering the admired narrative of Judaism, 36
   gathering as gentiles, 34
   God-fearer as, 3–4
   involved with Jewish ancestral customs, 6
   Isaiah's openness to, 56
   launching the mission to, 91
   Luke as a, 175
   moving out to, 21
   obstacles removed for, 65
   openness to in Luke, 152
   pagan as adversaries to Paul, 140
   Paul having confrontations with, 140
   in the text, 9–12
   times of needing to be fulfilled, 8
gentile reader, of Luke represented by Theophilus, 93
geographic description, on the road to Jerusalem, 83
geographical image, of moving from the provinces to the capital, 174
gift of tongues, 120
Gloria in Excelsis (Luke 2:13–14), 74–75
glossolalia, 50, 120
God
   defending Israel in the inner circle, 33
   delivering exiles from captivity, 57
   impossible to serve both mammon and, 91
   loving as not so far from fearing God, 4
   showing no partiality, 13, 15, 53
   working through the apostles, not the Sanhedrin, 126
God fearing, introduced in the story of Cornelius, 22
God worshipers, transition to from God-fearers, 17
God Yahweh. *See* Yahweh
God-fearer(s)
   as already members of the Christian community, 177
   attracted to the faith community, 23
   attracted to the one God of Judaism, 148
   as a believer in the one God, 4–6

as centurions in the Roman army, 10, 171, 177
contrasting with the pagans, 22
conversions among, 164
Crossan and Reed's view of Luke's, 23
from a culture valuing honor, 150
dilemma and the solution of, 10
entering the narrative, 23
eunuch representing the plight of, 11
exhibiting a profound devotion to the one God, 25
faith of in "the living God," 19
finding an avenue of entry into "salvation," 23
as a gentile, 3–4
as a gentile supporting the local synagogue, 8
Gospel narrative and Acts for, 93
hearers having first to be believers in God, 19
historical basis of attributing to gentiles, 5
implied reader as, 3–9, 118
invitation of, 32–37
Jewish representative of, 28
Luke as, 175
of Luke as a believer, not a pagan, 22
Luke enlisting in a conversion made public, 32
in Luke-Acts, 3
in Luke's text, 15–17
making one who is invited to repent, 172
making the centurions, 171
messianic hope bringing to the Jesus movement, 36
new phase in the story of conversion to Judaism, 35
non-conversion to Judaism, 6–9, 25
as a person of some status, 16, 17
perspective on Luke-Acts, 151–52
providing an entry into the Jewish tradition, 67
referring to an attitude of reverence toward God, 3
role in moving to the gentiles, 21
roster of in Luke-Acts, 9
social class of as prominent women and men, 17
standing outside the tradition admired, 176
survey of in the text, 21–22
variety of reasons for being, 5
God-fearing
  defined as equivalent to worship of God and righteous living, 15
  language of explicit for the gentile believers, 17
God-fearing reader, in the text as crowds, 93
"God-lover," Theophilus itself meaning, 4–6
gods, not made in the image of humans, 141
God-worshipers
  in Athens, 19
  God-fearers as, 20
  pagans and, 18–20
  Titus Justus as, 21
goel (redeemer), 57, 77
golah, identity of post-exilic, 62–64
good Samaritan, parable of, 87
good thief
  paired with the other, 29–30
  rebuking his fellow criminal, 25
  requesting entry into the kingdom, 110, 111
  testimony of, 109–10
  words of, 108
goods, practices of sharing, 124
gospel
  favoring those at the margins, 155
  reading from the center of the imperium, 157
gospel narrative
  as an invitation to conversion, 172
  pattern from edge to center, 173
  situating in the world of the Jews, 43–44
  treatment of as an "object," 46
Graeco-Roman gentile, reconsidering his cultural heritage, 172

Graeco-Roman tradition, teacher heroes of, 150n28
Graetz, Heinrich, 36
great commandment, dispute of, 49
great feast, parable of, 83, 90
Greek and then Roman thinkers, appreciated and admired Jewish aniconic monotheism, 5
Greek Empire, seen in the Septuagint translation and the Greek-language apocryphal books, 156
Greek Old Testament, the Septuagint, cadences and vocabulary of, 69
Greek territories, Paul turning to, 136
Greimas, A. J., 50–51
groups, dominant resorting to force, 159
guests, vying for higher places at table, 90

Haggai, 59
handwashing dispute of Mark 7, 84
Hannah's song, 72
Have you no fear of God. . .? 30
healing(s)
  becoming the setting for teaching, 84
  of Jesus, 52
  power of, 166
  taking place in the Galilee section, 78
  unwelcome result of in Lystra, 133
Hebrew scriptures, under a series of empires, 156
Hellenistic and Roman culture, found circumcision to be cruel and repulsive, 7
Hellenistic mode, Luke presenting Jesus as teacher in, 76
"Hellenists," as diaspora Jews, 134n13
Hermes and Zeus, hailing Paul and Barnabas as, 137
Herod Agrippa I, 130
Herod Agrippa II, 130
King Herod Agrippa II, 145
Herod Antipas, 107
Herod the Great, 42, 130, 172
Herod the Tetrarch, 108, 130

Holy Spirit
  appearing forty times in Acts, 121n5
  being received as a gift unwarranted, 121n5
  came upon Jesus, 31
  characteristics of, 121
  coming on the family of Cornelius, 14, 15
  contesting with the "unclean" spirits, 173
  continuity established by, 172
  demonic opposition to, 86–87
  instructing the Antioch community to set apart both Barnabas and Saul, 133
  Pentecost introducing a new role for, 121
  revealing the transcendent God, 31
  sending Paul to Jerusalem, 121
  transformation coming with the visitation of, 35
honestiores, 38–39, 154
honor, 106, 108, 150
honor-shame value system, 150, 153
host, reaching beyond his familiar circle, 83, 90
the "hour," Luke's Passion account, 102–3
house of David, promise referring to the entire people of Israel, 57
humans
  all are clean, 14
  each having an equal claim to respect, 39
  made in the image of God, 141
  serving needs of stressed by Luke, 152
humiliation, 108
humiliores, 70n3, 154
hypocrisy, 88, 89, 154

identity, 62
identity markers
  becoming important, 60
  defining Jews, 53
  interference with, 64
  of the Jewish community, 128

of Judaism, 164
as one wall of defense guarding the community, 63
providing boundary posts, 62
release from not the entire story of Luke-Acts, 153
removal of relating only to the gentiles, 65
setting Jews apart from that larger world, 77
idols
charges against worship of, 138
encounter with, 20
God-fearers not abandoning, 7
rejection of, 5
turning from to the living God, 19
images of God, conflict concerning, 140–41
imperial imposition of political control and cultural dominance, injustice of, 156
imperial judgments, last narrative in Acts concerning, 149
imperial power, made provisional, 141
imperial provinces, moving to the center from, 155–58
imperial reading, of ruthless king, 96
imperial visitation, under *Pax Romana*, 97
imperial world, of Jesus, 172
imperialism, 156
implied reader, 3, 4
inclusion, rather than conversion for sympathetic gentiles, 6
infancy narrative, added by Luke, 68
inferences, from anomalies in Luke, 44–48
initial sequence, as the narrative contract, 50–51, 51n12
intended reader, getting an idea of, 3
interpretation, gift of implying glossolalia, 120
invitation
of an insider addressing an outsider, 176
of Simon the Pharisee to Jesus, 26
Isaiah (book of). *See also* Second Isaiah; Third Isaiah

eunuch reading from, 11
evoking the political crisis of, 101
on Israel's relationship to the nations, 164
later chapters, promises of, 114
on a light to the gentiles, 33, 114
prophecies of opening the way for the Gentile, 176–77
reading in the post-exilic community, 55–64
sending a message from the edge to the center, 155–56
Isaiah 49:6, promise in, 74
Isaiah 53:7–8, pointing to Jesus, 12
Isaiah 56:3–7, on foreigners and eunuchs being admitted to the temple, 12
Isaiah 56–66, representing a prophet or school of prophets, 56
Isaiah 61:1, invoking Leviticus 25:10, 77
Isaiah 61:1–2, read in the Nazareth synagogue, 81–82
Isaiah 61:1–3, quotation from, 51
Isaiah scroll, reading in the synagogue of Nazareth, 79
Isaianic invitation to the gentiles, postponed, 64
Isaianic theme, including the gentiles, as gentiles, 36
Israel
in dialogue with the nation in the larger circle, 33–34
as priests to the rest of the nations, 58
itinerary, of Paul and his companions, 136–37

jail, miraculous release from, 124
jailer, 18, 19
James (brother of Jesus), the "brother of the Lord," 131
James (brother of John), death of at the hands of Herod, 130
Jason, hauled into court in Thessalonica, 138
Jerusalem
Acts 2:42–7:50, 123–27

Index

Jerusalem *(continued)*
  aid collection for, 137n17
  dire future for, 100
  Jesus lamenting over, 97
  new cast of characters appearing in, 94
  Paul returning to, 141–42
  procession-like advance toward, 149
  section of Luke, 68, 94–114
  stones of, 98–102
  witnessing in, 122
Jerusalem community of disciples, return to, 113
Jerusalem council, letter issued by, 142
Jerusalem to Rome (Acts 21:14–28:31), 142–47
Jesus
  accepting death, 166
  adding the witness of scripture, 113
  aligning himself with Elijah and Elisha, 81
  announcing "the Spirit of the Lord is upon me," 31
  anticipating what will happen in Jerusalem, 48
  apprehended and condemned as a teacher, 76
  arrest of, 103, 108, 111
  ascension of, 118–19
  baptism, introduction of as Son of God at, 78–79
  baptism, timing of, 43
  bringing salvation, 29
  as the coming Messiah, 73
  death of, 103, 149, 174
  debating the Pharisees, 85
  demons announcing the identity of, 18
  dialectical exchanges with opponents, 88–92
  dialogue partner of, 85
  enemies in the Jewish establishment, 93
  engaging the crowds, 86
  entering the temple and driving out the merchants selling there, 98
  farewell speech to his disciples, 105
  forgiving those who crucified him, 111
  freeing people from their various confinements, 52
  Galilee ministry, 68
  hand-washing, failing to perform the rituals of, 90
  healing the wound of Peter's sword, 107
  in his final hours, 96
  including the outsider as neighbor, 87
  instructing his disciples on prayer, 90
  introducing the motif of "stone," 97
  introduction of in a series of three pericopes, 47
  Isaiah 53:7–8 pointing to, 12
  kingship of, 73
  lamenting over Jerusalem, 97
  mission beginning in the synagogue of Nazareth, 79
  movement from edge to center, 155
  moving into the unrepentant towns and uncommitted crowds, 93
  moving toward his trial and death in a crescendo of humiliation, 149
  native place of, 53
  opening minds to receive the scriptures, 113
  praying at Gethsemane, 100
  as a precocious young teacher, 72
  proclaiming liberty to captives, 51
  as prophet and teacher and also Messiah, 110
  as protagonist, 75–76, 121
  raised by God, 168
  reading Isaiah in the synagogue of Nazareth, 77
  rebuking the bearer off the sword, 166
  rejecting the methods of violence in Mark, 161
  response at the Supper of "It is enough," 166n20
  as the servant, 106–7

silent facing his accusers, 109
speaking of his own kingdom, 105
story of, 42, 48, 114–15
suggesting in Mark that the Baptist is the expected Elijah, 54
task presented in the words of Isaiah 61:1–3, 51
teaching the disciples, 85
youthful, holding forth in the temple, 69
Jewish adversaries, Paul's dispute with, 140
Jewish barriers, removing to conversion, 148
Jewish component, among the community of believers, 118
Jewish institutions and practices, marginalized by the narrative of Luke-Acts, 127
Jewish practices, removal of in Acts, 25
Jewish sorcerer, encounter with, 133
Jewish tradition
 accommodating for the benefit of Gentiles, 153
 attack on, 65–66
 one being replaced with another, 77
 opened to foreigners, 151
Jewish-gentile communities, honoring sensibilities, 135
Jews, ten thousands believed, 118
Jews and Greeks, 16, 17
John Mark, 133, 135
John the Baptist
 on "all flesh shall see the salvation of God," 152
 call to repentance issued by, 153
 delegated to prepare the way, 73
 as the fulfillment of the prophecy of Malachi 3:1, 54
 narrative of concluding with his arrest, 78
 as the new Elijah, 73
 parallel sequence with Jesus, 69
 story belonging to the world of Judeans, 42
 time of over before that of Jesus begins, 43

John's baptism, 15, 31, 32, 116. *See also* baptism
John's Gospel, having Jesus showing his wounds, 113
Johnson, Luke Timothy, 31, 48, 49, 69n1, 95–96, 108
Joseph (husband of Mary), on the Anawim roster, 70
Joseph of Arimathea, 70, 71, 112, 169
Josephus, Flavius, 2n2, 42n1, 71n4, 175
journey to Jerusalem, 68, 82, 83
Jubilee, reference to the year of, 52
Jubilee era, people awaiting, 71
Jubilee liberation, 79, 82
Jubilee year, theme of, 77
Judah, returning to the land of, 57
Judaism
 authentic expression of, 62
 conversion first appeared in relation to, 7
 exposure to, 34
 God-fearers not converting to, 3, 6–9, 35
 "identity markers" guarding the community, 35
 mediating the revelation of the true God to the rest of the nations, 58
 as the world's priesthood, 58
Judas, 105, 116
Judea, geography of, 43–44
Judea and Samaria
 and Antioch (Acts 8:1–15:35) narrative, 127–35
 move beyond Jerusalem to, 151
 witnessing in, 122
Judean world, of John the Baptist, 172
Judeans, demographic expansion of, 56
Judeo-Christian morality, replacing noble morality, 39
judgment
 on Jerusalem, 100
 on Jesus as a judgment on Jerusalem, 98
Julius, centurion accompanying Paul to Rome, 145, 170

justice for the poor, giving shape to messianic hope, 36

kairos, 102, 102n19, 107
kathexes ("sequence"), 45, 46, 46n5
kerygma ("proclamation"), 14n20, 169
kerygma credo, 117
kerygma speeches, of Peter, 14n20, 112, 117n2, 124, 167
kerygma theme, structuring the Emmaus story, 114
Kiberd, Declan, 61
kingdom, like leaven, 154
kingdom of God, 85, 91
kingdom parable, 95–96, 95n11, 110
kingship, 95, 110, 111
kinsman, retrieving the fortunes of a relative, 57
Kirsch, Adam, 35–36
Kyrychenko, Alexander, 170

laments, over Jerusalem, 100
languages, hearing in their own at Pentecost, 120
Last Supper, Luke introducing the events at, 102
LaVerdiere, Eugene, 100n17
law (*nomos*)
   calculated wordplay regarding, 146–47
   debates with the Pharisees and lawyers, 65
   Jesus introducing the theme of, 87
   parable of the Good Samaritan on, 152
lawless (*ánomos*), being counted among, 107
lecture hall of Tyrannus, 20, 21, 139
legitimacy, concern for, 62
leper story, 84, 86, 173
lēstēs, meaning thief or revolutionary, 110–11, 160
Leviticus, specifying an alternative offering, 70
Leviticus 25.10
   discussing Israelite farmers who lost their land and were forced into indentured servitude, 51n13–52n13
   on Israelite farmers forced into indentured servitude, 52
liberation, Jesus' program of, 52
liberation theology, 155–56
liberty, proclaiming, 52
lifesaving teaching, Luke promulgating, 173
light to the gentiles, 34, 35, 74, 128, 133
light to the nations, 56, 58, 74, 127
linearity, in Luke's concern with calendar time, 45–46
liturgy of the meal, completing the Emmaus experience, 113
liturgy of the word, borrowing a pattern used in Acts, 112
locked gate, Peter not entering, 131
Lord's Supper, Luke's account of, 103–7
Lucan beatitudes, reversals proclaimed in, 157
Luke
   addressing his reader, 172
   adopting the viewpoint of the empire, 148
   arranging his narrative to take up one topic at a time, 45
   beginning different sections with programmatic episodes, 49
   on the biblical gift of tongues involving real languages, 120
   challenge to the reader, 24–40
   concern for sequentiality and chronological time, 102
   constructed his gospel narrative by adapting Mark's, 67
   contrasting two worlds, 172
   describing a popular and widely-known figure, 48
   distinct sections to his gospel narrative, 68
   distinguishing between near and distant events, 100n17
   eavesdropping as a feature of his writing, 1

elevated certain moments into paradigmatic events, 79
eschatological scheme of, 71
examples of his approach, 42–44
excepting the invitation to love one's enemy, 171
expanding the horizon to include the imperial world, 45
exploiting Mark's invitation to embrace the enemy, 171
exploiting the move from the edge to the center, 173
extended Jesus' journey to Jerusalem, 68
extending the time covered by the narrative, 47
extending the time on the road to nine chapters, from Mark's two, 48
failure to relate Paul's death, 146
favoring completing one story, 42
finding a path for the gentiles to enter the narrative, 65
forging links between the activity of Galilee and the teaching on the road, 84
introducing an array of centurions, 171
introducing his own version of a farewell address at the Supper, 99
making gospel available to the empire, 156
moving out into the empire, 158
not mentioning that John is sending a message from prison, 81
not subscribing to Paul's apocalypticism, 8
placing John and Jesus in their narrative contexts, 42
providing a programmatic episode for his narrative, 43
providing assurance that the gospel can reach the most distant gentile, 8
rearranged the sequence found in Mark regarding Peter's call, 44
reconstructing the second and third Passion predictions in Mark, 106
referring explicitly to the needs of Theophilus, 2
reorganizing the Gospel account of Mark, 46
replacing Galilee in Mark with Judea, 43
replacing Mark's pattern of nonviolent resistance, 161
reporting John's arrest, 43
repurposing of events, 135n14
saved the theme of Jesus extending his mission into gentile territory for Acts, 68
separating action from teaching, 98
shift in perspective from a resistance against the imperial forces to an invitation to include them, 161
showing a way for God-fearers to enter the Jewish tradition and its narrative, 176
situating the gospel narrative of Jesus in the world of the Jews, 43
softening Mark's picture of gentile authorities dominating by force, 106
surgical changes to the Mark narrative, 68
taking the gospel beyond the Jewish community to the gentiles, 7–8
transferring defamation of the temple to the story of Stephen, 127
translating the nonviolent confrontation of Marks's storyline into an invitation and challenge to the reader, 161
using the term *kairos* concerning Jesus' Passion, 102–3
Luke 7, as the most telling of Luke's adjustments in his Galilee section, 80–82
Luke-Acts. *See also* Acts of the Apostles
author of, 175–77
call to conversion in, 38
implied reader of, 4

196 INDEX

Luke-Acts *(continued)*
  interpreting as a repudiation of Judaism, 178
  moving from rejection leading to acceptance, 54
  presenting a portrait of Judaism open to the Gentiles, 151
  recognized as a coherent project forming a single narrative, 116
  repentance and conversion scenarios of, 164
  retaining its critique of the accommodations of culture, 178
  sequentiality in, 45–47
  study of the centurions in, 170
  versions of Theophilus appearing in, 9
Luke's Gospel
  alterations in the Galilee section, 78
  anticipating the Acts of the Apostles, 42
  ascension event, 117
  author of not an eyewitness, 175
  as a completed work, 117
  delaying the exorcism at Carpernaum, 43
  delaying the trial of Jesus until the following morning, 108
  divided into two books, the Gospel and the Acts of the Apostles, 67
  episode of the Nazareth synagogue, 51
  gentiles in, 9–21
  geography of Judea, 43–44
  lacking the focus provided by the implied reader, 178
  last chapter of counting as the first chapter of Acts of the Apostles, 112–14
  linear movement in, 122
  Mary returning home shortly before the birth of Jesus, 42
  opening chapters operating like an overture to a musical drama, 75
  as "an orderly sequence," 41–66
  Peter's call, 44
  placing Jesus in the role of Elijah, 54
  presenting Jesus' entry as a grand, gradual procession, 96
  properties/features of, 41–48
  reading, 67–115
  struggle between the two post-exilic expressions of Judaism played out, 64
  Theophilus addressed at the very beginning, 2
  timing of John's baptism of Jesus, 43
  timing of the births of John and Jesus, 42
  unfinished business from, 127
  unfolding in the Judean world, 172
Lydia, 17–18, 19, 20, 23
Lysias, Claudius, 144
Lystra (Acts 14:8–20), incidents in, 137

the Magnificat (Luke 1:46–55), 72–73, 157
Malta, storm and shipwreck on the shore of, 145
man with dropsy, setting up the meal lessons of Luke 14, 84
Mark's Gospel
  centurion at the cross, 168–69
  concluding interactions between Jesus and his antagonists as a three-fold movement, 110
  deliberate changes to by Luke, 44–45
  departures from regarding events in Jerusalem, 99
  dividing into two parts, 78
  as a drama of resistance against authorities in Jerusalem, 158
  elimination of two sections, 79
  evoking expressions of the resistance movements in Galilee and Judea, 75
  features in deferred to Acts, 116
  featuring a peasant Messiah, 75
  giving Luke's Gospel its determinative shape, 173
  instances of stones, 99
  Luke reworking the source of, 78–80

Luke's treatment of, 176
moving from the edge to the center, 47
narrative contract as the voice at the baptism of Jesus, 51
narrative moving from Galilee to Jerusalem, 155
non-conclusion of, 147
nonviolent Jesus resisting without causing harm, 158
as not a closed text, 117
occasion for Jesus' words about the first being last and servant of all, 106
opposition to imperial claims, 157
perspective reversing the viewpoint of, 177
of a provincial Galilean carpenter, 48
reading in the context of the resistance movement against Rome, 38
referring to the arrest of Jesus, 102
required deft and decisive surgery by Luke, 160–61
sections inserted by Luke, 80
showing a movement ranging from the margins to the center, 173
temple action of Jesus as the cause of the decision to move against him, 98
third Passion prediction and its subsequent teaching, 106
underlining the message of resistance, 47
marriages with outsiders, dissolution of, 60, 62
Martha and Mary (sisters of Lazarus), account of the meal at the home of, 87–88
Mary (mother of Jesus)
on the Anawim roster, 70
canticle of, 40
handmaid (*doulos*), 72
Magnificat, 153, 154
returning home, 42
visit to Elizabeth, 69

masters, contrasting God and mammon as, 83
Matthew
account of the dream of Joseph, 51
alterations by Luke to Matthew 11:2–19, 81
"inclusive story" of, 46
opposition to imperial claims, 157
perspective reversing the viewpoint of, 177
Matthias, 122
mature ministry in Galilee (Luke 8:4–9:50), 79–80
meals
series of Jesus shared with his disciples, 104
as the site of teaching, 88
merit, explicit appeal to, 27
Merton, Thomas, 163
message, from the marginalized to the authorities, 155
messengers, from John the Baptist, 80
Messiah, 167, 167n23–68n23
messianic ambitions, Jesus charged with, 166
messianic hope, 36, 37
messianic role of Jesus, dominating the Passion account of Luke, 110
messianic threat, showing the power of, 101
mighty, overthrow of, 73
military figures, in Luke's narrative, 38
miraculous work of Jesus, clustered by Luke, 80
mission
to the gentiles, 116
by Jesus beyond Galilee, 79
of Paul, 123
mocking, 29, 108, 110
Moessner, David, 46, 46n5, 48–49
moments and stages, in Jesus' progress toward Jerusalem, 97
monotheism, 37, 56
aniconic, 5, 9
ethical, 36, 63
moral system, Luke's proposed, 40
Moses, 126

"Most Excellent" (*kratistós*), Theophilus as, 3

narrative, generating Jerusalem-directed momentum, 48
narrative arc, of Mark inherited by Luke, 155
narrative conflict, surfacing in the account of Paul's mission, 140
narrative contract, 51, 54
narrative horizon, of Luke, 47–48
narrative movement, from edge to center, 155–74
narrative structure, of Acts, 122–23
narrative thread, of Luke coming from Mark, 67
narrative time, theme articulating by way of, 118
narrative world provided Jesus, related to the imperial world, 69
narrative world provided John, related to the Judean context, 69
narratologists, theories of, 50
nationalist hopes, deferred to the eschatological dream of a far-off day, 59
nations
　argument for converting, 178
　exposure to the Jewish belief in the one God generated conversions, 164
　listed in the Pentecost event, 120
Nazareth account, 52, 53
Nazareth synagogue, 49, 50, 152, 153
Nazareth villagers, overreaction to Jesus' announcement, 66
Nearchus, 109
Nehemiah, 60–61, 62, 63, 128
neighbor, defining, 87
New Testament
　conversion involving a personal change, 164
　written in the shadow of the Roman empire, 156–57
Niebuhr, Reinhold, 162
Nietzsche, Friedrich, 39, 39–40, 154
"noble morality," 39
nobleman, departure for the purpose of obtaining a kingdom, 95
nomikoi, the "teachers of the law," 27, 76, 82
nomikos, a lawyer, entering the road narrative, 87
non-conversion, setting the God-fearer apart, 7, 8, 35
non-cooperation, as non-cooperation with evil, 163n13
non-Jews, incorporated into the community of believers in Jesus, 5, 15
non-retaliation, 159, 160, 166
nonviolence, 160, 163
nonviolent action
　holding itself accountable, 159
　inspiring the opponent, 162
　"mechanisms" of, 161
　optimal result of, 163n13
　resolving conflict, 166
nonviolent activists, demonstrating the sincerity of, 165
nonviolent campaigns, dissolving authority, 159
nonviolent coercion, 162, 162n10
nonviolent conflict resolution, 111, 166
nonviolent confrontation, 159, 171
nonviolent demands, 172
nonviolent initiative, of Jesus, 160
nonviolent resistance, 160, 162
nonviolent resisters, 159, 160
Nunc Dimittis (Luke 2:29–32), Simeon's psalm, 74

oikos ("house," meaning synagogue), built by Julia Severa, 6n10
Old Testament canticles and psalms, format of, 72
On the Genealogy of Morals (Nietzsche), 39
one God, 19, 138, 164
openness to the gentiles, 65
openness to the opponent, nonviolent principle of, 171
opponents, inviting the nonviolent acceptance of, 165

opposition to Jesus, among the Pharisees, 82
outlaws, being seen as, 107
outsiders, 23, 86

pagan gods, parodies of, 56
pagan idols of the gentile world, aligned with demonic spirits in Acts, 93
pagans
   converted to Judaism, 56
   God-fearers as, 5–6
   hailing Barnabas and Paul as Zeus and Hermes, 18
   synagogue benefactors as, 6
parable of the kingdom. *See* kingdom parable
"parable of the Pounds" or "the Ten Gold Coins," 49, 95
parousia (advent), 96, 98
partiality, God showing no, 15
Passion, 76, 78n8, 95–96, 107–10
"passive resistance," 159
passive-aggressive personality disorder, 159n8
Passover feast, reinterpreted, 104
Paul
   affirmation that the Messiah must suffer, 168
   affirming that Jesus is the Messiah, 167
   amassing honor before his death, 149
   appealing to Caesar instead, 144–45
   arrested in Corinth, 136
   being a light to the gentiles, 33
   choosing in Corinth to go to the gentiles, 20
   concerns about reports of his missionary work, 118
   continuing in his mission in Rome, 146
   declared innocent and is treated as if guilty, 149
   encountering Lydia, 17
   experiencing an appearance of the risen Christ, 31, 118
   final statement on his shift from a Jewish to a Gentile mission, 146
   going to Jerusalem and returning, 130, 130n10
   gradually leaving behind the synagogue, 20–21
   growing in honor and stature, 149
   innocence regarding violation of Roman law, 146–47
   interaction with the jailer, 19
   invoking his Roman citizenship, 144
   issued a letter as authorization for his mission among the gentiles, 135
   linking up with Silas, 135
   Luke honoring, 131
   mission of as a threat to the empire, 141
   mission of "poaching" God-fearers from the diaspora synagogues, 5
   moving from the synagogue to an alternative site, 20, 139, 140
   not a direct threat to the imperial system, 141
   as a person of great honor, 150
   preaching about the one God, 18–19
   pushing back against those who claimed that he was preaching an easy gospel, 24
   raising of Eutychus, 54
   recruited by Barnabas, 127
   remaining in Ephesus for a couple of years, 136–37
   removing the requirement of circumcision, 152
   returning to Jerusalem, 141–42
   as a Roman citizen, 18, 138
   in Rome, 154
   selected to be a witness to the gentiles, 31
   on speaking in the Spirit, 120
   speaking to the Sanhedrin, 144
   speeches by, 19, 122, 133
   stoned and left for dead, 133, 137
   trials of, 143–45
   trip to Rome, 145–46

Paul *(continued)*
  trying as Saul to purge Judaism of sects, 143
Paul and Barnabas, disagreement over John Mark joining them, 135
Paul and Silas, jailing of and deliverance from prison, 18, 138
Pax Romana, 71
peace, on earth compared to Pax Romana, 75
Pentecost, as the programmatic event, 49–50, 119–21
Persian imperial regime, encouraged local identity, 59
persuasive arguments (*dialegomenos*), in the synagogue about the kingdom of God, 21n24
Peter
  abrogation of foods laws for Gentiles, 152
  arrest and imprisonment of, 130–31
  call of, 30, 31, 44
  citing the Pentecostal visit of the Spirit upon the family of Cornelius, 14
  community headed by in Jerusalem, 124
  confronting Ananias with his deception, 125
  demonstrating positive response, 44
  efforts in the coastal towns, 128
  encounter with Cornelius, 14, 65, 127, 129
  explaining himself to" those of the circumcised," 134
  identified as a Galilean, 173
  left stranded on the street at the house of the mother of "John who is called Mark," 131
  on obeying God rather than men, 124
  possessing the power of correction, 126
  prediction of the denials of, 105
  proclaiming Jesus as Messiah in Mark, 169
  resurrection *kerygma* speech, 14
  stories of, 30, 130
  testimony on gentiles, 134
  vision indicating all foods are clean, 13
  vision of establishing divine initiative, 15
Pharisee and the tax collector, parable of, 28–29, 91
Pharisees
  as believers advocating circumcision, 134
  false righteousness characteristic of, 71
  interacting with disciples, 87–88
  interacting with the crowds, 87
  Jesus debating, 85
  joined by representatives of the "teachers of the law" (*nomodidáskaloi*), 82
  making one last appearance as Jesus enters Jerusalem, 92
  rejecting the plan of God for themselves, 27
  requesting "teacher, rebuke your disciples," 76
Pharisees and *nomikoi*, recounting spiritual accomplishments, 29
Philip, 11–12, 128
Philippi, incidents in, 17, 137–38
piety, 70, 89, 90, 92
Pilate, 169
plot conflict, Luke resolving, 110–12
plot line of Acts, difficulties in delineating, 123
Plutarch, on Zeno biting off his tongue, 109n21
poor
  preferential option for, revising the Roman value structure, 153
  protecting from exploitation, 37
postcolonial criticism, 61–64, 156
postcolonial perspectives, 148, 172
postcolonial terms, considering the Gospel of Luke in, 68
postcolonial writing, initiation of, 61n27
post-colonialism, 148, 157

post-exilic *Golah*, identity of, 62–64
post-Jerusalem narrative of Acts, two parts of, 151
poverty, of the Anawim, 70
Powell, Mark Allan, 88
power
　Anawim peripheral to, 71
　emerging from the consent of the governed, 162
　finding in apparent weakness, 158
power of correction, as an attribute of authority, 125–26
praxis of Galilee, as the theme of Jesus's teaching, 114
praxis of Jesus, 52, 68, 76
praxis to theory, the road as the site of teaching, 84–88
prayer in the garden, Luke depicting as "agony," 107
Priscilla and Aquila, 136, 139, 146
procession, with praise and rejoicing, 97
procurators, as governors of the Roman army, 4
prodigal son, 25, 27–28, 83, 90–91
programmatic episodes, in Luke, 48–50, 75, 120
prologue
　expressing narrative continuity, 116n1
　Luke's Gospel beginning with, 69
prophecy and fulfillment, pattern of in Luke, 48
prophetic theme, in Luke, 75
prophets
　references to stoning in Luke, 99
　selection of, 121
proselytes, converting to Judaism, 163
proselytism, of the Jewish people, 34
protagonist, Jesus as, 75–76
proverb, on prophets from Mark, 52
Psalm 117 (LXX), on the stone which the builders rejected, 101
ptóchos (poor, destitute), as Luke's Greek term, 70n3
public baths, circumcised attending, 7
public order, of concern to Roman authorities, 147

purification rite, Paul's arrest in the final days of, 143–44
purity
　concern for, 62
　of the faith, 60
purity laws, 15, 22

Q Document, 67, 80n9, 99n16
Quirinius (Cyrenius), as governor of Syria, 42

reader(s)
　defined as a God-fearing Gentile in Luke, 176
　distinguishing intended, inscribed, and implied in a text, 2–3
redeemer, use of in the Old Testament, 57n20
redemption, having specific obligations, 57
rejection, of Jesus, 53, 54, 65
religion, as part of one's ethnicity, 7
religious conversion, history of, 163
repentance
　call to, 164, 171
　contrast with the sense of not needing it, 83
　contrasting with the avoidance of repentance, 81
　as a demand of discipleship, 37–38
　as a demand on the new adherent, 35
　figures of in Luke, 25
　gospel inviting the response of, 110
　granting to the gentiles, 14
　including even the military, 38n11
　invitations and resistance to, 83
　issuing a call to, 24
　John's baptism of, 27, 32
　in a meal setting, 90–91
　moving to social statement, 32
　narrow door of presented, 153
　presented as a change of state, 27
　scenarios of, 25–30
　Simon the Pharisee resisting, 27
　stages in Luke's understanding of, 31

repentance *(continued)*
   theme of added to the theme of resurrection, 113
repentant prodigal, approved over the obedient elder brother, 27
repentant woman, 25, 26–27, 80
repetition, 81
repression, forces of, 166
repressive reprisal, as a response by confronted powers, 159
repressive response, to Jesus, 160
resistance to repentance, dramatized in terms of wealth, 91
resurrection
   appearances, 118
   from the dead, 144
   validating alternative values, 153
resurrection and ascension events, announced by Peter, 119
reversals, 72–73, 83
revolutionaries, both Jesus and Paul aligned with, 149
Rhoda, neglecting to let Paul enter, 131
rich man and Lazarus, parable of, 91
riches, teaching on, 73
righteousness
   of the Anawim, 70
   as a major theme of Jesus's teaching, 170
   versus repentance, 85
   of the villagers of Luke's infancy narrative, 153
Ringe, Sharon, 52, 69, 69n1, 104
ritual purity, 14
ritual regulations, dismissal of by Luke, 32
road to Jerusalem section of Luke, 68, 82–94
Roman army, as the common image of the empire, 170
Roman centurions. *See* centurion(s)
Roman citizen, Paul as, 18
Roman courts, 143, 151
Roman Empire, 37–40, 157
Roman imperial social structure, 141
Roman ladies, prominent, supporting synagogues, 6
Roman law, required allegiance to Roman gods with an exception for Jews, 147
Roman officers, favorable treatment of, 148
Roman procurators, aligning Theophilus with, 7
Roman system, distinction between *honestiores* and *humiliores*, 39
Roman world, foray into, as an unprecedented opportunity for mission, 65
Romans, not understanding what the problem is with Paul, 147
Rome
   "light to the nations" leading to, 38
   move from Jerusalem to, 153
   narrative concluding in, 123
   Paul's trip to, 145–46
   turn toward contradicting the progress of the narrative, 174
Ruth (book of), as a dramatization of Exodus 22, 37
Ruth and Naomi, as examples of the concern for the poor, 37

Sabbath, 60, 62, 65, 152
Sabina, Poppaea, 6
sabotage, 159–60
salvation, Jesus bringing to the tax collector, 29
Samaritans, as foreigners, 93
Sanhedrin
   antagonistic to the apostles, 124
   having no power over the new movement, 126
   Paul speaking to, 144
   providing primary opposition to the apostolic church in Acts, 98
   providing primary opposition to the council of apostles in Acts, 94
   replaced with the council of apostles, 152
   returning to provide opposition, 143
Sapphira, 124, 125–26

Satan, showing Jesus the kingdoms of
    the world, 96
Satyagraha campaigns, showing Gandhi's "experiments in truth," 158
King Saul, anointing of, 72
Saul (Paul), 131–32, 133. *See also* Paul
scholars of the law (*nomikoi*). *See nomikoi*, the "teachers of the law"
Second Isaiah. *See also* Isaiah (book of)
    as the anonymous prophet of the exile, 55–57
    fulfillment of announced by Simeon, 74
    moving Israelite theology to new insight, 33
    promise to the family of David transferred to the people themselves, 58
sect, Paul rejecting the term, 144
self-achieved righteousness, 88, 91
self-awareness, 27
self-justification, 91
selfless service, 105
self-righteousness, 88, 92
self-salvation, 88, 89
self-suffering, Gandhian theme of, 165, 166
Septuagint, 11, 69, 120, 156
sequentiality, in Luke-Acts, 45–47
Sergius Paulus, 133, 133n12
Sermon on the Plain, 80, 84
servant, Jesus as, 106–7
serving at tables, image as a lesson of humility, 106
Severa, Julia, 6, 6n10
Sharp, Gene, 158–59, 161, 165, 171
silversmiths, riot of in Ephesus, 139
Simeon
    on the Anawim roster, 70
    looking to a light to the gentiles, 33
    promising Jesus' mother she will be pierced with a "sword," 107
    psalm of, 74
    vision of a light to the Gentiles, 153
    "waiting for the consolation of Israel," 71
Simon Magus, 121n5, 127

Simon of Cyrene, 109
Simon the Pharisee, 26–27, 27, 84, 90
sin, negative valuation of, 39
sinfulness, Peter's recognition of, 30
slave girl, exorcism of a demon from, 18
social dimension, in assigning honor, 150
social framework, as an alternative to the monarchical state, 55, 59
social hierarchy, separating elites from the humble masses, 38
social power, 159
social reordering, anxiety involved in, 62
social reversals, in the full narrative of Luke-Acts, 73
Socrates, 108–9, 139, 150n28
soldiers
    in Luke's narrative, 38
    taunting Jesus, 108
Solomon, 126
"son of Abraham," Zacchaeus as, 28
Son of Man, 106
speaking in tongues, by the disciples, 50
Spirit. *See* Holy Spirit
Spirit of Jesus, 121, 172
Spirit of the Lord, 77
status, 73, 83, 90
Stephen
    judgment on the temple, 151
    Luke honoring, 131
    major speech by, 122
    martyrdom of, 46, 126–27
    pronouncement of, 111, 111n26
    pronouncing judgment on the temple, 152
    story of, 110
stewardship, importance of honest, 91
stone(s)
    closing the tomb of Jesus rolled aside, 101
    falling upon and being crushed by fallen, 101
    image shifting to building blocks of envisioned as coming down, 100
    of Jerusalem, 98–102

stone(s) *(continued)*
  motif of, 97
  stumbling and living in Luke, 100
suffering, 107, 168
suffering Messiah, 114, 117, 165–68, 167n22
superiority, sense of, 92
Supper of the Lord, 103–7
sword(s), 106, 107, 111
synagogues
  gentiles who are sympathizers of, 5
  as home to Jews along with certain "Greeks," or God-fearers, 17
  mission to, 151
  moving away from to the public arena, 152–53
  shifting from to lecture halls, 23
Syrian Antioch, as the base of the missions of Paul, 128

tabernacle, turning from tent into temple, 126
talents, use of, 49
"Tales of the Tribe" (Kirsch), 35
Tattennai (Persian governor), 59
tax collector, beating his breast, 29
teacher(s)
  Jesus as bringing his message to the center of the Jewish world, 98
  Jesus of Nazareth as a precocious young, 75
  Jesus's role moving ideas of kingship toward acts of persuasion, 110
  selection of, 121
  suffering for his witness to the truth, 76
"teachers of the law" (*nomodidáskaloi*), 82
teaching
  contrasting true with false, 88–89
  projected by Luke's language of stones, 98–99
  rejection of coming to a fulfillment, 108
teaching of Jesus
  emphasis on, 88
  in Jerusalem centering on judgment and challenge, 101
  to the Pharisees and lawyers, 76
  on the road, 84, 85
teaching prophet, Luke's Jesus as, 76
temple
  charges reappearing in Stephen's witness in Acts 7, 116
  cleansing expanded in Luke's treatment into a time of teaching, 111
  heightened role of, 63
  as a house of prayer for all peoples, 12
  Mark's judgment of, 99
  "precious stone and votive offerings" in, 100
  receiving its own critique in Luke, 65
Tertullus, presenting the charges against Paul, 144
text markers, dividing Acts into three parts, 122
Theophilus
  addressed at the beginning of Luke's Gospel and the Acts of the Apostles, 2
  as already a Christian, 177
  being reassured in his faith, 4
  as a cipher, 3
  as implied reader of Luke's work, 148
  as likely a benefactor, 106
  as a literate and prominent gentile, sympathetic to Judaism, 8
  Luke providing with assurances, 24
  not a convert to Judaism, 7
  as the reader of Luke, 41
  sharing the title, Most Excellent (*kratistós*), with the Roman procurators Felix and Festus, 172
  as the sponsor of Luke's project and also a reader, 2
  as a symbolic name, 5
Thessalonians, describing Paul and Silas as turning the world upside down (*anastatoó*), 73
Thessalonica, 138, 141
thief

one joining in the mockery of Jesus, 30
reproving the first with the words "Have you no fear of God?" 108
Third Isaiah, 34, 57–59, 77. *See also* Isaiah (book of)
threads of dialogue, between Jesus and others, 85–88
time of the gentiles, 91, 119
timeline, for Jesus in Jerusalem indeterminate in Luke, 99
timing, of the births of John and Jesus, 42
Timothy, 16, 136
Titus Justus
  explicitly named as a God-fearer, 20
  helping to initiate the move to the gentile world, 21
  providing an alternative venue for preaching, 23, 139
  on the transfer of Paul's preaching from the synagogue to the lecture hall, 22
Tobit, praying for all nations to cast away idols, 8
Tower of Babel, as "the Tower of Confusion," 120
transfiguration, of Jesus, 112n28
"transvaluation of values," in the Western world, 154
trial of Jesus, 76, 149
trial of Socrates, apologia written to explain, 109n21
trials of Paul, compared with those of Jesus, 149
Tyson, Joseph B., 175

uncircumcised people, Peter eating with, 14
unclean spirits, possessing a person, 121

Valerius Maximus, 109n21
values, of the strong, 39
villagers, 69–70, 75
vineyard tenants, 99, 101
violence, refusing to respond to, 171
violent coercion, 162, 162n10
virtue, 27, 89, 92
the Vision, of Cornelius concerning food laws, 14
"voices from the margin," associated with postcolonial writings, 156
"votive offerings" (*anathema*), memorials by notable figures, 100
vulnerable, dedication to, 63

walls, destruction by collapse of, 101
warrior ethic, striving toward excellence, 39
"the Way," Paul speaking of, 144
way of the cross, Luke presenting, 109
weakness, finding power in apparent, 158
western imperialism, Bible and biblical interpretation used in support of, 157
widow of Nain, from Luke's source, 80n9
widow of Nain's son, raising of, 54, 80, 81
wind, introducing the Spirit, 120
woes, balancing blessings in Luke's beatitudes, 80
works, of the Spirit, 121
worship, implying a commitment to the one God, 17, 64
worshiper (*sébomai*), 16, 22
"worshiper of God," Lydia as, 17
"worthless things," translated "idols," 19n23

xenoglossia, 50, 120

Yahweh, 33, 56

Zacchaeus, 25, 28, 29, 97, 104
Zachary, 70
Zechariah, 59, 73
Zeno, 109, 109n21
Zerubbabel, 59

www.ingramcontent.com/pod-product-compliance
Lightning Source LLC
Chambersburg PA
CBHW070319230426
43663CB00011B/2181